Crafting the Travel Guidebook

How to Write, Publish & Sell Your Travel Book

Barbara Hudgins

The Woodmont Press
Liberty Corner, New Jersey

Published by
The Woodmont Press
P.O. Box 16
Liberty Corner, NJ 07938
www.woodmontpress.com

Disclaimer: This book is designed to provide accurate information with regard to the subject matter. It is sold with the understanding that the publisher and author are not engaged in rendering legal or other professional advice. If legal assistance is required, seek out the services of a competent lawyer.

Trademarked names, including names of destinations and publishing houses, are used in this book in an editorial context with no intention of infringement of the trademark.

LCCN # 2007926365
ISBN # 978-09607762-07

Manufactured in the United States of America

About the Author

Barbara Hudgins is best known as the original author and self-publisher of *New Jersey Day Trips*. This guidebook sold over 110,000 copies in several editions before she sold the rights to Rutgers University Press. She also co-authored the 10th edition put out by that press. She was the subject of a chapter in the book, *Make Money Self-Publishing* by Suzanne Thomas, as an example of a successful regional author.

Barbara's travel column, which covers both local and foreign trips, has appeared in The Madison Eagle, the Bernardsville News and other newspapers in northern New Jersey. Her day trip articles have also been featured in *Garden State Woman* and *New Jersey, Yesterday, Today & Tomorrow*. National magazines such as *Signature, Woman's World* and *Foreword* have published her free-lance pieces on a variety of subjects.

The author has lived in New York, New Mexico, Hawaii and Virginia, but has made her home in New Jersey for the past 30 years. She holds a Master's degree in Library Science and has worked at the New York Public Library, Hunter College Library and the University of Hawaii. A former English major in college, she began writing music, movie and theater reviews before gravitating to travel writing. Her two children, Lani and Robert, now grown and with families of their own, helped her to research the many destinations that appear in her books and articles.

Her background and knowledge of self-publishing give her the expertise to successfully market in the publishing world. Her experience as an author for a traditional publisher, as a self-publisher and as a freelance writer, positions her as a unique expert in all of these fields.

Acknowledgments

To Irene Rich and Carol Potter for editing help and suggesting necessary changes and to Sue Meehan for getting my footers and headers in the right place: my everlasting gratitude.

Many thanks to all the authors and publishers who allowed me to use their books as examples, or permitted me to quote from their works, including Troy Corley, Harry Pariser, Louis Hatchett and the many others.

To the reference librarians at the Bernards Township Library — thanks for the help in the research and in getting those books down from the top shelf for me. And to my daughter Lani and son-in-law Michael for kicking the computer when it wouldn't start, taking all those digital pictures on our trips and helping out in so many other ways, thanks again.

Table of Contents

Part One

Getting Started

Chapter 1

Introduction

So you've decided to write a travel guidebook! Perhaps you are a travel writer with a sheaf of articles about your trip to Australia and you feel you have a good enough angle to support a full book. Perhaps you're a travel editor who is fed up with the books coming across your desk since you feel none of them has really brought the reality of the place home. Or you could be an outdoor editor who notices there are more and more inquiries about mountain biking in your area but there is no guidebook on the subject.

Of course you may not be a writer at all. You might be a travel agent who became frustrated with the treatment of single parents by travel packagers. You might be the owner of a large Labrador who finds herself out in the cold on Cape Cod because there is not a motel in sight that will accommodate dogs. Maybe you're a volunteer guide on a travel website who is tired of giving away all your valuable insights and descriptions for free. If you've developed an audience, maybe there is a way to cash in on your work.

Travel books cover a wide variety authors and subjects. What first comes to mind is the traditional guidebook which features a mélange of descriptions, basic information and handy tips for the reader. But the travel category also includes the travel essay, which in the hands of an artist can become a meaningful adventure. The travel memoir is closely related to fiction: both need

narrative skills and a point of view. And then there is the vast
world of the how-to-do-it guides that ignore destinations altogether to concentrate on one aspect of traveling, such as packing
a suitcase or navigating around airports.

When contemplating the creation of the guidebook, the first
thing one must consider is its marketability. Ask yourself this
question: How many people will read my book? And the second
question: Where will I find this audience? Will the audience be
found in bookstores, airport gift shops, rugged-wear outfitter
retailers, gourmet food shops or at online bookstores? Many
guides can be found in more than one venue, since bookstores
have a limited amount of space. Local guides are often found
in neighborhood shops, while outdoor activity titles thrive at
Outfitter stores. The Zagat Restaurant Survey got its big start
when it appeared on the racks of New York newsstands.

Once you have an inkling of your audience, you then have
to think in terms of boundaries and general format. How will
you shape your book? How much territory will you cover? How
will the chapters flow? What will you consider important enough
to include and what will be tossed out. Will you include opinions and observations? Of course any non-fiction book has to be
researched, and you may have the beginning of your research
already on your laptop. Travel books are a combination of
personal observation, interviews with others and basic research.
It is the stitching together of all these elements that creates the
unique work.

Who will publish the guidebook?

If you are planning to send out proposals to a publisher you
have a few more steps to take. For one thing, you will need to
peruse a list of publishers that cover your field and there is a
full list of such publishers in this book. There is no sense is
submitting a proposal about kayaking in Canada to a publisher
who specializes in Florida titles. Or if you are trying for certain
big New York publishers, you will have to limit your search to
literary agents because those publishers will not accept unsolicited manuscripts.

On the other hand, there is the possibility of self-publishing since a large number of travel books belong in that category or started out that way before they blossomed into larger entities. Self-publishing now has a step-child in the form of POD publishers who dominate in numbers if not in quality. Today the stream of guidebooks comes from various rivulets.

The Accidental Travel Writer

Despite the fact that most publishers expect you to turn cartwheels before they will look at your endeavor, many travel guides were "birthed", as it were, by accident. The author never set out to be a writer, but came to the field because he found a void that needed to be filled. Many of the names we now associate with big-time series were created by happenstance. Here are some stories:

The 1930s: Duncan Hines. Hines was a traveling salesmen who criss-crossed the American hinterland as part of his job. Eating in local restaurants in many small towns was an adventure: sanitary standards were not what they are today. At the time more Americans died of restaurant food poisoning than they did from hit-and-run accidents.He began to keep a notebook of the best places he found. Since Hines' travels took him all over the country, many other salesmen asked him recommendations. He finally decided to put all his "discoveries" into a book called *Adventures in Good Eating.*

This self-published book, after national publicity, took off and formed the basis for a publishing "empire". His other travel books included *Lodging for a Night,* a vacation guide and a cookbook filled with recipes from the restaurants that he recommended. He eventually sold more than 2,000,000 of these volumes from his home over the next 19 years. He was so well-known that when Proctor & Gamble decided to enter the cake mix arena they purchased his name as a trade-mark. And so, although this early restaurant critic died and his titles went out-of-print, his name remains enshrined forever in the supermarket aisles.

(Thanks to Louis Hatchett author of *Duncan Hines: the Man Behind the Cake Mix* for this material).

The 1950s: Arthur Frommer. The Frommer series, now owned by Wiley Publishing, seems to cover every aspect of the travel world. But this stream of books all emanated from a single self-published guide. Arthur Frommer graduated from Yale Law School but entered the army during the Korean War. However, he was posted to Europe. While there, he wrote and self-published a guidebook called *The GI's Guide to Traveling in Europe* which emphasized budget travel. It sold well, and so Frommer restructured it into a book for the layman called *Europe on $5 a Day*. Published in 1957, it was considered revolutionary since previous guides had been aimed at the well-heeled traveler. Frommer's guide was invaluable to hordes of young Americans who visited Europe in the years when the American dollar really was almighty and could purchase incredible value.

Although Frommer practiced law back in the USA, he also continued to write and self-publish guidebooks. Destinations such as New York, Mexico, Hawaii, Japan and the Caribbean followed the original guide. In 1977, Frommer's trademark was sold to Simon & Schuster. In 2001 the series was bought by Wiley, but the author has kept a strong commitment to low-budget travel and to consumer advocacy. Still going strong, Frommer has his own radio show, a syndicated travel column and a magazine. Arthur's daughter, Pauline Frommer, now writes her own series of travel guidebooks and continues the family legacy. (Adapted from Wikipedia)

The 1970s: Tony and Maureen Wheeler. In 1973, a young English couple decided to record their lengthy journey across the continent from Turkey, through Iran, Afghanistan, Pakistan and India. The original book, *Across Asia on the Cheap*, was written and published in Sydney with scant money. Written with style and full of strong opinions, it sold well enough in Australia that it allowed the couple to expand it into *South-East Asia on a Shoestring*. And so the **Lonely Planet** series was born.

The early books catered to young people from Australia and Europe who followed the overland route between those two points via South-East Asia, the Indian subcontinent and the Middle East. This was becoming something of a rite of passage for young travelers and was known familiarly as the "hippie route". The new and rapidly growing market of backpackers and a guidebook company that catered heavily to this community meant that Lonely Planet's readers developed a kinship to the company.

The books' voice has changed over the years as it has entered other markets, such as Western Europe, where more competition exists. The series now caters as much to middle-class travelers as backpackers. As of 2005, the Wheelers no longer control the operation although they still own a majority of the company, and Tony Wheeler still writes a few guidebooks himself. Multiple authors and professional mapmakers now dominate the style of the publishing house. (Adapted from Wikipedia)

The 1980s: Rick Steves: Steves is another example of an accidental tourist who becomes a beacon of common sense to the traveling public. Rick became enamored of traveling through Europe after his first experience as a teenager, visiting piano factories with his father. By the age of 18, he was traveling on his own, funding his trips by giving piano lessons. In 1976, he started a business called Europe Through the Back Door (ETBD) and conducted guided tours throughout the continent.

He also gave classes in traveling to Europe at a local college. For each class he created extensive itineraries, replete with notes. He soon discovered that people were stealing these itineraries! Why not flesh out the itinerary and create a book?

The first edition of his book, *Europe Through the Back Door,* was self published in 1980. His later works were put out by a small company in New Mexico. Soon there were a number of country, city and regional guides. In the 1990's Rick's PBS travel series put his guides on the map as it were, and now Rick Steves name goes above the title. In 2001, his original publisher merged into the Avalon Travel Group.

In addition to his guidebooks, Rick has also penned six phrase books and still runs his tour company which now has a staff of 60 full-time employees. He lives and works in his hometown of Edmonds, Washington and goes off every year for a long European trip. (Adapted from the website: www.ricksteves.com)

The 1980s: The Zagat Survey: The Zagat Restaurant Survey entered the scene in 1979 and soon took New York by storm.

Up until that time, haughty restaurant critics from a few favored media could make or break a restaurant. The Zagat Survey was started by Tim and Nina Zagat, two Yale-educated lawyers who formed a circle of two hundred respondents to create a dining "club" in New York. The purpose of the club was to give ordinary people a chance to give their opinions on the places they liked to frequent.

At first, the survey was strictly a freebie for members of the club. Whether it was a deli, a watering hole for the famous, or a local eatery, when enough votes were tabbed up the place was rated. The rating system was devised by the Zagats. The tabulations were handed out and later collated and edited by the couple. What started out as a hobby was soon becoming too time-consuming and expensive, yet its popularity was unquestioned.

After several publishers turned down the concept, the Zagats went on to publish the small pocket-size guide themselves. At first they drove around New York personally stocking the newsstands and bookstores. After the guide hit the big-time, they hooked onto more professional distribution. One city led to another and soon there were Zagat Surveys out on all major cities. There are now guides for hotels, resorts and spas around the world plus a very active website. (Adapted from Wikipedia.)

As you can see from these stories, if you are the go-to person for voyagers off to the Andes, or if people keep stealing your list of the restaurants, or if friends ask you how you managed to drive your RV from Maine to Vancouver on a mere $20,000 for the year, then you are ripe for transforming yourself into a travel guru and writing a book on the subject. And certainly, if the website featuring your trip around the world is garnering multiple hits and queries from strangers, that may be the catalyst for your new book.

You may not end up as the head of a publishing empire. You may not even make a full-time living from your travel guide. What you will discover is a life fulfilled by doing what you love, even if it turns out to be on a part-time basis. (Travel writers who live on royalties and magazine assignments do not reside in fancy houses. They do sometimes linger in fancy hotels but that's because someone else is picking up the tab.) On the other hand, plenty of people make a very decent living by creating a series or combining their guidebook writing with magazine and newspaper work.

Some neophytes think that only way to enter the field is to be accepted by the big-name series editors and ascend from writing a short piece to becoming the co-author of a book that sells 50,000 copies a year. That is one way, but it is not the only way. There are hundreds of small presses, dozens of university presses, and an untold number of self-publishers whose books line the shelves of bookstores, fill the Amazon.com "river" and can be found in gift shops, wineries, RV and sports outfitting stores and museum shops near and far.

Focusing on your travel guide means first and foremost focusing on the projected audience for that book and how you plan to entertain and inform that audience. But it also entails creating a format for your text, placing boundaries on your coverage, finding a voice that mirrors the concept and a style that shows you understand the audience for whom this book was intended.

Travel writing may be an art, but putting a travel guidebook together is a craft. And because creating the guide is only half the battle, this book will also cover the areas of publishing and promotion. Hopefully your new guidebook will become a worthy contender among the many titles on the Travel Shelf

Chapter 2

What's Your Concept?

Dear Publisher:

I have always loved to travel and plan to spend the next year and a half backpacking around Southeast Asia and then on to Australia and New Zealand. I also plan to write up my travels as I go along, pointing out the interesting places.

Could you please advance me ten thousand dollars? In return you will get full rights to my diary and my adventures, which I will write as I go along and then shape into a book when I get back.

Thank you in advance.

Joe Doaks

10 Wishful Lane

Anywhere, USA

Think this book proposal is a little far-fetched? While most book proposals to travel editors and publishers are quite professional and competent, publishers do get letters from hopeful neophytes who think that all it takes is an itch to travel and a vague concept of a "book" to create an action-packed best-seller, featuring The Author as the intrepid globe-trekker, with maybe a few practical tips for lodging and eateries thrown in to assuage the buying public.

All travel guides start from the same source — that is, the facts about the place, or the cruise, or the food, or the type of traveler or whatever you are covering, just as all bread begins with some sort of flour. What you add to it, what you use to construct the whole, and how you shape it, is the nub of your book. It is what makes your book different, and hopefully, interesting enough to make the buyer reach for it rather than the offering of a competitor. If there is no competing book (and there may not be one if you have written the only guide to Podunk), then you must make the book compelling enough that a buyer will want to know all about Podunk.

First you begin with the concept. If the concept is as vague as the above letter to a publisher you're not going to get an assignment. Back in the 1860s, Mark Twain was able to talk his newspaper into shipping him off to Hawaii where he stayed a few months and sent back missives detailing his life among the savages, scoundrels and adventurers he met. But few Americans traveled far in those days and they depended on the highly embellished accounts of writers to get their dose of the exotic. Nowadays, everybody travels constantly.

The modern day travel guide has moved away from Twain. Yes, there is still a taste for armchair travel and those explorers who trek through New Guinea or Antarctica can still find an audience for their writings — if they are able to turn a phrase well and have developed a following. Start writing amusing accounts from all over the world on a popular website or a well-established newspaper, and when you've gained enough of a following, a publisher might take a chance on you.

But aside from interesting descriptions, travel guides also deliver detailed information about airlines, lodging and restaurants. They offer translations of foreign phrases, list emergency contacts, offer advice on everything from budget packages to luxury resorts, give you history lessons, culture lessons and sometimes etiquette lessons. They open new territory and track down out-of-the-way nooks, offer parenting and roommate advice and in many cases — photographs and maps to embellish the author's prose. So there's more to it than simply collecting those rollicking tales of your journeys and collating them into a book.

And now, for a few questions:

- What territory will you cover?

- If this is an outdoors book, what activity will you cover?
- If this is a how-to-do-it book, what subject will you cover?
- What are the perimeters of that territory/activity/subject?
- Is this book targeted to a general audience or one with a specific interest?
- What category will your book fall in?
- What is the specific format and organization for your book?
- How much of your own experience will you add to the mix?
- What voice will you use?
- How do you plan your basic research?
- If you are proposing a book to a series publisher, how well can you adopt your style into their pre-set format?
- What are your credentials for this particular book?

Well, you might say, I'm not going to look for a publisher! I'm going to self-publish. But whether you self-publish the traditional way (that is type-set, print and distribute through a wholesaler) the POD way (we'll get into that later) or simply offer an e-book download straight from your website, you are still going to face the above basic questions if your work is going to coalesce into anything resembling a book. So let's begin at the beginning.

The Concept alone may not be enough but you have a start with one!

For many years I operated as the Woodmont Press, the publisher of *New Jersey Day Trips*. My "office" was a tiny post office box in a one-time rural area called Green Village, New Jersey. In this box I would discover a book proposal every once in a while, although I had taken pains to keep my publishing name out of *Literary Market Place* or anywhere else a potential author might find it. Of the proposals sent, most were much too limited for any market. However, I received one that was very well thought out, gave a summary of the potential market for the book and a summary of the two authors' backgrounds. It was for a biking guide to

New Jersey. I replied that I was not interested in biking books but given their background (one of the authors was a graphics designer) their expertise (they were editors of a biking newsletter) and their understanding of the market they might consider self-publishing the guide. They did, and it sold at a reasonable clip for many, many years.

The other proposal with possibilities came in the form of a simple query letter. A mid-level executive from Summit, NJ enjoyed weekending in New York with his family. He wanted to do a book on The New York Weekend from the point of view of a suburbanite. Here, at last, was a viable idea. Even though I had sworn an oath never to do a New York book, I was still a little intrigued. After all, he had the money to sojourn in Manhattan and probably had sophisticated taste. I, on the other hand, had contacts with a local distributor and could get the book into stores in New Jersey, Westchester and Long Island, a very sizeable market. So I called him.

"How do you plan to approach this book?" I asked. "Are you going to do it by neighborhood? Are you going to do it by type of attraction? Are you going to include other boroughs such as Brooklyn and the Bronx? Will you include a range of different priced restaurants?"

"Gee, I don't know," he answered. "I thought you figured out all that stuff."

No, folks, the publisher doesn't figure out that stuff! The writer does that. Even series with pre-set formats like Lonely Planet or Frommer's or Fodor's all started out with an author (or two) who created the format, decided on the perceived audience and developed the voice to talk to that audience. In the case of my mid-level executive, he had envisioned his potential audience (suburbanites who weekend in the city) but nothing beyond that. Of course without any credentials or a plan on his part, we never went any further with the project.

If my author had sent me a detailed book proposal I would have known what his boundaries were: (Manhattan only or all five boroughs?) and how deeply he would delve into the subject (a short history of the geography and politics of the city or a paean to its diversity?). He would have detailed the organization (would he go neighborhood-by- neighborhood or separate restaurants, museum and theaters into different chapters?). I would know the voice he would use and what slant he will take from the tenor of his proposal and the writing samples he would supply. He would offer a Table of Contents, the approximate length of his book and whether he planned one index or more than one.

So you see, the author has to approach the publisher with a detailed plan of what he has to offer. What's more, in a majority of cases, the author also supplies the pictures and writes the captions for them, writes the index, compiles the glossary, and if maps are needed, he offers the source map with markings for the publisher or is expected to create the maps himself.

Needless to say, the self-publisher has to do all this anyway — including the pictures, maps and index — or has to pay for stock photos, professional indexing and typesetting and then the printing of the book. Then, again he might choose to learn various book design programs and hack through the job himself. And, in the end, self-publishers have to spend gobs of time promoting the book.

Finding a concept

So, how does one begin? Whether you are considering a book proposal to a publisher or proposing to do it yourself, here are some possibilities for your concept:

- Open a new territory
- Open a new category
- Create a new slant
- Find a new audience
- Find a new niche
- Create a new format
- Mix two categories in a new way
- Do a better job than the other books on the market!

Let's say you were flipping through some recent guidebooks and noticed that *Maui Revealed* has a chapter on weddings and wedding sites. You also remember that *The Unofficial Guide to Disney World* has a section on weddings. So, how many people are getting married at a travel destination where they and their guests can combine nuptials, sightseeing, swimming, snorkeling and honeymoon all in one happy week? There always seems to be an article on this subject in bridal magazines and newspaper inserts you find on Sundays. So maybe there's a book possibility on this subject.

Interestingly, no sooner had I written these words, than I discovered a book called *100 Best U.S. Wedding Destinations* which came out in 2006. There are a few similar titles on the market, so others have already noticed the trend. But this is only one of many angles that can be combined with the travel market to create a new book. The selling point of such a book would be that it could be marketed through bridal shops and the online bridal venues. Anytime a publisher can avoid the dreaded book-store return factor, he will become more interested in a book. (See the section on Publishing to learn about book returns).

Then there are all the personal experience authors who have either trekked to rarely- seen destinations or simply journaled their cross-country experiences on their website. While the adventurous travel book has long been the monopoly of well-known trekkers, or those that get an assignment from a prestigious magazine, the personal travel memoir has gained acceptance through the Internet. Expect more and more families to write up their hilarious misadventures in their RVs or SUVs and show them freely on a website. Sooner or later, the self- publishing bug will bite a few of them. There are already a number of RV road trip books that have been self-published (I mention two of them in this book) but each one has a different angle.

Sometimes, when a travel writer has a really popular website that is full of useful links and sustained by ads, a publisher or co-author will approach him with a book in mind. This happened to Johnny Jet (or to his real-life alter ego) who now has a book out. The co-author took care of all the details at the publishing end and put Johnny's information into book form.

But most travel writers come up with their idea when they notice a gap in the coverage of some travel subject — this might be a destination that has been overlooked, a niche for a specialized audience, a new mode of transportation, an expertise that nobody knew existed, or simply a plethora of bed and breakfasts in the local area that the author thinks is worthy of notice.

For many authors, it is simply a matter of looking at the same territory from a new angle or trying a different organizational format. For instance, when I first published *New Jersey Day Trips* back in the 1980s, all previous material had been done from the geographical angle — with sections of this small state divided into northeast, northwest, the Jersey shore and so forth. The few books available, and later the official state guide, all approached New Jersey from that perspective with names (such as Skylands and Gateway) given to each area.

I chose to divide my book by subject. So my chapters consisted of quaint towns, restored villages, museums, zoos, nature centers, amusement parks, gardens and so on, with an extra chapter for miscellaneous trips that didn't seem to fit in anywhere else.

At the time, a local wholesaler told me the book would never sell since all books about New Jersey must be written from the geographical angle. Guess what? My title sold for 18 years and over 110,000 copies before I handed it over to Rutgers University Press (where it still sells well). Let me add that three other New Jersey books have copied my general format. So there are no hard and fast rules that say a travel book must be done in a certain format. You have to choose the one you feel best fits your style and your material.

Certainly, some of the most popular series around began life because a new author looked at an old territory in a different way. And the number of travel editors that publish new titles leads me to believe that they must itch for a fresh approach when they see so many copycat titles come over their desk.

As for the big travel publishers — they not only rush to stake out new territories they also widen or narrow the scope of the territories they have already "settled". So Rick Steves not only has *Paris*, he has *Paris by Day and Paris by Night*, to say nothing of his volumes on *France* plus *France, and the Netherlands.* Publishers are also constantly on the lookout for a new audience or a new angle, so Fodor's has both a *Gold Guide to New York* and a *Guide to New York with Kids* while Frommer's has a *Guide to Las Vegas* and an *Irreverent Guide to Las Vegas*.

New combinations are another way to crack the market. You can combine a memoir of your RV trip across country with a "how to" on the pesky details of such a journey. You can combine a how-to on traveling with children with a specific destination such as London. You can combine a book targeted at art lovers with a destination such as Paris to create the Art Lover's Guide to Paris. In the chapters on categories, audience, boundaries and format, I will go over these ideas in detail. But here are the most common concepts:

Open a New Territory: One year, I talked to a woman who had written the first book on Costa Rica. This was back in the 1980s. It's not that other guidebooks hadn't covered Costa Rica as part of Central America; it was that nobody had devoted an entire book to this particular country before. When Eastern Europe opened up to tourism and later the Soviet Union broke up, travel publishers rushed in like gold prospectors to the Yukon.

Narrow a Look at a "Discovered" Destination: Let's say you're in the Virgin Islands and you notice that all the guidebooks around seem to cover both the British and the American Virgins, although the large American islands get more space. At the same time you notice that there are many long-term visitors, that condos and townhouses abound and many travelers come for at least a two-week stay. Why not write a book aimed at long- term visitors to St. Thomas, with daytrips to the other islands included, but concentrate on what to do on an extended stay?

Use a New Format: When Dave and Jennifer Marx decided to broach Disney World, there were a number of popular books on the subject that were already out there. The first was the Official Guide by Steven Birnbaum followed by the immensely popular Unofficial Guide. So one thing this couple did was to create a new format. Although most professionals will tell you not to fool around with size and shapes, they came up with a book that was a combination of guidebook, a journal, plus a daybook that had pockets to hold tickets and papers. It took several years and plenty of heavy marketing, but their *Passporter Guide to Disney World* is currently the one of the best-selling guides to that Florida destination. So taking a new tack does work! For most travel books, however, a new format simply means organizing the chapters in a new and interesting way.

Conquer a problem in a new way: "How-to" travel books are an expanding niche. There is always a new way to do almost anything and travelers are most inventive. This includes such disparate subjects as "how to invest so that you can travel the world" or "how to survive on a wilderness hike". You can solve an old problem in a new way (how to interest teenagers in traveling with their parents) or try to solve a new problem (long lines at airports, what to put in your carry-on, changes in travel restrictions).

Create a New Destination Interest: Everyone has done a book on wineries in the obvious regions, and the best spas, and the golf courses. But there are always weird places, or caves and caverns, or butterfly and bug centers that can be discovered. People are forever finding destinations of interest that have a common bond. Some of these books sell better than others, but if *The Sopranos* are hot, then a guidebook to all the spots featured in the hit HBO series will sell for a few years. And if "spiritual tours" are attracting customers, can a guide to spiritual places be far behind?

Once you are sure of your concept, you now have to decide where your book would fit in the imaginary travel bookshelf — in other words: what's your category?

Chapter 3

What's Your Category?

Travel books are usually sorted by categories in the bookstore. It's fairly simple to find geographical destination books since they are grouped together under Travel or Foreign Travel. Regional travel books may be grouped under the travel section or in a separate section called "Local Interest". Outdoor recreational books (those devoted to biking, hiking and fishing) are often found in a section called "Outdoors". Much depends on the size of the bookstore and the taste of the owner or manager.

The following categories are meant to help you in constructing your guidebook. They are offered simply to help you define your book in terms of seeing it as a marketable property and how it would fit into a certain shelf in a bookstore. They are not necessarily the category that would go on the back cover of your book nor do they particularly coincide with BISAC categories which I'll get into later. The sub-categories are put here to help you discern where your book stands in relation to your audience.

The Destination Guide

The most common and most popular type of guidebook is the destination guide. It doesn't matter if the destination is as large as China or as tiny as Disney World or Monaco: such guides give a roundup of everything there is to see and do within the circumference of the target area. There will be differences in tone and style, and in what is included, depending on the perceived audience for the book — but the general destination guide tries to pack in as much information as possible between the book's covers

There is usually a section for foreigners that explains the basic facts, a glossary, and a section on history, icons aplenty, advice and tips, and of course a rundown on hotels, restaurants, sightseeing, sporting activities and nightclubs along with optional chapters for specific groups like families with kids or senior citizens. This meal is followed by a dessert of calendar events, multiple indexes and appendixes. It's no wonder that most are written by at least two authors with several helpers who provide research, maps and other support services.

Guidebooks that are written for a particular niche audience, (such as the Art Lover's Guide to London or the Black Guide to New Orleans) I have put under the sub-categories of Special Interest and Special Audience. The general destination guidebook is dominated by a few names: Fodor's, Frommer's, Lonely Planet and some others. The main difference in these destination guides is the format (each of the above named publishers has a distinct format) and the tone (some will appeal to a younger crowd, some to a business crowd).

This doesn't mean that there is no room for newcomers. While smaller publishers tend to concentrate on regional guides, niche audience books, how-to-do-it guides or personal experience tales, there are always a few who storm the gates of the citadel and are successful.

The Eclectic Destination Guide

There's a bestselling book by Patricia Shultz called *1000 Places to See Before You Die* which doesn't fit into any of the usual categories. This is an example of taking an old magazine article idea and expanding it to the max. There are hundreds of articles every year on such topics as: "The Ten Best Spots in Las Vegas" and "Twelve Places You Should Not Miss in Tuscany". By expanding this concept to include the whole world, Schultz has created a work that can please everyone without getting mired down into details. Since she covers countries all over the globe she doesn't have to waste time on the manners and mores of each venue except in terms of the particular attraction.

This book is a best seller with over a million copies sold! And lots of travel writers are probably kicking themselves that they didn't think of the idea first. Although most of the destinations are too expensive for the average traveler, the title appeals to the retiree — and with Baby Boomers reaching sixty, scads of them will be retiring.

The Themed Destination Guide (see also Specific audience)

I'm not talking about the personal experience anthology which goes under the literary travel/armchair adventure category and resembles an anthology of short stories. The themed guide covers destinations that may be all over the map but they have one thing in common — an attraction that appeals to a specific audience. Sometimes these sell well, sometimes they are found only in special bookstores. Take for instance a book about factory tours I noticed at the gift shop at the Crayola Factory in Pennsylvania. I probably would not have noticed it in a regular bookstore because it might be shelved in any number of places. However, here it stood out.

Themed guides can be limited to a small geographical area in which case they might be shelved with regional books (e.g. *Amusement Parks of New Jersey*) or they may cover a wider swath (*Amusement Park Guide to the USA*). Themed guides do not sell as well as destination guides — at least in bookstores. But they have their adherents and can be sold in bulk to interested organizations, specialized catalogs and the Internet.

Some themed destinations popular at the moment are:

- Weird, Wacky, Houses
- Roadside Curiosities
- 100 Best Spas
- Ranch Vacations
- Villa Vacations across the World

The Regional guide

Regional guides come in all shapes and sizes and often cross over into other areas such as food and wine or outdoor recreation. The regional guide can encompass a small city, a cultural area or a state. Most regional guides are written for local residents, potential residents and long term visitors. They may include some history and culture, but they rarely spend time advising foreign visitors on money exchange, kilometers or embassies.

Subdivisions include recreational activities (50 hikes in Vermont) daytrip and weekend guides (Away For the Weekend, 52 Weekend series) restaurant reviews (The Zagat Survey) shopping guides, thematic guides (Historic Sites of Mississippi) and any number of other possibilities.

There are plenty of small and medium-size publishers as well as hundreds of self-publishers that put out regional travel guides as well as regional cookbooks, calendars, and histories. Regional guides do not always sell in the same large numbers as destination guides, but they usually sell at a steady clip. Sales of 3000 copies a year are not unusual for an individual title especially if it is confined to a specific activity such as hiking or fishing. However, many small publishers have a stable of books about hiking or fishing in the region which together add up to a respectable sales number. Most regional publishers do not require an author to be represented by a literary agent. On the other hand, they publish a limited number of titles per year, so there's heavy competition for a slot in the catalog.

The Regional Outdoor/ Regional Special Audience Book

Regional books are often coupled with outdoor themes (60 Hikes in Colorado, Fly-fishing in Montana) or they can be coupled with food and wine/history (The Best Historic Hotels in Georgia) or are "kid" oriented. Such books may give some background on the state or country or the author may choose to ignore the "orientation" chapter and concentrate only on what is important to the local reader. A book about Philadelphia for children was written primarily for people who live in and around that town. Directions were given from the heart of the city, mass transportation stations were included and there was no attempt to translate money or mileage into any other language or system.

Orientation chapters (or a page or two) in such books are given over to a general overview of the city or region and what it holds for the special interest of the reader. Here is also where information is given on how the book is set up and whatever special icons will be used within the text. Along these lines, a dog-lover's guide to Seattle would concentrate on explaining how the book is constructed, what the icons stand for, and would include a general chapter on the care of dogs in a large city.

Destination Outdoors

Most outdoor books are basically regional in that the publisher assumes that the reader lives in the area, and all directions are given from some mythical point in the center of the area. But there are also destination outdoor-activity guides like biking in southern France. And since outdoor books about a region may appeal to visitors as well as residents it is necessary to clue in everyone as to local laws. Tourists to Maine can find shelves of books on fishing, hunting, walking and hiking in the Pine Tree state both in bookstores and general stores. Most outdoor/recreation guides have sub-categories that are put on the back cover, so you might find: Recreation/hiking or Travel/Europe/hiking or Fishing/Minnesota on any of these.

Outdoor/Action/Adventure Travel

There is also a "how-to" style of action/outdoor travel book that concentrates primarily on the details of what to wear, how to pack your backpack, what roads to take rather than descriptions of specific trails. Specific destinations may be included as part of the anecdotal section of the book, but the main thrust is how to accomplish the task. Such titles as *How to Shit in the Woods* and *How to Snowshoe through the Mountains* along with basic survival guides will be found here.

The more adventurous the travel (mountain climbing, rappelling, kayaking) the more details the author has to give on the specifics both of the activity and the region where it is taking place. Maps are usually, but not always, an integral part of such a book.

Outdoor books sell well in non-bookstore venues such as Sports and Outfitting stores and in the General Store of a sport-friendly tourist location. The armchair adventure book is a separate category reserved for people who want to read about other people's dazzling deeds but do not want to replicate these adventures themselves.

The Special Audience Travel Guide

By special audience I refer to people who are part of a group by reason of their age, race, religion, sexual orientation or physical abilities. In other words, the very people one cannot legally discriminate against when offering apartment rentals. However, there is no law that says you cannot write a book which would appeal to any of these particular groups. Here are some categories:

Gay and Lesbian Guides: These concentrate on hotels, restaurants, bars and clubs where one can find common-minded folk at a specific destination such as a city or a country. However, there is usually a chapter or two on the cultural tone of the place and the general scene. Many destination travel guides have a special chapter devoted to this audience.

Handicapped Traveler Guides: Although most guidebooks nowadays include handicapped icons to show that a particular place has easy access and toilets designed for the handicapped, authors rarely check out that particular angle. A guide written specifically for the handicapped (and this may include the blind, deaf and otherwise impaired), would be particularly sensitive to the needs of this group. Handicapped or barrier-free guides are often combined with a destination although there are many general works on the subject.

Cultural & Ethnic Travel: Religious, racial and ethnic travelers may be searching for their roots or for something that relates emotionally to them. Devout Catholics visiting Rome will be looking for different things than an art lover viewing the Sistine

Chapel. So a single author can write two books: *Rome for the Catholic Traveler* and *The Architectural Wonders of Rome* and use the same basic research for both. What differs is the emphasis, the tone and the point of view that is directed to two different audiences. One is written for the "special audience" (members of a particular religion) the other for the special interest audience (people who like art and architecture).

Members of ethnic and cultural groups may also be looking for restaurants that cater to their taste or dietary restrictions and sections of town where they might feel more at home. Here are some typical titles earmarked for a specific ethic or religious group: *Poland's Jewish Landmarks, Guide to Black Washington,* and *Guide to Black New York* (all published by Hippocrene Books). In looking for ethnic subjects, it is important that you know the extent of your possible audience. In other words, Jewish Landmarks of Mongolia or a Black Guide to Iceland would be pretty slim books with zero marketability.

Special Interest Travel

This is a large category that includes Food and Wine, Literary Trails, Historic Places Travel (such as following in the footsteps of Hemingway, or Robert E. Lee) and any number of hobbies. One can always come up with a new category just as one can "open up" a new geographical territory.

Food and Wine: Often found in a special section of the bookstore, these guides include:

Restaurant reviews: The *Zagat Restaurant Survey* series and others like them concentrate on restaurants within a defined geographical area. Each venue is reviewed either by an individual food guru or by a group of homegrown critics who send in their comments which are thereupon transmuted by an editor.

The Chef's Special: Here some intrepid soul runs around and collects recipes from the best-known restaurants in New Orleans or the Maine coast. This person has to know how to cook, how to write recipes, and how to coax secrets from the top chefs. However the author can add plenty of history and local color to the mix. Often accompanied by photographs, these books tend to be pricey and can be found in gourmet stores as well as bookstores.

Winery guides: Many more of these are sold in wineries than in bookstores. Whether the locale is the Middle Atlantic States, the Napa and Sonoma Valley, Australia or France, such books strike a balance between advice for discerning drinkers and a description of particular wineries, their histories and their tours.

Food Emporiums: A new and growing sub-category that includes regional farmer's markets, gourmet stores, food festivals and outings that are food-related. Generally found in the regional section of bookstores and in country stores as well as some gourmet and kitchen-stuff stores.

The Historical/Literary/Biographical Tour

You will always find such titles in the gift shops of historical sites and restored homes, as well as in general bookstores.

Historical: Very often this is a step-by-step reenactment of a historical journey such as Lewis & Clark's expedition, or Civil War battles. These guides sometimes, but not always include modern day hotels and restaurants as stopovers.

Biographical: Whether it's the childhood homes of presidents and military leaders or their graveyards, this is a sub-category ready to be mined. Usually done in anthology style (if it includes several different people), these books can also be written as a personal road guide or in chronological order if you are tracking a single famous person.

Literary: Discovering the literary haunts of famous writers such as Hemingway or Fitzgerald, or the homes they lived in, or their graves, or all three is the focus of this type of guide. These guides are often accompanied by literary analysis plus some biography.

Fictional: Tracking down fictional haunts such as Tara, or the real Scotland Yard that appears in so many mysteries is fun to some. The English countryside is dotted with mansions that could fill in for the great estates that dominate the British classics. Settings of movie and TV classics show up in this field also.

The self-fulfillment/soul-searching/holistic/mystical tour

Here you will find:
- Actual religious venues such as monasteries and convents where you can stay overnight.
- "Sacred" places such as ashrams, Native American lodges, and sites for pilgrimages for any and all religious groups.
- Natural areas where the traveler becomes "one with nature"
- Health resorts and retreats where one can find renewal.
- Finding oneself through travel — a combination of self-fulfillment and travel guide.

Hobbies and other special interests:

Whether we're talking about old standbys like art and architecture, golf courses, and gardens or the latest fad, guides for special interests run the gamut from simple directories to full-fledged guides. They can be combined with a destination (The art and architecture of Rome) or be a local or regional guide (A green guide: the Gardens of Virginia and Maryland). There is a guide to writer's conferences for aspiring authors and a compilation of the best railroad trips in the world for those who love to go by track. Anyone with a fervent interest in theater-going, flea markets or whatever can combine that with a specific destination and create a new book.

There are also romantic destinations — a small slice of the travel guide pie. These books include such titles as *Best Places to Kiss*, wedding destination guides and compilations of romantic inns and hotels.

Other Segments

College students, families with kids, budget travelers, luxury travelers, single women, business travelers, and senior citizens/

retirees all have travel books aimed specifically at them. The budget traveler, whether a college student or not, has been a prime consumer of travel guides ever since *Europe on 5 Dollars a Day* was published. Whether it's Cheap Eats, Cheap Sleeps, the Let's Go series, or the many how-to books on traveling for free or low cost, this is a category that can be sliced and diced six ways to Sunday.

The retiree market is getting bigger every day as Baby Boomers begin to cash in their pension checks. For many this is a luxury market, but others are looking for interesting long-term destinations that are not overly expensive. Baby Boomers are also taking up a larger portion of the RV market. Families with kids are a huge market and regional books that emphasize trips in and around home base do well, as do mild activity books such as biking with kids. Frommer's has an Irreverent Guide series that offers a flip, sophisticated tone that is geared to the twenty to forty-something set.

Road Guides

Directory style: The best known road guides were started by companies associated with the automobile: Michelin Tires, Mobil Oil, and AAA. These companies were interested in getting people to get out on the road. Their most important function was to identify decent hotels and motels along the way. For no particular reason, these guides used an alphabetical format within a stated territory and no index, although that format has changed over the years.

Road Trip Style: Road guides do not have to be done in alphabetical style. A book such as *On the I-75* begins outside of Chicago and ends up in Florida and then goes back up again. Road trips can be a specific listing of what your find on the road or morph into a travel journal or memoir.

Road Guide –essay or journal style: These can range from literary works such as John Steinbeck's *Travels with Charlie* to the journals of anyone who has set out from home in search of himself or the back roads of a country. They are often cross-over works, so a book about traveling in an RV with children could go under Travel/Children or Travel/RV –both would be sub-categories. If the content of the book concentrates on the musings and observations of the author about the random towns he encounters, then this road guide would go under Travel/Essays.

A book called *Discover America Diaries* by Priscilla Rhodes is typical of the memoir/essay road guide in that it follows a trip from the northeast to the northwest in a truck-pulled trailer. It is based on a website that sent postcards to school classes.

Travel/ Memoir/Essay

Authors like to write memoirs because it gives them a chance to indulge their literary expression while bypassing the drudgery of researching factual material. Sometimes the public will take to a travel memoir in a big way and a few of these reach the best-seller lists. In a typical travel memoir, the author records his personal reactions to a particular place, adds wonderful descriptive passages of cities or mountains and offers insight into the culture of the people. The humorous memoir (basically a retelling of misadventures along a certain route) is also popular. The travel essay may be personal but it concentrates more on reflections and a thematic idea rather than personal reaction alone. Many books contain both styles. Recently publishers have been receptive to the year-long destination memoir, whether it takes place in Provence or Tuscany.

Armchair Adventure

Back in the 19th century, almost anyone who ventured beyond the confines of the civilized world could publish a book about his travels which would be scooped up avidly by an adoring public. I suppose the original armchair travel book was the journal of Marco Polo back in the 13th century.

Since so many more places are accessible nowadays, and since people can see videos of almost any corner of the world, armchair travel usually consists of personal experiences of very harrowing or inaccessible places or meeting with inaccessible people. So anyone who spends a year dog-sledding with Eskimos or living with headhunters in Borneo has a book in him. A well-honed style helps in getting such a book accepted by a name publisher.

Anthology Travel Stories

Anthologies based on personal travel "adventures" often use the personal memoir style and are written by a gaggle of writers and later woven together by an editor. Anthology travel is a good place for the unpublished writer to find his way into print. These compilations follow the *Chicken Soup for the Soul* model in that they are a collection of different types of tales with an omnipotent editor deciding where to place each piece. The stories can be threaded together by a particular theme (humorous mishaps, dangerous assignments) or a particular destination.

For instance, the publisher, Traveler's Tales, will pay a small sum for those articles they pick for their personal tale series. But they also have a space on their website for selections that go into their online story section. Recently a new publisher asked online for contributions from backpackers for personal stories for a book called *Italy from a Backpack*. The Internet is fast becoming the place for editors of anthology compilations to find writers.

The How-to-Do-It Travel Guide

The How-to-Do-It book covers a wide area. One is what I call the technical "how-to", which is usually written by an expert specialist or an insider. Whether it's the travel editor who decides to divulge the secrets of upgrading hotel rooms and airline seats, or the flight attendant who writes a book on packing light for air travel, or the travel agent who is going to teach you how to become a home-based agent, veterans of travel occupations all feel they have a book to share.

The main thrust of this how-to-do-it is not the trip itself, but how to achieve the trip in the most successful or perhaps the cheapest manner. The book usually answers a specific question such as: how do you travel around the world for a year on $20,000, or how do you get the best comps in Las Vegas, or how do you get upgraded seats on airlines or upgraded rooms in hotels?

The problem with most of these books is that the topic may be easily covered in one long article. How does one flesh out the rest of the book? Sometimes the author simply writes a smaller book and publishes it using Print-on-Demand. The more common method is to use anecdotes from various trips to flesh out the story, or to expand the concept by bringing in allied subjects. So the suitcase packing book ends up with chapters on wardrobe selection, important documents, health, safety, weather and checklists galore.

Then there are the business-oriented travel books that are meant for men and women who are traveling for corporations. These are basically etiquette books for Americans abroad (especially women) in regard to foreign customs. They may sometimes be found in the Business section of a bookstore rather than the Travel. Typical titles are: Etiquette for Foreigners in Japan/How to Travel without Stepping on Toes/The Business Woman's Travel Companion and so forth.

Personal Experience: How-to plus Memoir

The personal experience "how-to" is often loaded with stories and anecdotes of how we did it and you can too. If the author has a good writing background, he or she will probably add stories that include other tourists as well. The personal experience "how to" should always be enhanced with factual information the reader can use. For instance, if you found that in traveling in an RV, certain rest-stops or certain roadside food chains have particularly good coffee, or that certain motel chains discourage RV travelers, such material that should be noted. Typical personal experience titles would be: The RV Family Robinson/ Cruising with Kids/ How to be a Happy Camper/ How I Kayaked around the World. The how-to can always be combined with a destination book that includes traditional travel information (what to see, when to see it) so that you end up with a book like Let's Take the Kids to Paris.

The Travel Pictorial

The photography book about foreign places isn't a true travel book at all. In fact, it is as likely to be found in the art and photography section of a bookstore as in the travel or regional. Very often these books are subject centered and might be titled *The Great Fountains of Rome* or *The World's Best Golf Courses*. Others might simply be called *Views of Scotland* or *Scenic Vermont*. These are gift or coffee table books and don't really fit into the travel guide category.

However, publishers of straight travel guides often do a pictorial series that parallel their other lines. Because color photographs are expensive to reproduce and require special paper, these books have high price tags. Sometimes you can earn your credentials by writing the captions and fillers between the photographs in a pictorial travel book if you have the expertise and the photographer simply hates to write. Or, if you are the established author of The *Travel Guide to Vermont*, you might get an assignment to fill in the blanks for the same publisher's photography series.

Travelers Aids

There is a whole field of traveler's aids: language dictionaries, money converters, and directories. A dictionary of common phrases or a directory of hospitals, consulates, and American Express offices, can be a book in itself. Often these aids are published in the form of mini-books of no more than 32 or 64 pages and are sold at airport gift shops and over the Internet. They are designed to fit into a pocket or pocketbook and are used for quick reference. They are not true guidebooks but are often put out by travel publishers as a mini-version of the full guidebook at a cheaper price.

What Are BISAC Codes?

These are categories designated by the Book Study Council and can be found at www.bisg.org. There you will find categories and subcategories. A code accompanies the main category selection. The code number usually does not appear on the book itself, but will be used by publishers when dealing with whole-salers such as Baker & Taylor and Ingram. If you have a publisher, he will take care of it.

Some publishers also put a category on the back cover to help bookstore clerks shelve the book in its proper place. However, I notice they do not use the long or unwieldy designations offered by BISAC, but often revert to the general designation of "Travel". Publishers are given the choice of category. Here is an example

Major category: Travel

Sub categories: Travel/Europe/France
Travel/Caribbean
Travel/South America

Major Category: Sports/Recreation

Sub-category: Sports/Recreation/Hiking

The BISAC categories are based on the publisher's subjective concept of what the book is about. The same book may be cate-gorized in several ways, which is great when you are choosing categories for online bookstores like Amazon or bn.com. There, the same book can show up under a number of keywords.

Positioning Yourself within a Category

Once you know your category you should start to think about positioning your book. Whether you are preparing a book proposal for a travel publisher or self-publishing your work, you must consider this: where does your book stand in the spectrum of books on the subject? Does it encompass more or less than other books that cover the same territory? Does it open up new territory, and if so, where would it fit on the shelf in a bookstore? This is why the authors' guidelines from publishing companies ask you to list competing books and to state how your book differs from those already on the market.

Of course if you're the only game in town, you have it made. The author who wrote the first guidebook to Costa Rica had the field to herself for a few years. But once a travel destination becomes popular, Fodor's, Frommer's and a whole slew of others are sure to widen the path to that prize which the first travel writer hacked out for herself.

Guides such as The Rough Guide Series discovered new territory by catering to the post-hippie generation that was searching for a closer look at the people and the land of other countries. Probably the biggest swath in travel writing today is given over to distinct types of travelers — gay & lesbian, single parents, handicapped travelers, senior citizens, solo travelers, and other groups.

In the regional guide area, the paths seem to be narrowing — more and more books come out on smaller slices of the regional pie. Bike riding in northern Vermont, kayaking in southern Connecticut, fly-fishing in Missouri, and ten scenic rides around Albuquerque are typical titles. In such cases, the number of sales may be limited, but there will always be sales and they will be steady. Outdoor activity books, such as mountain biking, kayaking, canoeing and hiking are of ever growing interest.

While the outdoor travel book section has been burgeoning for almost twenty years, the personal journey, the holistic healing journey, the travel to mystic places and the "woman finding herself" travel book has blossomed only recently. For many years there was a stigma against an account of a trip that was "too personal". However personal accounts are more acceptable now — primarily because of the Internet where daily dairies in the form of a blog are quite the thing.

When it comes to positioning, there are always niches within niches. The "Let's Go" series is written specifically for college students (and written by college students). However, when my daughter went to France for her junior year of college and I bought her a copy, the book seemed geared primarily for the summer student traveler, not the student who would be staying on the continent for an extended stay. A year later, I found a book written for "Junior Year Abroad" students but this one was simply a list of which schools ran what programs and how to register for the programs. Another book for Americans abroad was geared toward workers who lived overseas and while it gave some practical advice about money, banking, and health services, it was written specifically for employees, not students.

So there was obviously a niche open for a guidebook for

American students living and studying abroad, one that would include both sites to see, places to shop, how to travel by mass transportation, what to do in emergencies, how to live cheaply, how much foreign language you need, and perhaps an interview with the leading education abroad services for important tips. Within the last five years, several books have appeared to fill that niche. So when a need appears, it will be filled sooner or later. It's up to the nimble author to find that niche first.

Look for your imaginary position: Go to a local library. Go to a large chain bookstore such as Barnes & Noble or Borders. Go to an independent bookstore (if you can find one in your area). Check museum stores, nature center bookstores, adventure outfitting stores. See how they have their books arranged on their shelves. Check the category listing on the back cover of the book (usually upper left or right hand corner).

Where would your book fit in among the others? If you have a specific destination, how does your approach differ from the others? Positioning is relating to a new and untapped audience, opening a new territory, creating a new combination (travel and odd architecture/ecotourism and cruising) or anything else that puts your book in a unique position so that it covers something the competing books do not. Maybe you simply have the only up-to-date guide to Patagonia because the last one was written in 1992. If your work fills a need that has been ignored by the competition, then it has a good chance of finding its place on the travel bookshelf. So know your category, and know your niche and understand the importance of finding your audience.

Chapter 4

Finding Your Audience

Everything you envision, your concept, your category, your boundaries, your format, all circle around one basic question: Who and where is your audience? What can your book offer to that audience that differs from the books currently on the market? Let's say you set out to do a book about Paris. Here are some possible questions from potential customers:

- How do I see Paris cheaply?
- How do I see Paris quickly?
- How do I make my friends envious by staying at the best hotel in Paris?
- How do I stay at a good hotel but pay budget prices?
- How do I meet a guy/girl in Paris?
- How do I meet other people like me? (I'm young, or gay, or old, or arty)
- How do I get into the best restaurants without looking like a rube?
- How do I find a restaurant where the locals eat?
- How do I stay away from other tourists and look like a native?
- How do I see everything with my disability?
- How do I make them understand what I'm saying?
- Should I spend my time going to museums or to shops?

And the "I" person here is not you, the author, but the customer, the final reader. He or she is interested in what you have to say only insofar as it pertains to his or her likes and dislikes. If you are contemplating a book with a specific audience or interest, such as *The Best Wedding Sites*, or *The Black Guide to New Orleans* you know exactly who your audience is — and the publisher's main job is to find those special outlets, either in brick and mortar stores or online retailers, where that audience can be reached.

But assuming your book is not that specific, there is still an optimum audience that would be interested. Whether you realize it or not, your book is probably aimed at budget travelers (who may be young or old) adventurous travelers (who may be young or middle-aged) well-to-do travelers (or people who like to go First Class when they travel) single women, single men, senior citizens who have time to spare, business people who have no time, families with children, families with senior parents, people who love foreign places, people who like to stay with the familiar, or any combination of the above.

The wider the circle of these potential customers the more possibility you have for higher sales. On the other hand, if you try to please everybody you often end up pleasing nobody. And the next question is: Aren't most of the reader's questions already answered by books currently on the market? What does your book bring to the reader?

Defining the audience for your book and positioning your book alongside the competitive titles is all important for your success. You might consider what trends are currently in vogue among other publishers. For instance, is there really an appetite among readers for first-hand stories from travelers? From the number of online publishers who are looking for short pieces from traveling vagabonds, one would think so.

On the other hand, if everybody else is doing the short length traveler's tale, or the all-inclusive guidebook, maybe you should concentrate on something different. Cultural tours, cooking tours — certainly somebody could do a directory of all those hands-on tours that seem so popular.

Pinpointing your audience: Even within the specific category and general boundaries, every guidebook has some sort of angle that differentiates it from the others in the field. It may cover a wider or smaller geographical area (i.e. there is a book called "Wineries of Long Island" and one called "Wineries of the Tri-State Area" and one called "Wineries along the Northeast coastline"). And those differences have everything to do with the perceived audience.

Not only is a wider area covered in the last book listed, but also the target audience for that book is specifically people who travel by car (and who like wine of course). Whereas the first book mentioned would appeal primarily to residents of Long Island and New York City, and the second to NYC and suburban residents who like to take trips, the third would appeal to travelers as well as residents. In other words, various travel writers not only cover a smaller or larger parcel of ground, but they can also cover the same ground from different audience viewpoints.

Your hook, your angle, even your voice depends very much on the audience you are writing for, and the amount of expertise you yourself possess. If you are someone who likes to visit wineries, you will notice immediately that there is no guidebook to the wineries of Podunk. There may be a good reason for this. Maybe there are only two wineries in Podunk and perhaps they do not particularly encourage visitors. Then again, Podunk may get an average tourist rate of 2500 a year, which not enough of an audience to warrant a book on wineries or anything else.

On the other hand, if you see an article in a travel or wine magazine about the growing number of wineries in Podunk, or the number of antique shops and restaurants that have opened in Podunk because of the fabulous wineries there, then you know there is enough interest there to develop tourist traffic. And with enough traffic, a guidebook is feasible.

When I wrote the first edition of *New Jersey Day Trips*, I did not cover half the territory of what I have in the present edition. My scope widened over the years. However, from the very beginning, my perspective was from the point of view of a New Jersey resident family, with children in tow, who were going to drive to most of the attractions. All trips would be within a single day's time, and that would include getting there and back. Therefore,

for out-of-state destinations, I did not want to go beyond a two-hour drive beyond the state border nearest to that attraction. I also included trips that would be interesting to senior citizens and singles, but my primary target was a family with children.
Here is a sample of different NYC guidebooks slanted to different audiences.

1.   A popular guide to New York museums includes almost all of the museums in the five boroughs. It gives full write-ups plus all particulars of hours and prices, but gives directions only from NYC busses and subways. There are no driving directions for car owners.

2.   Zagat's Restaurant Survey lists selected restaurants alphabetically and then has a geographical, ethnic type, BYOB, and cost category listed in the back index. Its largest audience is the local one.

3.   General guidebooks such as Fodor's cover NYC from the point of view of an out-of-towner and try to include as much general information and history as possible and hit all the high spots at the same time. They also give general information on buses, subways and so forth. Because the Fodor series also sells well to foreigners, the books include information on money conversion, passports, airport facilities and menu items. Fodor's also publishes a special NYC edition just for kids.

4.   Frommer's guides started out as a budget series, so there is still an emphasis on price. In Frommer's guide to NYC, chapters include "Shopping" "The Club Scene" Outdoors, Accommodations, food, etc. Hotels are divided by price (High, Medium and Low) and then rated by stars as to accommodations within their own price category. Frommer's also offers a more sophisticated slant in its Irreverent Guide to NYC

5.   The D&K series emphasizes graphics, maps and interiors, so a fully sectioned interior of the Metropolitan Museum of Art is part of the book. While there is a more limited selection of attractions, those that are included (the top spots) are given a thorough going over with excellent illustrations.

6.   There are many guidebooks for hikers, runners, joggers and/or bikers that concentrate only on the parks and trails within

New York City. These "green" guides may leave out the major tourist attractions altogether but will give minute detail on directions to finding the parks and green oases, and often include simply drawn maps.

7.   Guide books for city walkers tend to keep to the streets and point out the museums, historic buildings and other sights that include both well-known and out-of-the–way places. It is assumed that the reader is walking for pleasure and a desire to see the city up close.

8.   Any number of small and large publishers now put out guides for specific cultural or age groups such as the "20& 30-something" crowd, gay and lesbian travelers, pet lovers, shopaholics, theater lovers, art lovers and so forth. There are several NYC guides slanted to one or the other of these special interest groups.

One's audience is always part of one's slant. So a book called "Chicago for Kids", for instance, would cover such things as how many bathrooms there are and where kid-style food is available. It would answer questions about stroller rentals, the length of the waiting line, and anything else of interest to parents. In fact, such books are often written by parents or grandparents because such folk realized that the other books that cover Chicago were deficient in exactly that area.

I picked up a travel guide to weekend excursions in northern California recently. It turned out to be written by a hearty, healthy backpacker type who assumed everyone's idea of fun was to trek to the rim of a volcano. Although the book included a few restful weekends, it was written with a very active audience in mind, a group that would be in tune with this particular author's interests.

Now if I had written a weekend book for that region, I would have concentrated on the winery tours, visiting the beautiful college campuses in the area, eating at romantic inns, checking out the architectural gems in the neighboring town, hanging out at the beach, antiquing, and that sort of thing. Of course I would throw in a mild hike or two for the active bunch, but mine would be a completely different book, and it would appeal to a different audience.

This is where subtitles come in. It is always a good idea to add a subtitle: not only does this increase your visibility for Google searches and Amazon links, but it helps the potential customer find exactly the right fit for his tastes. Here are a few possible subtitles for a potential book:

- Vacation Weekends: 52 exciting activities for the outdoors lover
- Vacation weekends: 52 leisurely trips through the beautiful countryside
- Vacation weekends: 52 romantic spots for you and your lover

What's Your Competition?

Obviously many travel books were born when a traveler saw that there was a gaping hole in coverage for a particular place or interest. The first person to write a book about Costa Rica, the first person to collect the names of motels that accepted pets, the first person to follow in the footsteps of Lewis and Clark, all fall into this category. They had no competition — they only had to worry about finding their audience. However, the majority of travel books have some competition. This is where your slant, your angle, your voice, your format and organization can make the key difference.

How-To-Do-It books often have little competition because the subject is something that the author feels has not been treated adequately by other guides. A parent traveling with children may feel frustrated that books geared to traveling with kids are aimed at a particular destination, or perhaps aimed at parents with school-age children. Come up with a book entitled "Traveling the World with Preschoolers", and maybe you've created a how-to-do-it book with an untapped audience.

On the other hand, what happens when you take on a really popular subject? For instance, how were *Oahu Revealed* and other books in the "Hawaii revealed" series able to capture a strong audience when they had to battle against a veritable army of heavy-hitting competition? The two authors kept pointing out how they were different in their approach and their coverage. They covered each island separately so that they had more space for individual site descriptions.

The authors tell you over and over again that they experience everything. They eat in every restaurant, they sleep in every hotel and they snorkel in every dive site! They also point out that they go to out-of-the-way places that other travel writers ignore and they don't take freebies. In this way they give the reader the feeling that they are insiders who really know the score, while the visiting travel writer is just a hack grinding out material to be fitted into an already established framework. And it works!

Finding the Competition: How do you discover what books are out there that cover or even approach your subject? The most comprehensive listing of books in the United States is *Books In Print*. Most libraries have a copy. But what you really want is the *Subject Guide to Books in Print*, one of the volumes in the set. This is the one that lists books by subject so you only have to turn to the pages with the heading Travel and then peruse down the subheadings until you hit your subject area.

Look under all variations of a heading. You will find listings under the name of the country — e.g.: Ireland: Description and Travel. But this list will include not only travel guides but pictorials and histories that cover travel destinations, so you should also search under "Travel Guides" "Restaurant Guides" "Outdoor Guides" and any other heading you can imagine.

Of course what many people do is simply log onto Amazon. com and check through certain key words. Down at the bottom of the page you will notice categories such as Travel > United States > Southwest > Arizona as a guide to find other books on this particular topic. However, many books fall through the Amazon net, either because the publisher didn't put it into the right category or the title keywords didn't match Amazon's, so I would check the Subject Guide to BIP anyway. What you get from Amazon.com is the competitor's cover, the write-up from the publisher (called the editorial review) and any other reviews the book received. If the book has a "Look Inside" feature you can also check out the Table of Contents, the index, and a few pages of text to get an idea what the book is really about.

Certainly you should also visit your local library and book-store. There you will find the guidebooks that are popular enough to be shelved (Listings in BIP cover practically any book currently in print, so there are voluminous entries). Look at all the travel titles and notice if any come near your subject and in what manner or style they cover it.

How many competitive titles are there? There may be plenty of books on your subject, but are they competitive? Are there one, two, ten, or twenty? Are they all direct competition? If you want to do a nuts-and-bolts book about traveling cross-country in an RV, is a hilarious memoir of a couple's adventures on the road really a rival for your audience? Is a directory of Trailer Parks and RV stations competition? Not really, although that book also might include some handy RV tips. These titles are actually complementary to your guide. As Carol White discovered when she returned from a very long trip with her husband in an RV, friends were more interested in how the two got along in close quarters and how they managed their household affairs from afar than in the actual trip destinations. And so *Live Your Road Trip Dream* was born — because other RV road trip books did not cover that aspect of the journey.

On other hand, if you find a book entitled "Mexico: Every-thing the Traveler Has to Know" you'd better check it out if you had your sights set on Mexico. If this is one of those volumes that tries to cover everything, and does a decent job of it, you'd better start looking for chinks in the armor. Is the book too big to be carried around? Is the type too small to read easily? You can research travel trends and discover that most travelers visit only certain parts of Mexico. Therefore, you could change your concept from the whole country to the following title: "From Cancun to Acapulco: The Ten Best Vacation Spots in Mexico".

By narrowing your focus, you can concentrate on a fuller explo-ration of the destinations that most tourists visit. That way you'll have more space for Acapulco and Cabo San Lucas, with a little history and lots of descriptions of hotel, eating places and attrac-tions for each town. Or you might try approaching Mexico from the other angle: the least touristy spots. You could begin to assess the best arty towns, the healthiest places, the undeveloped beach areas, and the single fancy resort in the middle of nowhere until you have a compendium called the "Hidden Gems of Mexico". Either book would commence with a chapter or two on history, a glossary for language and an explanation of the money exchange and then go on to explore a particular approach.

In analyzing the competition, you have to figure out what you can do that is different from the other titles on the shelf. Sometimes, this is easy. You may have entered the travel guide field because there was so little on the subject — or what there was is so badly done — that you felt absolutely compelled to write a better book!

More frequently, it's a case where the competition is geared to a different audience than the one you contemplate. You may notice that all the books about destination X are targeted toward families with kids, and you feel there are plenty of singles and couples in the 18-to-35-age group who could use a guide created with them in mind. Or you see that there are plenty of books about biking and hiking in a certain foliaged state, but there's nothing for the walking and browsing crowd that actually comprise the majority of tourists there.

There is always some corner of the map, some activity, some angle, or some group that has not been covered by the competition. That is where you have your best chance of creating a book that has a solid audience.

What if there is hardly any competition? It may be that the book you contemplate involves an activity or a destination that simply has a very limited audience. Perhaps then, you should consider a Print-on-Demand edition to sell to a select audience through the Internet. Sometimes there is a topic that is of great importance to a small number of people (such as traveling with a specific disability or accompanying a disabled person) and the best way to approach this niche market is through an e-book or POD volume. There are also small, unique destinations that appeal to a limited audience. The book may sell less than 1000 copies a year but it will sell to interested readers. So you can either self-publish a POD book or look for a niche publisher that services a small, particular audience.

How current are the competing books? This is another facet you should research. If the last book about traveling with children was written in 1986, it means that either there isn't much of a market for a book of this kind or that nobody has tried it recently. Maybe the field has been superseded by specific destination guides for families with children.

Remember that series like Frommer's and Fodor's expect to sell several thousands of copies per year and if a particular title falls short of that expectation, they will not do another edition. So while a big brand name publisher may not choose to pursue a title that will sell only 3000 copies for the year, a small or regional house might be happy to take on such a book.

For whatever reason, just because a large publisher has let a certain title lapse doesn't mean that you cannot enter the field. There are many books that never sell out their original print run of 5000 copies. There are a number of factors such as timing, book promotion (or the lack of it) and a change in public taste that can affect sales.

So if you see that books on your topic came out twenty years ago and then disappeared, check out the reason. Call the publisher and ask. Because publishing companies merge all the time and editors play musical chairs with all the houses, it is not uncommon that a book simply falls between the cracks. If a whole generation has passed since the last book came out on this particular subject, you may have a best seller on your hands.

Is the Competitor's Slant Different from yours? Take for instance, a book called *Amusement Parks of New Jersey*. The book was written by a real aficionado of such places. The man is a historian and the book teems with information on the background of each and every park. There is the history of the family that started the place, the rise and fall of their fortunes and changes in the landscape. There are also a full descriptions of the fourteen or so parks covered, listing each and every attraction. This is a great book for amusement park and roller coaster buffs and a wonderful historical resource guide for anyone doing an article on theme parks and smaller amusement parks. But it did not tell me what I wanted to know!

The descriptions of the rides were clinical and there was nothing on such details as to the length of the lines for the major attractions, whether food was allowed to be brought in, the cleanliness of the restrooms, the comparative rudeness (or courtesy) of the crowds that frequent the park, how to reduce the customer's cost and a million other things that most theme park patrons want to know.

This is not how I would have written a book about amusement parks, and so it is not really a direct competitor. My book would have had much less history and much more hands-on opinions on everything from the quality of the hot dogs (and whether they are hot enough) to the length of time it takes to schlep from one roller coaster to another. I would note the high cost of parking and locker rentals. I also might consider widening the borders of the book to include both New Jersey and Pennsylvania.

When checking out competitive titles of theme parks or anything else, the first thing you should ask yourself is: does this book cover the subject in the way I would cover it? What does it leave out that I would put in? Would I use the same tone or slant? Would I change the perimeters? How would my format differ from this author's format? What section of the audience has been ignored — and how would I include them?

Once you know your boundaries and format, once you have established a primary audience and the slant and tone you will use to address that audience, you know exactly how your book would differ from others in the field and whether it has a chance to succeed.

Non-Bookstore Outlets

And now a question all publishers ask, but very few writers think about: where will your audience be able to buy your book? Your immediate answer might be bookstores, but there are many other venues out there.

In setting up your book proposal or your sales plan if you are self-publishing, you should always consider where the audience for your book may be found. The category of your guide is all important when targeting a particular audience! Here are some of the retail outlets where certain titles sell far better than in bookstores:

Outdoor Outfitters Stores: Along with the backpacks, canvas vests, and rugged shoes, these stores regularly stock books about hiking, biking, fishing and general regional recreation. Don't forget the Nature Centers found inside public parks and forests and Audubon bookstores — they also buy the outdoor category.

Wineries: Most books about winery tours (or those dedicated to regions such as the Napa Valley where wineries predominate) sell more copies through the gift shop at these venues than they do in bookstores.

Gourmet Food Shops: Along with traditional cookbooks, these shops will feature restaurant guides to their local city or area.

Newsstands and drug stores: These carry standard directories like the Mobil Travel Guide and The Zagat Survey as well as local guides and maps to the area.

Airport Book stores: They are more likely to take traveler's aids such as money converters and phrase books, but they may take one or two destination guides.

Religious Book Stores: Did you know there are over a thousand Christian Book Stores? And there are many bookstores that concentrate on Judaica as well. Whether your title is *Walking the Bible* or *A Guide to Kosher New York* don't forget these outlets. General travel titles that appeal to wholesome family values might also be accepted by these stores.

Museum stores: Art museums will take a limited number of guides they consider worthy. Science and nature museums are pretty liberal in picking up both general guides to their area and specific guides to rain forests, exploration titles and field guides to practically anything.

Historic site gift and book shops: Along with historic titles (often geared toward children) guides to battlefields, restored villages and other historic attractions as well as regional guides will show up here.

Specialized stores: A children's toy shop might take a book on trips with kids. There are gay and lesbian bookstores and New Age bookstores (where anything about spiritual renewal through travel might sell) among other specialized bookstores. A guide to destination weddings will do better in a bridal shop than in a traditional bookstore. RV books (both road guides and road trip stories) sell at RV provision stores. And then there are the gift shops that cater to railroad buffs, theater aficionados, and any other interest or taste that might possibly be translated into a travel guide.

Travel book stores: There aren't too many of these around — the one that Julia Roberts slipped into in the movie *Notting Hill* was a rarity even in London, but it does make the author's heart swell with pride to have a book in such a store. The Rand McNally store in the posh Short Hills Mall in New Jersey sold my title for many years.

Bulk sales to corporations: Restaurant guides like Zagat's feature a custom-made cover for corporate clients so that the company can hand out free copies to employees and clients with their name on the cover. But even small presses can sell to companies who transfer employees around the world. Whether it's a how-to book on foreign etiquette, a general guide to the new city or country or just a relocation book, certain titles entice corporations to buy direct from the publisher and usually at a better discount than they would get at a bookstore.

Wal-Mart, K-Mart and Costco: They will only take big sellers and the return rate is said to be horrendous. Many publishers avoid them, but it is a path to volume sales.

Book Clubs: The History Book Club, the Travel Book Club (if there is one), The Gourmet Book — there are a host of book clubs that might be prime targets for your title. Book clubs pay a set price which is far lower than the usual discount price to retailers and wholesalers. However, book clubs give you free publicity and bragging rights. For authors with a royalty agreement there is usually a clause in the contract which gives them a lower percentage on book club sales.

Re-sales through associations: Can you get your local Chamber of Commerce to buy your area guide and resell it customers? It's been done. Think about your angle and your audience and consider which organizations might be interested in your particular slant. Newcomers Clubs, ski clubs, bicycle clubs, garden clubs — there are many organizations that might take 40 or 50 books to re-sell to their members. And then there are the ethnic organizations — the Polish American club in your neighborhood, the Chinese American school and so forth — who might be interested in selling your related guide at their annual fall festival.

Direct sales to audience: If you are someone who regularly gives talks or slide lectures on your travels to Borneo or your trip across Canada on your motorcycle, back-of –the- room sales might account for a good portion of your income. Sales may not be large as they are in bookstores, but you make much more per book. If you are a self-publisher you can garner a hefty profit this way. If you are an author who buys back his book from the publisher at 50% discount, you make more selling direct than you do from royalties. And in most cases, speakers do get paid, so there's a double income here.

Premium sales: This is when a bank or a newspaper offers a free book to any customer who signs up for an account or a subscription. If you can negotiate a reasonable discount with the company, this is a wonderful way to get free advertising while someone else is selling your book for you!

The Internet: The great equalizer — here any book can find an audience! Online stores such as Amazon and bn.com afford limitless space so that any title has a chance. But the Internet also offers the opportunity to sell direct from your own website. Many authors, particularly self-publishers, do just that, and it is the prime way that How-to-Do-It Travel books are sold.

Chapter 5

What Are Your Boundaries?

After you have decided on your category and have a clear concept of your book and your audience, you must now consider your boundaries. Exactly how much territory will this book cover? What places within this territory will be covered? How much depth will be given to each place? If it is to be a themed destination book, how many destinations will you cover: Fifty? One hundred? If it is a road guide will you cover every single spot you pass or just concentrate on the interesting ones?

Even a simple directory needs some borders and some cohesion. A travel memoir also needs to have definition — you may want to skip the boring month in between your sojourn in Morocco and your hike up the Pyrenees. Whether you are self-publishing the book or making a book proposal, you must begin with defining your boundaries.

When you consider the borders of your guidebook, think both of geographical borders (e.g., you decide to cover Boston and three of its suburbs) and the limits you put on attractions (e.g. you will cover restaurants, theaters, nightclubs, historic spots, shopping and some water sports, but not tennis, athletic clubs, or golf). You may find that some juggling becomes necessary as time goes on. For example, perhaps you were not planning to include spas but you find that your write-up of Budapest would be lacking without a mention of their beautiful spas.

Even as specific a book as "Bicycle Trips in Northern Virginia" has to have some clear geographical delineation. Where will you draw the line, literally, on the map to decide what towns you will include? If there is an interesting park just south of your "line", maybe you should bend your boundaries to include it!

How deep do you go? In general the depth of your coverage depends on the width of your coverage. If you try to include every restaurant, every hotel and every sideshow attraction you are not going to have much space left for depth. Now some of the newer guidebooks are coming out at over 600 pages and they do include lots of details as well as a plethora of extras such as seasonal festivals, maps, photos and a heavily weighted appendix.

The category and style of the book has a great deal to do with its depth. If your personal interest runs to history, you might spend several pages delving into the history and sociology of the land you are exploring. Certain series, such as Moon Handbooks, are known for the depth of their historic and ethnic coverage and they would expect an author writing for them to follow that lead.

What Are Your Criteria? Then there is the matter of selection. You could spend forty pages on Florence and go into every nook and cranny of that great Renaissance city and then stuff the rest of Tuscany into ten pages. This is what makes one guidebook different from another. If your book were a guide to the gold route of the Golden West, you would probably spend a chapter on the history of prospecting, as well as the actual sites where the public can visit gold mines and ghost towns.

On the other hand, if your style runs to the personal essay you might go into reams of speculation as to what you would do if you were a gold prospector or you might interview a modern version of a gold rush pioneer. Depending on the length of your text and how much you need to cover in order to make the book salable, you should consider the following questions:

1. Should you expand the concept? For instance, there is a book about New York City museums that includes the major zoos and gardens in the metropolis using the notion that a zoo or garden

is a "living" museum. This widens its scope.

2. Should you expand the territory? If there are child-friendly museums nearby, such as a science center in Jersey City and a hands-on museum in Long Island — shouldn't they be included in a child-friendly museum book about New York City?

3. Should you expand the background? How much of the text do you allow for history or biography?

4. What about extras? Will there be recipes to augment your book on the Best Bed and Breakfasts in Georgia? Will there be a chapter on how to play blackjack and craps in your book on Las Vegas? Such details as interviews with personnel, subjective observations and anecdotes all add to the depth of your coverage of a destination. Sidebars and call-outs also add to the visual aspect of the book.

Specific geographic perimeters: This is your first decision regarding the guide. Where do you draw your borders? If you are covering activities in San Francisco and the Bay Area exactly how far does the Bay area extend? One restaurant guide goes as far as Lake Tahoe!

If you're doing Disney World are you going to sneak in a few pages about Sea World and Universal Studios or leave them for a second guidebook you plan to write? If you're covering Paris, will you include the usual side trips to Versailles and Giverney or venture further out? When you make your first outline for your book, list your geographic borders!

It is also the prospective size of your audience that determines your scope. Very few writers do a book just on St. Thomas in the Virgin Islands. Most guidebooks cover either the three American Virgins (St. Thomas, St. Croix and St. John) or both the British and American islands. That doesn't mean that a niche book aimed at the resident population and long-term visitor might not do quite well even if it were limited to St. Thomas (with side trips to other islands on a random basis). But such a book should cover such things as condo rentals and undiscovered nooks as well as the usual attractions.

Subject Boundaries: This concerns the scope of your coverage. You're doing a book on Copenhagen but you are not sure exactly what subjects to include. Hotels, yes, but how many? Just the expensive and moderate ones or are you going to search out the cheapies?

Make a list of how many hotels and restaurants you think you will include. (Some guidebooks keep hotels to a strict nine per venue: three luxury, three moderate and three cheap.) Create a value system for restaurants — how many will be top-tier (the ones that every other guidebook will mention) and how many unknown gems will you discover? If this is a book slanted to the budget crowd, then you can increase coverage of moderate and cheaper hotels and try to hunt down as many freebies as possible.

Criteria of Inclusion: Will you include such places as gyms, bicycle shops, tattoo parlors, amusement parks, department stores or monuments? This depends on the subject of your book and your audience. A guide to cycling trips might well include a list of bicycle shops in the territory while a historical guide would probably include all the statues and monuments in the same area. A book aimed at the 20-something crowd might include tattoo parlors. On the other hand, a general guidebook might ignore these or simply list them at the end of a chapter.

There will be some lines drawn when it comes to the quality of the establishment, the danger of a venue and other possible criteria you will use for your book. If you are working with a publisher who has an established series, they will tell you their criteria. It can be as simple as a bed-and-breakfast series where the publisher includes only homes with a minimum of five bedrooms. Or they might demand that all motels include air-conditioning. (This will not work well on an island where the populace depends on the evening breeze to cool the room.)

If you are offering a proposal for a completely new, independent book (or self-publishing) it's up to you to decide on your criteria. How far will you stretch your limits? If you are listing freebies, do you include only absolutely free places, or places that are free on Thursday from noon to eight p.m.? If you include nightclubs do you only note the ones that are downtown and easy to reach or do you include out-of-the-way nightlife?

Although you should set up your goals at the beginning, you will find that you will make exceptions to the rule as you go along. At the edit stage you may have to throw out certain places because they don't meet the criteria for your book. It's easier to do this later, than to try to decide everything while you are amassing your research.

Thematic Borders: Let's say you're doing a book on the gardens of British Columbia. Does this include public gardens only, or are you going to mention some beautiful private gardens that only open up once a year? How about parks without gardens or sculpture gardens without any flowers? Much depends on how much space you need to fill up and how much space is allotted to each entry. Readers want more than fifteen or twenty entries within a guidebook, so you'll have to add a list of "other gardens" whether you have seen them or not. You may even start incorporating government buildings and private mansions because they happen to have a small but interesting garden in order to fill up the book.

Political Correctness: Sometimes you have to widen your scope to include certain entries simply due to the necessities of political balance or political correctness. You're contemplating a book on restaurants? Better make sure there are several vegetarian eateries between the covers! The same goes for museums dedicated to ethnic and cultural minorities — be sure to include as many as you can.

Doing historical sites of the state? Don't forget the western corner or the southern rural area even if it has a paucity of mansions and forts — throw in a ruin if you must in order to give geographical balance to the text. This is true of countries and even continents.

You can, of course, spend more time on one section of the country than another. There are always industrial cities that have very little interest to the passing traveler and these tend to get lumped together in a "throwaway" chapter

Chronological Boundaries: When you do a chronological book based on calendar listings you are pretty much free to expand your pages during July, August and December with more events likely to be going on. But if you're writing about 52 Weekends in the San Francisco Area, what happens if you have a superfluity of possibilities in the summer and fall but you're coming up short for January through March?

This is where a balancing act comes in. The author will probably throw in those destinations that are climate neutral such as indoor spas, and museums for the winter months. If there are close-by ski areas, so much the better. But because it is difficult to come up with something for every weekend, most of these books are sectioned into seasons, with lots of trips appearing on the cusp of each seasonal change.

If you are doing a personal road trip book, however, you can just follow the road wherever it takes you and describe the different seasons as they unfold. Since many road trip books are based on a day-to-day journal of what the author experienced, the coverage will be based on the actual territory that he traveled. It is during the editing phase that the author decides what stays in and what is thrown out.

Money Limits: If the concept for your book is a budget guide to New Zealand, you may automatically limit your coverage of lodgings to hotels and other accommodations that charge $80 a day or less. Your restaurant section may be constrained to those eateries that charge $40 or less for a full meal (including one glass of wine) and those would be your criteria for selection.

Other Criteria for limits: If your book is about the 100 best golf courses in the world you have effectively limited your entries to that group. Other possible criteria:

- Resort hotel must have a swimming pool (for a family fun vacation book)
- Handicapped access must include automatic doors (for a handicapped book)
- RV camps must have noise limits after 10 p.m.(for a book for retirees)
- Personal guides for tours must speak fluent English (for referrals in your foreign travel series)

Some publishers have specific criteria for what they want in a particular series. This may run the gamut from demanding that you include twelve dog parks for a city-wide guide for dog-lovers in Seattle to an insistence that you personally check out every den in the sex scene in Bangkok for a book about Thailand.

Expanding Your Scope: Sometimes, when the subject of your book is somewhat limited in scope (for instance you are going to cover only the Bed and Breakfast lodgings in a certain town known for its B&Bs), you must add depth to your text. Each Bed & Breakfast must be described; its owner interviewed, its history recorded, and details given as to its amenities and the best season to visit. The lace curtains, the quilts, the antiques in each room would also be included.

Assuming there are 70 B&B's in this town, each one will have to take up two pages, at least, if you want to attain a book with a minimum of 140 pages. Add ten or twenty pages of attractions in the town itself and a few pen-and-ink drawings and then drop in ten full-page recipes for the cinnamon scones or cheese omelets that are served in these establishments and you have now added another 50 or so pages to the book. That, together with six or eight pages of front matter (a map, an Introduction in which you rhapsodize on the virtues of B&B's in general, a Table of Contents, the Title page, acknowledgement page, etc) and another ten or twelve pages of back matter (the index, the appendix, a few pages advertising other books by the same publisher) and the book has now reached a respectable page count. If need be, you can always cut down on the pictures or text if you have over-reached your intended count.

Personal anecdotes and essays: The personal anecdote and the thoughtful essay are common ways to add depth. In fact, travel guides that concentrate on self-fulfillment through travel would undoubtedly be filled with personal anecdotes, and/or essays on the value of whatever experience the "journey" brings. But a standard travel guide can gain value by the occasional anecdote or personal musing. A meeting between the author and a fisherman at five o'clock in the morning or the art of haggling with a rug merchant in Egypt is certain to interest the reader whether he is an armchair traveler or someone about to set out on a trip.

In looking over a Fodor's guidebook to a shore destination that came out several years ago, I was surprised to find a chapter devoted to "insider views". Actually the chapter consisted of "personality pieces" of the type found in the Feature Section of Sunday newspapers. One piece was about a longtime lifeguard who had started the lifeguard races between the shore towns. Another was a history of a gambler who had made his mark in the area. The rest of the book was filled with factual information, lists of hotels and restaurants, plus short histories of the various places; the usual Fodor compendium. I can only surmise that the editors included the chapter to offer a personal touch.

Special Audience

When the guidebook is directed at a specific audience, many authors spend more than fifty percent of the text on issues of interest to that audience. In *A Travel Guide to the Jewish Caribbean and South America,* author Ben Frank spends much of the time giving the history of the Jewish enclaves and congregations in all the countries he covers. The percentage of coverage in books targeted to special audiences or special interests often depends on whether the book is partly biography, (such as a book following the footsteps of Lincoln) partly how-to, (such as how to take a road trip in an RV) or partly autobiographical/ mystical, (how I found my soul at the ten most sacred places in the world). Obviously there is a lot of leeway in balancing the subject and the minutiae of the tour.

Scope of the how-to-do-it book

This is a little different. You really have to invent your own boundaries here. Some subjects are easily covered in a magazine article (e.g. *How to pack a suitcase,* or *How to keep kids interested on a long trip*) so developing an entire book on the theme means expanding both depth and width of your coverage.

For instance, in *Trouble Free Travel with Children: 700 Helpful Hints for Parents on the Go* by Vicki Lansky and others, there are chapters on planning, entertaining, sleeping and eating but these are subdivided by the age of children and mode of transportation. So there's a chapter on cruises, on short car trips and longer destination car trips, on airplanes, trains and buses. But whether it's the manner of getting there, the type of hotel or resort to choose, or the restaurant or fast-food place to eat, the advice pertains separately to infants, toddlers, pre-schoolers, school children and the dreaded teenager phase. As with many how-to books, this volume is less than 150 pages including the index, but the author had to decide from the beginning how she was going to organize this topic.

The author of a one-topic, "how-to" has to find creative ways to fill up the allotted number of pages. This is usually done by adding funny anecdotes, or a history of the subject or widening the subject so you include much more than you originally intended. For instance one author of a "how-to-pack-a suitcase" book actually spends more time writing about coordinating outfits and how to ship accumulated stuff back from your destination than on the basic subject. If the book didn't include wardrobe selection, picking out the correct suitcase, where to store documents and other assorted subjects, the page count would be much too short.

Because how-to-do it books cover such a wide range of subjects, the scope may vary widely. Many authors stretch out the basic information with sideline chapters and a passel of lists. In a book on exchanging homes, or house-sitting in foreign countries, one would expect lots of anecdotes and interviews with veterans in the field to give texture and value to the basic information. On the other hand, a book on airline upgrades and frequent flyer miles would be filled with charts and checklists and the names and addresses of airlines.

Insider information is the backbone of many a how-to book, whether it's advice on how to get the best travel bargains written by a travel consolidator or a book on how to get published by an editor or literary agent. They all spend several chapters divulging how the system works and then devote the rest of the book to explaining how the reader can best use that system.

Personal experience "how-to's" usually strike a balance

between "how we did it" and "how you can do it". This is often done in chronological order. Carol and Phil White in their *Live Your Road Trip Dream*, devote the early chapters (and some back pages) to the logistics of planning a long-term cross-country trip while the middle section concentrates on the trip itself. The authors spend almost half of the book showing the reader how to prepare for an extended trip in an RV using very concrete steps. While the description of the road trip across America is based on journal-like entries, it is the chapters on the very specific preparation that really sells the book. Such important details as how to rent your house; what to do about mail and bills; how to handle health emergencies and mechanical breakdowns; how to keep in touch with others, plus a large dose of checklists, creates a blueprint for others considering a jaunt onto the wild blue highway. For every writer doing such a book (like how to finance and structure a vacation escape) the parameters and balance between the how-to-do-it section and the personal experience will differ.

You will also find, as you continue, that your scope may shift a bit. Perhaps there's an editor who wants more coverage of a particular aspect of your trip. Or you may visit a much-vaunted castle or seaside resort and find it doesn't live up to your expectations and that the main attraction there has ceased to exist, and you have to scuttle the chapter you had planned to built around it! You may have to add extra pictures or widen your coverage of another destination, to fill up the void.

But just as a jigsaw puzzle lover starts with the outside framework and works toward the center fitting each piece in place, by setting up your boundaries first, you will find it much easier to complete the work.

Chapter 6

What's Your Format?

Once you have set up your boundaries, you must now go on to consider the basic organization of the book. In order to lay out your chapters you have to decide on the general format. How will you structure the book? How are you going to arrange the information you have at hand?

The format includes the actual look of the book (including the size and shape); how you will organize your chapters (by subject, by geography or alphabetically); whether you will include one or more indexes; and the space you will devote to photographs, maps or other illustrations. You also have to figure out whether you need a glossary and a host of other questions. Such things as title page, copyright page, table of contents, the index (or indexes) and appendix are part of the general format. It is also common to include an orientation chapter that explains how to use the book. The publisher will decide the physical format of the book, including the size, the look and the general layout.

As for maps, photographs and other illustrations: the subject matter of the book will define your needs to a certain extent. One cannot imagine a book on the scenic wonders of New Zealand without photographs.

There are franchise books like Frommer's and the Rough Guides that have a pre-set format. This is why the submission guidelines state: "You must read one or two of our books to understand our style." If you are submitting a proposal to such publishers, you would have to indicate what you intend to cover within the pre-set organization of the book.

A typical pre-set format might start with Chapter One "Orientation" or "What You Need to Know" or "The History of the Place"; and Chapter Two "Hotels" with Chapter Three as " Restaurants", Chapter Four, " Shopping" and so forth. Some series are so formatted that they already have boilerplate pages that are dropped in to explain the format and icons to the readers. As a writer for that series, you will be given an outline informing you how to code your headlines, titles, subtitles and captions.

However, if the territory you are covering is well known for its flea markets, you may want to indicate a sub-division under shopping for "Flea Markets". So even with those publishers, you will find flexibility accorded to the author on the basis of the subject matter. And even with pre-formatted books, destinations have to be divided according to the lay of the land and the accepted definitions of that particular place. If you were writing about night clubs or food markets only, you would still have to come up with your own way of organizing the information.

What about self-publishing?

Here, you may have to invent a completely new format. You will have already staked out the length, depth and width of your territory much as a gold prospector stakes out his claim. When it comes to the format, you can do what you want, but the fact is many new guidebooks use the organizational style of previous tomes.

Very few people attempt to invent the wheel all over again. Of course you don't want to slavishly copy somebody else's format either! (There is actually a publisher called Jetlag that puts out fake travel guides to places like "Slovenia" as a satire of certain Brand Name series). But when it comes to the details there are pretty standard conventions as how to indicate price, credit card acceptance, telephone numbers, whether biking or hiking or camping is permitted, and so forth. These can be synthesized into handy little icons that are available from most software programs. It is in the overall format of the book that you will have to invest the most time and effort.

Look at competing or similar books. You would want to structure your manuscript in a different way from those currently on the shelf or you would simply be producing a clone. In fact, the main impetus for writing the guide may be that you hated the format of the other books written on the subject. I have known people to throw a guidebook across the room because they were so frustrated with the way the information was offered.

On the other hand, if you are hacking out uncharted territory, you may already have a stack of articles or journals and need some way of fashioning those bits and pieces into a fascinating whole, but you don't have a clue as to how to begin.

Here are the most common formats:

1. **Activity**: Hiking, skiing, walking, biking, antique shopping. These may be sub-divided by geographic areas and/or ease of activity for each chapter.

2. **Subject matter**: Museums, zoos, restaurants, motels, historic sites and other attractions. For a specific interest guide to food travel for instance, the subject chapters might be roadside stands, gourmet shops, food festivals, wine festivals, ethnic groceries and bakeries, all within a prescribed geographic area.

3. **Alphabetical Listing**: A common method used in directories or a single topic book such as a restaurant guide to Chicago.

4. **Geographical**:
   a. Divide the sections/chapters by commonly acknowledged terms such as the wine country, the desert region, the North Shore or the Lake Country.
   b. Divide along legal lines such as countries, counties, states, provinces, boroughs, and such.
   c. A combination of both.

5. **Daytrips**: A series of defined circuit trips that start from a single point and include major points of interest such as shopping, hotels, restaurants and historic sites within specific geographic boundaries.

6. **The Road Trip**: That is, driving in a straight geographical line. Used primarily for trips by car, RV or other

vehicles that go from one point to another. Also used in travel memoirs.

7. **Seasonal**:
   a. Sections are divided into spring, summer, autumn and winter and then subdivided into subject destinations and/or activities.
   b. Straight calendar listing by day, week or month

8. **Personal interest**: The essay or personal diary may use some of the above divisions but also has the freedom to jump around. A personal travel essay book might have random samplings that vary from autumn in Vermont to summer in Cape Cod to winter in Australia with the coalescing theme being the eye of the beholder.

9. **The How-to-do-it Book**: Usually unfolds in a sequential manner.

Note: There is often a "leftover" chapter for miscellaneous trips or facts that didn't fit into the main format plus an introductory chapter that explains how the book works.

Let's look more closely at these options.

Alphabetical Format: Most often found in restaurant guides, directories and "resource" guides. The *Zagat Restaurant Survey* series is one of the best known alphabetical guides. All the restaurants are listed alphabetically, but the book is balanced by a number of indexes that include the geographical section of the city or area, the ethnic style of restaurant, the price (cheap, medium, expensive), places that allow BYOB, and so on.

The basic directory and the annotated directory usually proceed from A to Z. There is often a general introductory chapter to such books that gives you information on the subject and on how the book is organized. For instance, Mobil Travel Guide's *On the Road with Your Pet* includes sixteen pages by a guest expert that concentrates on how-to material for vacationing with pets and which type of pet is most suitable for a trip. But the body of the book is done in Mobil's directory style which is divided alphabetically by states, and then by city, and then by name of motel.

One editor who spiced up the alphabetical listing was Jim

Leff in the *Chowhounds Guide to San Francisco*. In this maverick restaurant guide, listings are alphabetical but the entry titles are chosen in a random manner. They may go under the name of the restaurant, the name of the town (Sausalito) the section of San Francisco (Fisherman's Wharf) the type of food (Italian) the type of eatery (lunch wagon) the specialty of the place (burritos) or anything else that seemed to pique the editor's fancy. Of course there are several indexes at the end of this compilation to sort things out.

Geographical region: The most common form of destination guide is the one that commences with a large geographical area and then divides the book into smaller geographical regions. For instance, France would be divided into provinces with perhaps a full chapter devoted to Paris. The book would then be subdivided into smaller geographical regions or into subject areas (restaurants, attractions, hotels, landmarks, etc.) A guide to Paris itself would be divided into arrondissements with a few trips beyond to attractions such as Versailles added at the end. There may be an introductory chapter on history, culture, and basic information, but the bulk of the book would be geographically sectioned.

The geographical subdivision is also used with themed destination guides. So a book on American factory tours or destination weddings can be chopped into specific geographical areas such as the East Coast, the South, the Midwest, the West Coast and Hawaii.

Type of activity: If the full subject of the book is an outdoor activity, then the major organization is usually by geographical area with a possible subdivision by the ease or difficulty (or the length — in the case of hiking and biking) of the activity.

Hiking, walking and biking guides can be done in a circuit (or loop) style or by starting at point A and going to point B (in the manner of Road Guides). The loop or circuit is the most popular. The assumption is that the reader will be driving to a certain point where he will park, take his water, food, map and/or guidebook and start the circuit. Many guides will give a time frame for the walk (or bike ride) so that the reader can estimate how long it will take him to make the loop.

Bicycle tours with groups, or a book on hiking from Massachusetts to Maine would be done in the Point A to Point B format. Hiking, biking, antiquing and kayaking are often chapters in a book about a destination or a "What to Do on Weekends" guide. These sections are usually subdivided by geographical region and/or the roughness of the activity (easy, moderate, and most active) or both.

Walking guides to cities are often done in a square block format and include detailed descriptions of the buildings or monuments that you pass by. These guides may be accompanied by grid maps of the area. You can then pinpoint each place by calling them A and B and C and noting them on the map. For instance, you can say: "Start at 3rd Avenue and 54th Street. Walk one block west to Smith House, (144 W. 54th St.) then south to Grant's Department Store on 53rd and 3rd." You can then use letters or numbers on the map to highlight the Smith House and Grant's Department Store. The *Access Guide* series uses a large grid style for sections of the city. They then use numbers to flag particular sites and color codes to denote whether they are hotels, restaurants, historic sites, museums or parks. This is fairly complicated and requires a professional book design team. (However, I find their use of red for hotels and orange for historic sites confusing).

City guides often differ from country guides because after taking a walk along the Strand or through the historic part of town, the reader always has a choice of returning to his hotel or point of departure by taking a bus, a train or a taxicab. Therefore these guides can use the point to point system (see below). *Walking Shakespeare's London* is a case in point.

Type of attraction or subject: Commonly used with city guides or vacation spots that encompass a small area, these attractions might include museums, beaches, outdoor activities, shopping, nightclubs, wineries, historic houses, gardens and so forth. Most geographical guides subdivide their chapters into a type of attraction format anyway. And of course a "type of attraction" guide will often subdivide into geographical districts, but not always. But it is quite common to simply name your chapters after the subject covered. For instance, *Frommer's Irreverent Guide to Las Vegas* is divided into chapters called Hotels, Restaurants, Casinos,

Diversions, Side Trips, Night Life and so forth with summaries of the prices and other facts at the end of each chapter and a general index in the back. A book dedicated to a beach resort might be divided into such chapters as Beaches, Water sports, Hotels, Restaurants, Casual Dining, Night Life, Day Trips, Shopping, Special Sights, Boat Rentals, and Long Term Accommodations.

Seasonal/Chronological: Regional or local guides are sometimes divided by season or even into month-by-month calendar chapters. Fall trips, winter outings or even monthly fairs and festivals are another way of approaching the division of chapters into an easy-to-comprehend guidebook. Other seasonal approaches are the weekend-by-weekend and even a holiday-by-holiday organization. In *Free L.A.*, chapters are divided by month in one section (using calendar style), by holiday in another, and by venue in the third. In the *52 Weekend* series, the books are divided seasonally with weekend destinations most appropriate for spring, summer, fall and winter. Road trip memoirs may combine calendar divisions with a point to point trip, resulting in April in Paris and May in Barcelona.

Point to Point Format: Used most often in road guides, walking guides, and traveling in RV guides, these books cover a trip that goes from one point to another. Subdivisions are usually specific attractions. *Along the I-75* is an example of a point-to-point book with this directory-style guide starting out in Chicago and ending up in Florida and then going back north again. Although *Discover America Diaries* by Priscilla Rhodes is primarily a trip memoir with many flashbacks, the book follows the couple from Maine to the West Coast with stops at state capitals along the way in a point-to-point fashion. Leisurely literary travel memoirs often use the point-to-point construction but in a novelistic way.

Timeline: Historical and biographical travel books are sometimes structured along a timeline. If you're visiting the battlefields of the Civil War you might start with the firing of cannon on Fort Sumter, South Carolina and end with the peace signing at Appomattox Courthouse in Virginia. Or you might organize the tour along geographical lines (the battle of Fredericksburg and the siege of Petersburg, Virginia might be easier for a tourist to visit on succeeding days than a side trip to Gettysburg, Pennsylvania) with a timeline chart in the back. The anniversary of the Lewis and Clark expedition has produced some timeline-style books based on their trek.

You also have to decide how much space (if any) you will spend on facts about accommodations for sleeping and eating in the surrounding areas when setting up the format of your book. This should be part of your original concept.

General Information: In addition to a basic format, most destination guidebooks (and certainly such brand names as Fodor's or Rough Guides) spend two or three chapters on basic information such as transportation, money exchange, customs, history, etiquette and lists of important contact numbers (such as the nearest embassy or consulate). These chapters often appear in the beginning of the book before the standard format begins, and are called "Orientation" or "Introduction" chapters. Indexes, appendixes and resource lists are always placed at the end. Even local guidebooks, which often forgo information meant for foreign tourists, spend at least a few pages explaining how the guidebook is set up and how to use the index (if one exists).

Special Audience Guidebooks

There's much more freedom of format here. A general "how-to" book about travel for lesbians might be set up in any way the author feels like (e.g. introduction, followed by which cities are most "user-friendly", then, how to find roommates) whereas a book such as *A Lesbian's Guide to Paris* would probably morph into either geographical subdivisions or subject subdivisions (hotels, nightclubs, restaurants, etc.) after the introductory chapter.

A Travel Guide to the Jewish Caribbean and South America, by Ben Frank, devotes more than fifty percent of its text to history although the format is geographical, with each country sectioned into historical information first, with "guidebook" style information (names of hotels, restaurants, tourist spots) coming afterwards. Naturally, everything is selected to inform a special audience.

Special Interest Travel

The majority of special interest guidebooks adhere to a geographical format but there are often variations in the subdivisions and a few quirks thrown in here or there. A book called *The 100 Best Cruise Vacations* is sectioned first by geography (Caribbean cruises, Alaskan cruises, Mediterranean), but then each chapter begins with a rundown on the largest ship available, on down to the smaller cruises by barge and sailboat. Wedding destinations that go from east to west may move from large, expensive venues to small, inexpensive ones within each chapter. Factory tours may be divided by type of factory (food, auto, or toy) and then subdivided geographically or vice versa. Food festivals can be sectioned by type of food or by season, while a guide to learning vacations usually falls into chapters devoted to different specialties in the field.

History/biography/literary travel can be organized in several ways. There is the "following in the footsteps" type of book where you simply visit every place that was important in, let's say, Lincoln's life. After you have finished your travels you can redeploy your chapters so they match the chronological order from birth to death to burial place of the famous person you are following. Or you can place them in geographical order so it's easier for the reader to drive from one place to the other.

Themed anthologies, where you visit the boyhood homes of perhaps twenty-five famous writers, can be re-arranged by the chronological order of the artists' lifetime or by the country where they lived. If by country, then all English poets, dramatists and novelists would get thrown into the English pot before you embark for Russia and Dostoyevsky and Tolstoy. Special interest and special audience books allow for forays in many different directions. The main thing is to remain consistent once you have decided the way you are headed.

Travel Memoirs, Travel Essays, Literary Travel, Armchair Adventure

The format here approaches the fictional style. In fact, many travel memoirs would have been published as autobiographical novels or collected short stories thirty years ago. The only difference is that nowadays the material is deemed to be true. Otherwise, the richness of the writing, with an emphasis on description and/or the unusual adventures of the real-life hero and his observations, are cut from the same cloth that fiction writing teachers hold up as an example to their classes.

What some people call literary travel such as the title *Rowing to Alaska* is more closely aligned to a collection of short stories than a travel book. While several of the short narratives are connected by a similar venue (they take place in Central America and Alaska) they could each stand alone as a traveler's tale. The main theme that connects them all is the author's adventures, his grizzled companions, his point of view and his particular style of description. In fact, in many cases, such books are comprised of articles or stories that appeared first in literary magazines or upscale travel journals.

Memoirs tend to be chronological with the author starting in February and ending in May of the following year. Or they may have a geographical format with the author spending two chapters in Florence and three chapters in Africa. Of course a travel memoir that covers a year in the life of the author will usually follow a geographical and chronological order with Africa taking up January to June, and Spain, Florence and London the following seasons.

Armchair adventure books often read like novels except that the characters are real people. Travel essays, on the other hand, are compilations of one wanderer's musings, or a collection of various opinion pieces from a variety of writers with different backgrounds. The editor simply picks a theme that brings them all together. One edition of Traveler's Tales used the central theme of dangerous places and included reports from war zones and hurricane spots written by a variety of authors.

How To-Do-It Books

Whether you're writing about how to fly anywhere for free, how to pack a suitcase or whatever else in the vast "how-to" category, you'll find you are really writing a basic non-fiction book rather than a travel book. Therefore, you will probably lay out your chapters in a sequential form.

So it's mostly a matter of step A and then step B and so forth; but what those steps consist of is up to the taste of the author. For instance, a How-To-Pack Book might be divided into chapters on packing for cruises, airplanes or automobile rides and/ or packing for long trips, short trips, and business trips, and/or packing for different climates of different countries, or all of the above, sectioned into some sort of order.

With a How-to-do-it book, the outline becomes the table of contents and defines not only the limits of your coverage; it also demonstrates the way you intend to cover your material (your basic format). As an example, here is the Table of Contents from *The Traveling Woman: Great Tips for Safe and Healthy Trips* by Catherine Comer and Lavon Swain:

1. Researching your destination
2. Choosing Safe Transportation
3. Booking accommodations/fire safety/types of accommodations
4. Finances, phone cards& travel documents
5. Staying healthy while traveling
6. Starting a travel file
7. Packing
8. Your personal safety
9. Dealing with emergencies/finding help
10. Favorite websites for women

Appendix:
1. Authors' biographies
2. Travel resources
3. Index

As you can see, the chapters are in order, but — as with many non-fiction books that tell you how to do things — the progression from one topic to another is often a matter of personal choice. There is no exact order, as there would be in a book about constructing a house where, I assume, you start with a foundation and work your way up. Here the packing could have come before the staying healthy chapter, Chapter 2 and Chapter 3 could have been interchanged and Chapter 6," Starting a travel file" might have been placed practically anywhere. Like many other instructional books, this one features lists, checklists, to-do lists and a large appendix devoted to other resources.

When it comes to insider information books, the set-up may be a little different. Here the author may spend one-third to one-half of the book explaining how the travel industry does it (consolidate trips, kick people off airplanes, hold hotel reservations, train travel agents, pay couriers to lug documents around the world) and devote the rest of the text showing the reader how he is supposed cash in on this knowledge. The construction of the first half depends on the particular expertise of the author. The second half is the how-to-do it part — although sometimes when an expert tells you how to browbeat the help at a hotel or whisk through an airport it sounds a bit farfetched.

But since the how-to-do-it book category covers such a wide sphere and is often combined with some sort of destination or activity guide, the structure will vary considerably. Some "how-to" authors, especially those with a single thesis, (getting through airports, finding the right travel agent) discover that they come up short on the length of words. Using examples for their points, writing a few peripheral chapters and filling up the end space with a huge resource list is one way authors have found to enlarge their text. But many books in the how-to-do-it department come up with peculiar lengths like 78 or 118 pages.

Note: Details of the format such as giving directions, prices and hours, and such necessities of book construction as the index and appendix will be covered in Part Two: Creating the Framework.

Extra Values

These are extras that some publishers add to spur sales of their travel books:

CDs: Should you add on a CD of all those beautiful pictures you took? Some small presses and self-publishers include these placed in a slipcase that is pasted onto the inside of the back cover. These are costly and many bookstores and libraries do not like to handle books with inserts since they can easily be stolen. Travel guides with CDs are most often sold from websites where the sale is direct to the customer.

Coupons: Certain national guides such as the Mobil Travel Guide and the AAA travel books have a history of including coupons inside the book. These are discounts to attractions or free entrance for one person when accompanied by a paid admission.

Coupons work best with a directory-type book (such as the free guides given out by state tourism offices) that do not pretend to make value judgments or with well-trusted guides such as AAA or Mobil. However, many small, local guides use coupons as a form of added income, since local businesses usually pay a small fee to have the coupon inserted.

Website Updates: More and more guidebook websites are adding updates as an extra value to customers. Updates are particularly important in warning customers that a particular attraction has closed down or that a certain destination has become dangerous. Some also promote travel bargains from affiliates.

In chapter 9 and 10, I will go over those little details of the format that make travel guidebooks different from travelogues or essays

Chapter 7

Your Voice, Your Tone, Your Slant

In fiction writing, teachers often talk about one's "voice" and point of view. In essay writing there is no question that the voice belongs to the author. In fact, newspapers and television programs often hire particular people simply because they represent a political or social voice (left, right or center) that reflects the values of a certain portion of the population.

There is also the personal voice that comes through in one's writing. Staff journalists are often asked to subordinate their voice to the official tone of the newspaper they work for. Feature writers are allowed more leeway. And travel writers belong in the feature-writing category. In fact, travel writers are allowed to use the "I' person and their own unique voice more than other newspaper feature writers.

Since travel books are often a collaborative effort, a particular book may have three or four "voices". They all will have the same general tone, though. The tone of the book might be sophisticated, or enthusiastic or ultra-knowledgeable (as with the outdoor/ adventure author who cautions as well as explains how to rappel down the mountains) but all the contributors to that particular collection will add a slightly different flavor to the whole.

As you probably remember from elementary school grammar,

the voice is defined as the first, second and third person, better known as I, you and he/she/they. Travel writers use all three.

First Person: Used in memoirs, armchair travel, adventure travel, and humor. "I" was often eschewed in early guidebooks, and certainly in newspapers, but is much more accepted nowadays.

However, most guidebooks allow a slipping in and out of the first person so that one paragraph may start with "I" and another with "you". The author can move back and forth easily between the second person voice, the third person and the first person with ease. Whereas fiction writers are warned to keep to a single point of view, non-fiction authors are given a wider berth.

First Person plural (We): "We" is used when there is a family or group traveling together. In rare instances you might find the imperial or editorial "We" used in a pronouncement, but 95% of the time it's the travels of the couple or the gang of enthusiastic backpackers who constitute the personal plural. For instance: "We camped out under the stars at the foot of the cliffs that we hoped to conquer the following morning".

Second person: You and the understood "you" are found very frequently in travel writing and in guidebooks in particular, both in giving advice and commands. "Be sure to bring suntan lotion for the sailboat" or "wear a money belt beneath your shirt" are frequent admonitions one finds at the end of a paragraph. There is also the casual "you" that replaces the first person in imparting information to the reader.

Here is an example of the second person voice where much of the text was done in that mode. The guidebook *Free O.C.* lists free events and venues in Orange County, California. All entries show the basic information at both the top and the bottom of the write-up.

Last Thursdays Art Walk
Avenida Del Mar, San Clemente 92872
949-218-5378
www.lastthursdaysartwalk.com
Stroll the streets of this quaint Spanish Village by the Sea and delight in an evening of art, wine and cool sea

breezes.

Fourteen galleries and studios, most located along Avenida Del Mar, open their doors to visitors for three hours during this event for showings of art and demonstrations of their creative process. Many of the 16 local restaurants have wine tasting with the requirement that the wine be consumed inside the eatery. A FREE shuttle delivers you to one of five stops along the walk route. A map of the walk area, including shuttle stops, galleries and restaurants is on the Web site.

WHEN: Last Thu. every month May to Sept.

(Courtesy: *Free O.C. Orange County: The Ultimate Free Fun Guide to the California Riviera*)

The omniscient third person: In travel guides, the omniscient (or all-knowing) voice is found most often in sections concerning the history and culture of the place, but it also is used along with the first and second person as in the above paragraph about the last Thursday walk. Here is an example of the omniscient voice as used in standard narratives:

> "Taos was well established long before Europe emerged from the Dark Ages. The present pueblo of multistoried adobe apartment buildings has been occupied since about A.D. 1450.With about 1,100 residents, Taos Pueblo is governed by a council of 50 men who are members of the secret kiva religion. The economy is based on government services, tourism, arts and crafts, ranching and farming."

The quoted authority: One way travel writers get away from too much third or first person material is to quote an authority. The quote is of course given in the first person voice, but it almost always parlays information that would otherwise be given in text form. An example:

> "I've been serving guacamole sauce on my burgers since we opened," says Sid Guffey of Denver's **Charcoal Sid's** eatery, "and the people keep coming back for more. Maybe it's the chopped onion I put in, and just a little bit

of red pepper."

Guidebooks allow the author freedom of "person". Unlike a novel where you may be locked into the hero or heroine's point of view, travel writing allows for an easy flow back and forth from one person to another. In shorter travel articles, the writer usually chooses one (or at the most, two), and stays with that voice throughout the piece.

What's your background?

Your background also influences your voice. Travel writers come from all walks of life, but the most common background is one of the following:

Journalism school or journalistic training: Whether by attending college courses or by apprenticing to a local newspaper, the journalist has certain maxims stuffed into his brain. These include getting the facts straight, interviewing two or three experts on any subject, writing a good lead, coming up with a good article title (the rewrite guys used to do that) and other axioms.

The travel feature article has a specific slant with a beginning, middle and wrap-up final paragraph, usually about a single subject. It could be as narrow as the new scuba diving-spot in the Caymans or as large as "How to Do Moscow in Three Days". Writers with a journalistic background are more likely to depend on an authority for background material and less on their own personal reaction.

The Review style: Movie reviewers, restaurant reviewers, theater reviewers and ultimately travel reviewers come from a different corner of the world. They may have been English majors or journalism majors, or simply have expertise in some field. Restaurant reviewers often have cooking expertise, while theater and movie reviewers may have backgrounds in those fields.

Reviewers for newspapers and magazines are rarely staff members (except for major newspapers). They do their work from home or from the field, e-mail their story in and get paid as "contributing writers". Reviewers cast an analytical and sometimes caustic eye on the world, but their summations can be very important both to the reader and to the place reviewed.

The advisor/guide: Rick Steves became the everyman's guide to Europe by accident. Although he gives plenty of history and background for each country, it is his timely tips and his ability to plan itineraries for various folk that keep him popular. Of course he also writes very well.

How-to-do-it books are heavy on advice: the author often comes from a field of expertise, so a travel agent will write a guide on how to book your own travel, while airline personnel, hotel managers and such all come up with their own version of the inside scoop. Their writing skills vary, but since their books often amount to a compilation of checklists, it doesn't matter very much.

The Editor: The annotated directory needs an editor who can pull all the elements together and rewrite information from various sources, so that it melds into an organized whole. Themed anthologies that were written by various authors need an editor to pull all the pieces together and group them into consistent chapters. The editor's voice is either neutral or non-existent; it is his ability to shape the stories into an entertaining compilation that counts. As it happens, travel editors also become the authors of guidebooks simply because they pick up so much knowledge from the material that crosses their desks everyday.

The literary essayist or memoir author: In this genre of writing, the author's voice becomes more important than the subject he writes about. The literary essayist is often plucked from the field of fiction by a publisher who is looking for the literary slant. National Geographic Directions Series is an example of this; they approach the writer and ask him or her to do a book on a favorite destination or form of travel.

Imagined London by Anna Quindlen comes to mind. The book is a mélange of personal memories, biographies of the English literati, and a description both of modern London with its multi-cultural mix and the city of the past. A few visits are made to what is left of those tourist destinations that evoke the presence of Charles Dickens and Sherlock Holmes, but this is a book for people who enjoy Quindlen's style. The basic theme could have been covered in a travel magazine essay.

The adventurer journalist: (Also, the adventurer- photographer). This is a role that goes back hundreds of years to the days of Marco Polo. While some adventurers write an advice guidebook on how to live in the jungle or kayak down white-water rapids, most of these books fall into the armchair adventure realm. Non-fiction bestsellers about climbing Mount Everest, or sailing around the world belong in this category. Obviously this slant requires both an ability to write and the nerve to go out and live the adventure.

The amateur enthusiast: this could be anybody or everybody. This person is usually immersed in his subject. The subject could be traveling in the footsteps of literary heroes, discovering all the minerals in Yellowstone National Park, living in houseboats around the world, touting the virtues of bed and breakfasts, following theater festivals around the country, or hiking the northwest corner of some mountain that nobody else has hiked. Sometimes this person has an immense audience; sometimes a tiny one. The amateur enthusiast may have no background in writing and may need a co-author or a heavy dose of editorial guidance.

Your Personal Background

Aside from your professional and socio-economic background there is always a personal history. Bits and pieces of sights and sounds remain in the consciousness. All your experiences and memories become part of your expression on paper, so a little incident that occurred years before can flower into an observation in the present. Just as your economic class, your ethnic background, your nationality — in short, the culture where you grew up shapes the way you see things — so do the incidents in your life, large or small.

Your voice is your own. You may adopt a tone suited to a particular travel series (exuberant happiness or sophisticated cool) but the voice that comprises your thoughts, your memories, your observations and your way of seeing things, that is what makes your work different from another work that covers the same ground. Whether you are passionate about the environment or the indigenous peoples, whether you really blossom when writing about shopping, or art or scuba diving, or if it's the night life that sets your inner muse on fire, it is your taste and your outlook that inform your writing.

On the other hand, most writers tend to slant their prose to match the tone of the magazine or book publisher they are working for. This isn't difficult because the writer is drawn toward certain markets that are in tune with his voice. Very few authors maintain a pure personal voice that has no relation to the audience for which the piece is intended.

So if you write for an irreverent series your tone will be more caustic; if you write for a luxury series there will be opulence in your prose that is reflected in your descriptions. Books slated for a youthful crowd may employ a jumpy, jazzy tone filled with lots of today's lingo (I won't even try to give an example — it changes so quickly). Books intended for business folk employ a no-nonsense, practical tone.

There are also standard voices that the travel writer takes on. Just as the Italian street performers in the old days had set characters such as the clown, the harlequin and the flirt, certain persona appear in all travel writing. Crafted, of course, to conform to your personal voice, still certain postures show up in travel literature. Here are some typical voices:

- The funny, beleaguered Mom
- The funny beleaguered Dad
- The competent Mom/Dad/Grandma
- The sophisticated snob
- The cheapo college trekker
- The hip earth woman/man
- The no-nonsense single woman traveler
- The dog-lover (who assumes we all love Fido)
- The knowledgeable mentor (for wine, food, museums, antiques or whatever)
- Older sister to younger woman
- The party dude
- The hearty backpacker

- The ecological guru
- The professional expert (for how-to-do-it books)
- The just-the-facts-ma'am style
- The retired leisurely walker
- The outdoor leader

In travel writing, the author not only has a particular voice — he also sees things in a certain way. It is, after all, his vision that gives substance to the book and makes it more than a compilation of facts and figures. If he is interested in the spiritual, then he looks for spiritual meaning in anything from a rock to a sunset. If he is interested in the culture of the region, he will spend time offering history lessons and introducing you to places where you can meet real people in a foreign country. If he is interested in ecology, he will fill pages with descriptions of rain forests and desert trails.

So start doing some writing exercises (you'll find a few in Part Three) and see how your voice, your tone and your slant flavor your descriptions of a favorite subject.

Chapter 8

What Are Your Credentials?

Okay, you know what kind of book you are going to write and where you will find the audience. So the next question is: why are you the person to write this book? Whether you are proposing a book to a traditional publisher or publishing the guide yourself, you need to present some sort of credentials. This may be nothing more than the fact you took a trip and know how to write or that you have a platform in the shape of a website or popular blog. You have credentials if you are:

- A freelance travel writer
- A regular travel columnist for a newspaper or magazine
- An editor for the travel section of a magazine or newspaper
- An editor for a travel book series
- A published novelist with a background in travel
- A travel newsletter author
- The owner of a popular travel-related website

For the non-writer, acceptable credentials would include:

- Professor (e.g.: history, geology geography, ethnic culture)
- Airline Pilot or other airline employee
- Travel Agent or other travel professional

- Tour guide in a specific locale
- A hotel owner or manager
- A hiking or rafting guide
- Odd job that takes you around the world
- Travel website host

Expertise

Your expertise on a certain topic may be the needed credentials for the job. Let's say you are a professor of geology with many scientific papers to your credit. However, you want to write a trade book for the general public about the beauty and variety of the rock formations in Yosemite National Park. Now your expertise in geology is unassailable, but are you able to write good, clear, explicit prose? Academics tend to get bogged down in jargon. Can you write physical description? If not, perhaps you could find a co-author.

Are you an editor? Some editors can write, but frankly, others are better at editing someone else's work than creating their own. If you are an editor of a magazine or newspaper who is great at working up an article from a bunch of press releases, you are prime material for an annotated directory or anthology travel book.

Are you the right person for the subject matter? It doesn't matter how wonderful your credentials are, or how many articles have appeared under your byline, or how many magazines you may have edited — if you are ignorant on the subject that has to be covered, forget about it! You may be wonderful at describing action adventure, but when you enter a field of flowers, do you know a daisy from a dandelion?

Availability: At the other end of the spectrum is the college student or graduate who wants to travel around the world and make some spare cash while taking the journey. The *Let's Go* series uses only Harvard students. There are also several adventure-style series that utilize both students and young backpackers to track down the off-the-beaten- path nooks and the sometimes scary streets of major cities. In these cases, an ability to get the material in on time and a fearless attitude can get the assignment even if there is no track record. Usually, a neophyte author will be given only one section of a book to do, leaving the editors back home to ratchet up their prose.

Your clippings: If you read the guidelines from most publishers that do accept book proposals you will notice that they almost always ask for samples of your writing. And by that, they mean published samples, commonly known as clippings.

Does it matter that the sample appeared in your college newspaper rather than the Travel Section of the New York Times? Not really, if the piece you send is super. Does it matter that your "clippings" are all on travel websites on the Internet? That depends. If you are the official Guide for "Travel in France" on About.com you probably have more readers than the top travel writers for Travel and Leisure.

What publishers and editors really want to see is how you handle a subject, how well you can fit the information into the allotted space, how well you use language, how accurate your descriptions are, and whether you lean toward the cutesy or the serious. Publishers will often assign fledging authors a 1000-word article on the proposed destination to be considered for the job.

What if you have no clippings? Luckily, nowadays there is the blogosphere where anyone can post their writings and opinions, their travels and travails, and ultimately find an audience. Of course, if you can get some excerpts onto other people's blogs and websites, particularly travel websites, that's an extra. And there's always YouTube and MySpace for inventive types who know how to get their 15 minutes of fame.

Your background: If you are proposing a book about the fountains of Europe, the fact that you have been photographing fountains for the last five years and have done umpteen articles about them in various magazines around the world helps. All you have to do is persuade the editors that there are enough readers out there who are willing to buy such a book. If you are an expatriate who has lived in Egypt for the last ten years writing reports on the cotton trade and you see that Lonely Planet Publications is looking for ex-pats to do a book for long-term residents, then you are already in an enviable position.

Websites

To pump up your credentials post some travel pieces on an established website. There are several that accept travel pieces from free-lancers. In most cases they do not pay, but you may be able to wangle a free press trip on the basis of an assignment. The writers who send in pieces include professional freelancers and authors who offer excerpts from their books for publicity. Neophytes who write excerpts from their travel diaries during their treks to some far-off outpost also post in the hope of catching some editor's eye.

The following websites take some travel pieces, but be sure to follow their rules for submission. Since they get writers from around the world, the competition is stiff. There are also hundreds of small websites and e-zines where writers can post whatever leftovers they have — and this includes travel essays, destination write-ups, and restaurant reviews.

www.bootsnall.com
www.europebackpack.com (also a book publisher)
www.travelerstales.com (also a book publisher)
www.travellady.com (slick magazine style pieces)
www.gonomad.com (very popular — query first)
www.worldhum.com
www.frugalfun.com (their travel review section)
www.vivatravelguides.com (also an e-book publisher and a nascent print publisher).
www.independenttraveler.com has staff writers, but they take "trip reports" from free-lancers.

There are also the travel forums on such sites as Frommer's, Fodor's, Expedia, AOL, About.com and others. A well-written answer to somebody's question on a forum can be used for exposure if you mention that you are a travel writer. But be aware that the copyright for your words on these forums belongs to the owner, not to you!

I would also suggest you subscribe to the free newsletter at www.travelwriter.com which alerts writers to the needs of magazine and guidebook publishers for short content. The regular subscription price to their full newsletter (which is reasonable) gives professional writers access to editors and newspapers looking for stories and travel bureaus looking for coverage of special events. You don't get the free junkets unless you can demonstrate an assignment from an editor.

Create Your Own Website: Lots of people do it for fun, for profit or just because they have the technology to do it. One man documents his travels with his wife and mother-in-law all over Europe. Another makes a business of his travels by creating a free directory of airlines, cruise lines, hotels, resorts and linking his site to every conceivable other site. He gets loads of ads and free travel around the world. Of course, all self-publishers and many travel writers create a website as a way to sell their books.

Create Your Own Travel Blog: A lot easier than a website and absolutely free. Such places as wordpress.com and blogspot.com make it easy for almost anyone to have a blog. Getting people to read it is another matter. In many cases, authors who have websites simply add a running blog to the site.

There are also travel blog communities. These cyberspace venues act as bulletin boards where anyone can post a piece — amateur, professional, reprints or whatever. Two places I found are www.travelblog.com and www.travelblog.org. One of them sports much more professionally written work than the other — or maybe it was that I just happened to hit on a piece that was so full of misspellings and terrible grammar that I assumed that all of the articles on the site would be as bad. I won't tell you the name of the blogspot where I found the offending piece — check them both out yourself.

Whether it's used for resource material, a place to gain credentials or the premier venue for publicity, the Internet will play a greater and greater role in all publishing and particularly in travel publishing. Use it to its fullest. And if you proffer a piece, run it through an automatic spelling and grammar check before you hit the send button!

Part Two

Creating the Framework

Chapter 9

Nailing the Details

And now, for the specific details of your book, I going to assume that you are starting from scratch. Of course if you are doing a book for a publisher with a standard format many of these problems will have already been worked out. Or you may be in a 50/50 situation where you have to take care of certain details, while the publisher has pre-set icons and chapter headings. Here are the details I will cover:

- Icons
- Directions
- Price and hours
- Foreign exchanges
- Punctuation and grammar
- Sidebars and callouts

Icons

First you should make clear which icons will be used. Standard ones are those denoting wheelchair access, credit cards, airports, restrooms, subway or railroad stations, and dollar signs for price — but many guides go way beyond the standard few to create unique icons. If the author or editors have developed special icons for the severity of the hike, whether the wait staff at the restaurant is friendly and whether shopping bargains abound at a certain store, these should be explained to the reader.

For instance, stars, or the asterisk sign, (***) are commonly used to denote the quality of the hotel, restaurant or attraction, but some guides use specific icons such as a paw print to show dogs are allowed or a waving child to denote the place is kid friendly.

Somewhere in the front or back of the book you should have definitions for all your icons, even the obvious ones. A few publishers have developed very "personal" icons — do not attempt to use them, they may be copyrighted! On the other hand, inventing silly icons that don't really fill the bill just to be unique can become irritating to the reader.

If you are working for a travel series, the editors will give you their icon format.

Directions

How will you give directions? How would they be set out — would they come at the end of the paragraph, be put in a sidebar or be integrated into the text? When I wrote the first edition of *New Jersey Day Trips*, I instituted a set of rules. Driving directions were to be from the closest highway. Only one highway would be chosen, so that if a destination were equidistant from the Garden State Parkway and the New Jersey Turnpike, I would choose one and only one. Some books go into great details on directions; others simply give the address and a map. Some city books only give directions by public transport, while road guides may only use numbered roads and highways

You also have to decide on abbreviations for streets, avenues, roads and highways. Most publishers have their own style sheet for these. If you have no publisher's guidelines, then use a style manual. Here are some of the most frequently used abbreviations:

Avenue = Ave. or Av. First letter usually capitalized
Street = St.
Road = Rd.
Highway = Hway
Interstate = I
Route: Rte.

County = Cty.
State = abbreviation for that state, i.e.: Rhode Island = R.I.
S = south, W = west, E = east, N = north

Abbreviations should be consistent with the language. Consistency and conformity are the bedrock of editing, so streets, avenues, boulevards in any language should have the same abbreviations. When writing about a foreign country, follow their custom in abbreviating streets. In English it may be Fifth Ave. but in Spanish it may be Av. De la Colon. When it comes to Canadian provinces, Swiss cantons, Parisian arrondissements and other such subdivisions, a glossary of abbreviations at the very front of the book is helpful.

Hiking and biking: In books devoted to hiking and biking, detailed directions are fifty percent of the book, and are often part of the text with directions to hiking up a hill mixed in with descriptions of the foliage, musings on nature, bird sightings and other such things. Here are simple car directions that allow the reader to find the place where he can start his hike or walk. This sample is from a book called *"Natural Wonders of Virginia"* by Deane and Garvey Winegar for a place called the Smith Mountain Lake State Park:

> **"Where**: North Shore of Smith Mountain Lake in Bedford County, about 35 miles east of Roanoke. From Roanoke drive east on State 24 to State 43. Follow State 43 to County 626 at Woodford Corner. Go southwest on County 626 to the park."

In these directions, the starting point is Roanoke. State roads are called "State 43" and county roads are called "County 626". Whether they are designated as such on the signs in Virginia is another matter. Maybe the actual sign says VA 43 and Route 626. The authors use compass directions when one comes to an intersection, rather than left or right. Someone else might have written the last part of the directions as: Follow State Road 43 to Woodford Corner, then turn left onto C 626 and continue to the park.

Whether you use left and right or south and north, County or Route, depends on the common usage of the place. When I lived in Hawaii on the island of Oahu, it was common to give directions in terms of the Hawaiian words for "toward the ocean" or "toward the mountain" and east and west of a certain landmark.

Directions in bike book: In *25 Mountain Bike Tours in New Jersey*, author Peter Kick gives very specific directions for a circuit ride beginning at Peters Valley Craft Center in the Delaware Water Gap National Recreation Area. He tells you where to park your car and then (taking your mountain bike with you) turn toward Kuhn Road. He gives the directions using mileage readings on a cyclometer based on one-hundredth of a mile starting at zero.

"00: Head west on Kuhn Road, climbing uphill. This short section of road is paved.
0.50: Pass a wetland area on your left.
0.70: At a T, go left on Old Mine Road
0.95: The road turns to dirt and descends slightly."

Directions in a city: Here you might use such directions as right and left, downtown or uptown or possibly east and west. Since most guidebooks to cities chop the destination into distinct "bite-sized" districts, it is not uncommon to start with the best-known landmark in a particular district and then radiate out from that point. Or you just might trek, street by street, from your easternmost point. For example, for walking directions in New York City: Follow Fifth Avenue south for eight blocks until you come to the Empire State Building which is on the corner of 34th St. From there you can proceed three long blocks west and one block south to the Penn Station/Madison Square Garden complex (33rd St. & 8th Ave).

City guides will also include public transportation. There will usually be an introductory paragraph which describes the various public routes, what they are called, how often they come, what they cost, whether you have to buy a token and how to use the automatic token machines. Once you have told the reader that BART equals The Bay Area Rapid Transit and that the subway system in both Paris and Washington D.C. is called the Metro, you can then go on to give the exact name of the station when giving directions.

In *Walking Shakespeare's London* by Nicholas Robins, the author sets up twenty walks each of which encompass an historical area of note (although many of the original buildings no longer exist). Each perambulation starts at an Underground Station and most of them end at another stop along the Tube. The bulk of each chapter is given over to the history of the various landmarks the reader will encounter, their relation to Shakespeare or to the theater, plus all the directions for turning right or left, crossing the street, and going down this or that alley.

Time is approximate for each venture and when there are public attractions included (such as the Tower of London) extra time is allotted for those who want to enter and take the tour. Here, for instance, are the directions for the walk between one Underground (subway) station and another.

Start: Blackfriars Underground Station
Finish: Monument Underground Station
Length: 2 km. (1 1/4 miles)
Time: 1 hour
Refreshments: The Old Wine Shades, Martin's Lane (1653)

(The book goes on to list a number of stops within this walk)

Suppose you are doing a book on a large city like New York or Chicago. These cities are easily broken down into cultural or ethnic sections such as "The Loop", "Broadway" "The Village", "The North Shore", "The Museum Mile", and "The Historic District". Within the chapters for each section, some books include a grid map showing the streets.

As with its other series guides, the *Access Guide to Chicago* takes this to the extreme with each city section getting a grid map and all sites given a number. Because a hotel may be close to a museum or historical building along a particular avenue, each type of attraction is given a different color. Restaurants and clubs are red, shops are orange, hotels are purple, historic and cultural attractions are blue (that is, their headings are done in colored type). <u>Because the grid map has clearly labeled streets and avenues on it, there is no need to give street-by-street walking directions.</u> A book like this obviously needs a skilled cartographer.

Directions from Highways: Look at a website for a popular attraction and you will see that four or five directions are usually given. These include directions from the north, south, east and west. They always start with a large well-known highway and then trickle to smaller roads. Are you going to put all of these options into your book? Some authors give all directions from the best known highway. Others simply give the address, the phone number and the website so that the reader can find all possibilities themselves. And still others pick the most prominent highway and give directions only from that point. Much depends on the space you have available.

I urge anyone desirous of writing a guidebook to a foreign country to read the customer reviews of all books written about that country. One of the most common complaints is that the directions are useless or absolutely misleading. People complain of being lost for hours because they followed the travel writer's directions. What can one do? Municipalities do change the names of streets. Restaurants do disappear or turn into bakeries. Here are a few suggestions:

- Give walking directions as left or right rather than east or west. Most people walking in a city don't have a clue as to what direction they are going. Give driving directions to include east, west, north and south because most road signs include a compass direction.
- If a road has a number such as C-28 (County road 28) use that rather than the name of the road (Honeysuckle Highway). Or use both.
- Don't use landmarks that might change, such as a BP station or Dolly's Chop House.
- Give both the names and the numbers (if there are any) for metros and subways, such as: Place Vendome (stop # 34)
- If you feel that the official directions to a

particular destination sends the traveler through dangerous streets or rough back roads, figure out your own directions and offer them instead.

- Don't write "slide-over" descriptions that connote the wrong impression. Read "Accurate but Misleading" in Part 3 of this book.

Hours and Prices

Hours: These can be formatted as part of a sidebar or included in the text. When an attraction is only open for a limited time, it is simpler to incorporate the hours into the text. For instance: "The balloon festival runs annually the last weekend of July, starting at 3 p.m. Fridays and running from dawn to 10 p.m. on Saturday and Sunday."

When used in a sidebar or underneath the entry, the hours should always be consistent. For instance, if you abbreviate Sunday as Sun. or use p.m. or pm, keep that usage constant. Decide from the beginning whether it's going to be "Hours: Sat. & Sun.:12-3 pm." or "Open Saturdays and Sundays, 12 to 3 PM".

Prices: When I first wrote *New Jersey Day Trips*, I included exact prices and hours and assiduously changed them for each edition. But because prices became so volatile my co-author and I decided that for the 10th edition we would switch to dollar signs. Some publishers avoid the whole problem by simply stating that there is an admission fee (or that admission is free).

Here is the simple code we used for range of prices. Some people would have made the break point at 9.99 so that an attraction that charged $10 would appear in the $10 to $15 dollar range.

$ = up to $5
$$ = $5.01 to $10
$$$ = $10.01 to $15
$$$$ = $15.01 to $25
$$$$$ = $25.01 and above

What about Foreign Phrases?

When it comes to writing a travel guidebook to a country where a foreign language is spoken, you're going to have to make a decision as to how many phrases and words you are going to include, and where you will put them. Should they all go into a separate Glossary? Should they be dealt with as you go along, so that food translations appear in the restaurant chapter and questions about bed and board go in the hotel section? You could create drop down lists at the beginning of each chapter with common phrases that the tourist is likely to ask. Rick Steves in his guide to Paris incorporates a few important phrases right into the Orientation chapter and also includes the phonetic spelling, so that the first-time tourist has some grounding. He also has a back-of-the-book phrasebook section.

The more foreign the language (in terms of alphabet, and whether it is written from left to right or right to left or up and down the page) the more the author must translate the basic words. In *Lonely Planet: Vietnam* (7th ed.), eleven pages are given over to a chapter titled "Tastes of Vietnam". Here you get a dissertation on manners, history and type of food in each section of the country, but there are also food glossaries bunched within the chapter so you learn that *Nuoc mam* is a fermented sauce and *com* is the word for rice. Side dishes are named and explained. The back of the book includes a glossary of common terms and a guide to pronunciation for each region of the country.

In the *Rough Guide to Vietnam,* general information on eating and drinking and a quick glossary of common food terms are part of their Basics chapter which appears at the beginning of all Rough Guides. In "Contexts" at the back of the book, a glossary of common phrases and acronyms needed for tourists takes up three pages.

Another thing to remember is that certain place names are different in the mother country than they are in guidebooks written in English. For years, the capital of China was called Peking in English until everybody agreed to write it as Beijing. Then there is Lake Lemans in Switzerland, which we call Lake Geneva but the Swiss insist on calling by their own name. So a tourist would be perplexed by the fact that the towns of Montreux and Vevey are situated on Lake Lemans according to the local map, while his guidebook informs him that these towns are on Lake Geneva. Here it is best to put the translation in immediately, so the text would read: "The docks at Lake Geneva (called Lake Lemans in Switzerland) offer boat rides to many ports along the Swiss Riviera".

As for phrases to include in your own guidebook, undoubtedly the following would be necessary:

- I need the police
- Where is the bathroom?
- Where is Hotel (blank?)
- Where is a telephone?
- I need a doctor
- Do you speak English?
- Is there a restaurant nearby?
- I need to find a pharmacy
- I need a taxi
- Where can I buy (toothpaste, suntan lotion, pills, etc.)?
- Please/pardon me/ thank you
- What time is it?
- How much does this cost?

A list of important foods in the foreign language such as: milk, coffee, tea, beef, pork, chicken, vegetables, fruits, plus the names of dishes you are likely to eat such as chicken paprikash or *pot au feu* plus all the words for coffee, sandwiches, various fruits, bread, wine and water should be mentioned. A reminder that if you want steak in France you should order entrecote, not bifstek, or that the tip is included in the bill, is the sort of thing that might go into a sidebar in this section.

When it comes to languages where both the alphabet and the pronunciation are foreign to the English-speaking tongue, there will probably be a greater reliance on phonetic spelling and/or a visual example of some important written words. For such countries you might mention those hotels where the visitor is most likely to find English spoken.

General Information for Foreigners

A destination book always has to include some basic information that would be important to travelers who come from a different part of the world or even of the country. For world travelers, you have to assume that the tourist knows very little about the country he is visiting. So it doesn't matter if you are writing book about Chicago or Katmandu, to the person who is a total stranger, certain matters are a mystery.

If you are covering a country where religious observances and cultural mores vary in the extreme from American or Western culture, you need a chapter devoted to those specific differences. However, let's say you are writing a book about one of the states in the United States. You would still need to include certain basics even if you assume that your primary reader is an American. Most Frommer's guides list the following topics for the foreign visitor in a special chapter. This list includes:

- Necessary documents (passports, visas, etc.)
- Medical requirements if any,
- Standard hours for banks and businesses
- Currency and exchange rates
- What you can bring through customs
- Information on postage and mail
- Tipping
- Electricity currents
- Local and state taxes, and a few other things

Money conversions: This is usually put at the front of the book. You can easily establish what is reasonable/medium/expensive and very expensive by translating the foreign currency into dollars and then establishing the ratio.

Miles, Kilometers, and Liters: The mileage problem is going to come up since most of the world uses the metric system. The Fodor guides use the metric system when it applies to the country they are covering and put the equivalent amount in miles in parentheses. They do this consistently, so that in reading the text you will come upon this sort of thing: "the distance between City A and City B is 40 kilometers (34.5 miles)". The DK Eyewitness Travel series, a British publication, handles it thusly in their book about Egypt: "Greater Cairo covers an area of 457 sq. km (178 sq. miles)"

The easiest way to include information about kilometers, liters and such is to place it in the Orientation chapter or the appendix. Here are some common translations of measurements:

One mile = 1.6093 km (kilometers)
One acre = 0.4047 ha (hectares)
One quart = 0.9463 liters (liquid measure)
One gallon = 3.7853 liters

Grammar and Punctuation

Whether you are using an outside editor or not, it's important to consult one of the many guides to style and usage when you go over your grammar and punctuation. Check your spelling, but if you use Word's spellchecker system go over their corrections carefully. Mine has a tendency to substitute "you're" for "your" and "its" for "it's" for no logical reason.

Bold and Italic: Most manuals of style contain very short lists of words that may be italicized. These include ships and titles of books. However, in most guidebooks there is a carte blanche approach to using both bold and italic type when mentioning attractions. If you want to recommend the Via Veneto restaurant which happens to be located at 15 Via Veneto, you have to put the restaurant's name in bold or italic so there is no confusion. For example:

> **Via Veneto:** 15 Via Veneto, Rome. Famous bistro with oodles of outside tables for people watching. Fairly pricey drinks, reasonable food, good veal dishes, and a collection of tourists from all over to sample them.

Capital Letters: When it comes to canals, turnpikes and castles there is a difference of opinion. In most usage books, the Panama Canal is capitalized. But if you refer to it in a sentence further on in the paragraph do you say Canal or canal? According to *The Elements of Grammar* by Margaret Scherzer, you capitalize. Let's say you are spending two pages on the wonders of Blenheim Castle. After your first introduction do you keep referring to it as the Castle? It's a matter of the stylebook you follow.

Political Correctness: There is also the problem of political correctness in questions of grammar and style. Many publishing houses, especially university and textbook houses adhere to the non-bias gender rule. While the old-fashioned rule of grammatical agreement says that a singular noun must use a singular pronoun, new rules state that the general *he* should be replaced with *he/she*. This can become pretty awkward when it comes to descriptions such as "Anyone who sees the sun set over the Grand Canyon feels that thrill in his or her heart." Perhaps one reason that first-person descriptions have come back into vogue is that they solve the problem of "he/she" political correctness.

If you are writing for a publishing house, they will give you their stylistic format. They may have a rule that you use serial commas at all times, or that non-English phrases are not put in italics or that their icons have to be coded in. If you are self-publishing then all these rules have to be decided beforehand. You may ask a line editor to go over your work with just these rules in mind.

Sidebars, Boxes and Callouts

If you have only 3 Days in Paris, see:
The Louvre
Musee D'Orsay
Bateaux Mouche
Sacre Coeur
Napoleon's Tomb
Notre Dame
The Latin Quarter.

In the old days there were simply sidebars. These were on the side, of course, next to the regular text, and they were used to place the basic facts (price, hours, telephone number) about the restaurant or hotel for easy reference. Then newspaper travel articles began to sprout sidebars with expanded information that included driving directions, "best time of year to visit" and the website. Then the USA Today format with "factoids" in pink-tinted boxes became popular.

Soon every non-fiction publisher had gone beyond the simple sidebar and was putting lists of "top ten choices" and short anecdotes into boxes or gray areas with borders. If you look at 2006 edition of *The Unofficial Guide to Disney World*, you'll see this phenomenon taken to the extreme. There are little "unofficial tips" callouts popping up everywhere. Then there are the words of wisdom from readers that are put into red type rather than black. There are also picks and reminders showing up in sidebars, grayed areas and boxes. There is no law saying you have to use sidebars but they are very popular right now.

Sidebars: Here is a typical example of the sidebar that puts information in a boxed area below the running text. This one is for quick facts:

> Hotel du Garde. 45 rooms. Three-star hotel three blocks from the Gare du Nord RR station. Continental breakfast included. Elevators. A/C. TV. $160 night summer season. 141 Rue de Plessis. Telephone:

Callouts: Callouts refer to text inside a balloon shape that sports a little point — the familiar way cartoon characters speak to each other. Some publishers prefer the callout for small nuggets of information:

The full or half-page sidebar: Nowadays, the large sidebar has many other uses. I call this format "drop-downs". They are used for fillers such as a list of top ten places. The large sidebar also jazzes up what might otherwise be a heavier tome. For example, many books have a "drop-down" within each chapter with titles such as the Top Ten or Best Bets.

- The Top Ten Beaches for Surfing
- Best buffet bets in Las Vegas
- Ten Best Bars for Mixing and Mingling
- Where to find the best views of Mt. Baldy

You may create a list yourself, or the publisher may tell you he wants a list of "top ten" in each chapter. These can be boxed at the beginning or end of the chapter or used as a drop-down box in the middle.

Ten Reasons to Have a Top Ten List

1. It calls attention to what you are saying
2. Book designers love them because
    they cost more money
3. You can repeat facts that might
    have gotten lost in the text
4. It uses up a lot of space
5. You can throw in anecdotes that don't fit in the text
6. You can put in quotes that you
    cribbed from a quote book
7. You can put in historical facts so people who
    hate historical facts can skip over them.
8. It makes the book seem more valuable.
9. You can make a list on any topic.
10. Everybody else is doing it.

Drop-Down Recipes: Let's say you are doing a book on the "Carolina's Best Bed and Breakfasts" and intend to drop in at least twenty recipes. You should probably try to keep these recipes all to one size so that they can be "dropped in" using a particular format. Perhaps they will take up a full page, maybe less. These can then be spaced throughout the book to liven up the text. The effect of such "down home" recipes is to impart the flavor of Southern hospitality to the entire work.

When You Are Working For a Series

Series producers have very set rules for their sidebars, boxes and callouts. A glance at the 13-page *guidelines for authors* for the series The Dog-Lovers Companion shows that the company expects authors to come up with one "callout" for every 2400 words. And this particular publisher wants the callouts to be new and different from the regular text, not just a summary of previous material.

Now different publishers have different rules, and the same publishing company will often have a variety of styles for each of its series, so who does what and how he does it should be made clear from the start. Other series producers may be less formal and expect one or two boxed anecdotes per chapter or a list of at least ten "Best Picks" throughout the book.

If you are self-publishing and are setting up the text yourself, you can use boxes, callouts and sidebars to your heart's content. If you are preparing a book proposal for a publisher that does not have a set rigid style, you can mention that you intend to pepper the book with anecdotes, histories, or side information, and that you plan to have these set off separately from the main text. It is up to the publisher to decide how these will be formatted and his book production crew will take care of the details.

Note: Editors, printers and publishers often use terms such as "callout", "pull-out" or "sidebar" to mean the same thing: placing information outside of the regular text for emphasis.

Chapter 10

Structuring the Material

Although you know by this time how much your book will cover and how you will approach the material, getting down to detailed construction of your format is the next step. You may have decided to divide the chapters by subject or by geography but how will you subdivide them? Here are some specifics of various formats as used in several guidebooks.

Subject Format: The example I am using is *The Food Lover's Guide to Paris* by Patricia Wells. The chapters are divided by Subject (in this case, the type of establishment) and then subdivided geographically (in this case the arrondissements) of Paris. As Ms. Wells explains in the opening chapter, Paris arrondissements are numbered from 1 to 15. Therefore she starts with the lowest number and goes up until the highest. Within each arrondissement, the establishment (whether a restaurant, a wine bar or a bakery) is listed alphabetically using the French name and applying French rules of usage.

Each listing gets a paragraph or two, usually with a picture alongside. Necessary facts (address, phone, hours, and prices) are done in sidebars next to each paragraph. This style is varied slightly in later chapters. For extras there are anecdotes and factoids that appear in boxed format and twenty recipes are dropped in at intervals.

There is no index, but a full table of contents and running

heads for each chapter makes it easy for a reader to look up a particular restaurant or café. However, a very large glossary exists. In the front matter there is a definition of the varied types of venues that will be covered such as bistros, brasseries, cafes, wine bars, and restaurants. The glossary in back translates French culinary terms and menu items into English and runs 37 pages.

Seasonal Format: *52 Great Weekend Escapes: Northern California*. This book is sectioned into the four seasons. Under each season there are thirteen chapters. These chapters are subdivided into five easy, five medium and three difficult weekend excursions. As you might surmise from that kind of division, the book is heavy on outdoor activities. The easier ones are simple climbs in Yosemite and hot air ballooning over Napa Valley while the more difficult ones involve climbing sheer cliffs and kayaking down the rapids.

Circuit Format: *Day Walker: 32 Hikes in the New York Metropolitan Area*, published by the New York/New Jersey Trail Conference, begins in Manhattan as a central point and branches out to Westchester, Connecticut, New Jersey and Long Island. While there are interesting history and geology lessons in the book, there are also specific directions to each of the 32 locations with full descriptions of the scenery as well as turn-by-turn directions.

The Geographical Format: While these vary, the basic format can be seen in the Rick Steves series and the Access Guides

In *Rick Steves' Germany & Austria 2005*, the first thirty pages are given over to basic information. After that the division is geographical with Germany coming first. Within that country, Munich is first, then Bavaria and Tirol, which is then subdivided into Fussen and Reutti. Berlin comes toward the end of the book and of course takes up many more pages. But there is methodical coverage of all the towns and villages in the country. Larger cities garner their own chapter. Smaller places are bunched together under titles such as Baden-Baden and the Black Forest.

A more general geographical format is used in books concerned with special destinations. So that *100 Best U.S. Wedding Destinations* simply starts out on the east coast and ends up in Hawaii.

The Know-It-All Format: Popularized by such series as Lonely Planet and Fodor's, this format sections the book into chunks of important knowledge such as Getting There, Getting Around, Top Attractions, Best Budget Bets, and so forth and then subdivides the work into both geographical chapters (the Northside, the Eastside, the Westside) and subject chapters (hotels, nightclubs, restaurants, sightseeing).

The Unique Format: If you are doing a book called The Best Bed and Breakfasts in Atlanta, you can create your own divisions. You could start with the B&Bs that are closest to the center of town, or those with the most rooms, or go from the most expensive to the cheapest or the most historic to the most modern. If you search the libraries and bookstores you will find many books that use a unique format to cover the material.

How will your chapters flow?

Once you have decided on your format, you must now plan out how you will create the flow of your chapters. Will you go from east to west or from north to south? Will you start with highlights first and then backtrack to general information? Will there be asides, and sidebars that show up in all chapters or just a few? Will you try to balance pictures throughout? Sometimes this is difficult since certain subjects are much more picturesque than others. Maps may be an integral part of the text or placed in the front or back matter — publishers choose either way.

Should you begin your chapters with a general premise, a point on the compass, a personal point of view, or a historical summation? You decide. Some chapters may go under fanciful headings (like Roses and Chocolate Bars, Where Washington Slept, Ate and Fought, Bicycling and B&Bs). Others may be clear and direct like "Architectural Chicago" or "Outfitting Your RV before the Trip".

Many authors try for a uniform length in chapters, but that is not always possible. You may find, as you go along, that a particularly large or unwieldy chapter has to be chopped up into smaller, bite-size bits. On the other hand, you may have to cobble together a few leftovers (like canoeing and kayaking) into a single "potpourri" chapter. Whether you have too much or too little depends on your subject matter and how wide a circumference you have chosen to encompass. Beefing up or chopping down the text will occur at the first edit stage when you realize that you have either overwritten or underwritten the book.

Depending on the general organization you use, chapters may flow easily from one to another with some reference to previous chapters (i.e.: unlike the Piedmont section of Virginia, the flat broad eastern section offers easy biking if you stay away from the cities.) Other books, divided by subject, can have chapters that can easily be interchanged and moved around to support a more balanced look or room for more photographs. Since there is no relation between zoos and museums, there is no reason that a book that includes both should have their chapters placed close to each other.

Your scope should also include such factors as interviews with personnel at the destination, illustrations and extensive sidebars relating history, personal observations and/or anecdotes. It is not unusual to have an in-depth coverage of a city or an event (for instance, Mardi Gras in either New Orleans or Rio de Janeiro), while offering cursory coverage of other destinations within the same book.

On the other hand, I have seen "off-the beaten track" guidebooks that spend pages of material on little known parks and dusty towns. With these "off-the beaten track" books it is particularly important to unearth interesting anecdotes about these places. Murders, ghosts, pirates or a restaurant situated in a mansion that once was a brothel, all help to bring color and intrigue to many a small town or far-flung outpost.

Details of individual entries

After you get into the heart of the text, there is the matter of treating your individual entries. These tend to be a paragraph or two in size and they offer a synopsis of the attraction. It could be a museum, a forest, a casino or a sports arena. But whether the entry is long or short, you have to determine its exact scope. This will vary with the subject, but most authors maintain a similar approach to all their entries within a chapter if not within the whole book.

I'll use the **Musee d'Orsay** in Paris as an example. Assuming this was a book about Paris that was sectioned geographically and I was writing an entry for that museum, I would include the following (aside from basic facts such as hours and price):

- The type and importance of the collection (referencing a few well-known paintings).
- A description of the building itself.
- A history of the building's transformation from a train station.
- The eating areas.
- The escalator and elevator, and how easy it is to get lost here.
- The proximity of the Louvre and the Metro stations.

How do you begin your medium sized entry? Here's an example:

Musee D'Orsay: 62 Rue de Lille, Arrondissement 13, Paris. Tel.: 01 40 49 48 14.

Hours: 10-6 daily. Admission fee. Free first Sunday of month. Half-price other Sundays. Restaurant-open 12-3 p.m. Paris City-card? Yes.

Want to savor an omelet within view of a Tahitian princess painted by Paul Gauguin? Try the café on the second floor of the Musee D'Orsay where the largest collection of Impressionist and post-Impressionist paintings in Paris is housed in a converted railroad terminal. Whistler's Mother in grey and black — Toulouse-Lautrec's vivid red-lipped prostitutes and Manet's Picnic on the Grass are all on view. Since the collection includes everything of note from 1814 to 1914, you will also see works by Picasso and Matisse as well as the academicians of the 19th century. (I would put in another paragraph or two here.)

Restaurant Format: Many travel books will use a separate format for all pertinent information on restaurants and place that on one side of the page, as a sidebar or underneath the entry, often using bold face type for the first word. Here, for instance, is a common style of roundup information as it would appear beneath the entry for an imagined eatery called **The Phony Pizza Palace:**

Location: 141 West Fourth St.
Ambience: Pizza parlor with class
Price Range: $14.00 — $19.00
Dress Rule: Casual
Best Bet: Margherita pizza
Alcohol: BYOB
Hours: Mon.-Fri.: 12-9. Sat., Sun.: 12-11.
Telephone: 212-555-3446
Website: www.phonypizzapalace.com

Another common format is to have the information split — with the name, address and telephone number on top, the review in the middle and the other information at bottom. An example:

The Phony Pizza Palace, 141 W. Fourth St. Tel. 212-555-3446
Regulars rave about the thin crust Margherita pizza here although you can also partake of calzone and standard spaghetti fare. Prices range from $14.00-$19.00 for an elaborate pie. They even have a decent salad and desserts.
Ambience: Pizza parlor with class
Price Range: $14.00-$19.00
Dress Rule: Casual
Best Bet: Margherita pizza, antipasto Bolognese
Alcohol: BYOB
Hours: Mon,-Fri..: 12-9. Sat., Sun.: 12-11
Website: www.phoneypizzapalace.com

Restaurant formats vary all over the place and if you are writing an independent book it is a good idea to create your own format. Of course, it should be easy to comprehend.

If your book specializes in a specific type of food consumption (vegetarian, vegan or whatever) you may have to invent icons or abbreviations to simplify your entries. Just make sure you alert the reader as to what your symbols mean.

Text format: Whether it's a restaurant or some other attraction, many guidebooks use the internal textual format to inform the reader of what to see as he ambles down the street. When using the running text it is common to place the name of the attraction in bold letters so that it stands out from the rest of the paragraph.

Here are some details from my write-up of New Hope, Pennsylvania which begins with a general synopsis of the town and then mentions specifics as part of the running text:

Another warm weather attraction is the **New Hope Mule Drawn Barge Ride** which offers one-hour rides down the old canal works. It is a slow and easy way to see the town. It departs from the barge landing at New Street and several rides are offered during the afternoon. Call 215-862-0758 for details. A popular pontoon ride is **Coryell's Ferry** which offers scenic rides on the Delaware. It loads behind Gerensee's Exotic Ice Cream Store, 22 S. Main St. (Telephone: 215-862-2050).

Chapter 11

Front Matter

After the main text of the book has been written, you turn to the front matter, which in most books consists of:

- The half title (optional)
- Title Page
- Copyright page
- Foreword/ Preface (optional)
- Map or picture (optional)
- Acknowledgements (optional)
- Dedication (optional)
- Table of Contents
- List of illustrations or maps (optional)

The half-title (or bastard title) page contains only the title of the book. The title page includes the title, subtitle, author's name, edition (if a subsequent edition), the name of publishing house and the city where the publishing house resides. Some trade paperbacks discard the half title page as a relic of old time printing practice.

Titles and Subtitles

Most books on writing will tell you to get a short and snappy title. This isn't always possible with a destination book when every possible title seems to be taken. You can come out with a zingy title like *The American Virgins*, but you would have to subtitle it: *A travel guide to St. Thomas, St. Croix and St. John* if you want your target audience to buy it. So try for a title that is self-explanatory.

Subtitles: Subtitles have two functions. One is to further explain what the book is about or what territory it covers to the prospective reader. The second is to contain keywords so that Internet search engines will put the title under a variety of headings. Take the following book: *The Rough Guide to San Francisco: Includes the East Bay, Wine Country, Marin County and Silicon Valley*. Now there's a subtitle! Not fascinating, not witty, but clear enough to interest the search engines. Type in the words: wine country, Marin county and Silicon Valley and this title should appear somewhere along the line. Its purpose is to attract as many readers as possible from any direction.

The keyword has become an obsession with publishers. When Globe Pequot put out a new version of a book published ten years before by a different company, they changed the subtitle. The first book was called *A Walker's Guidebook: Serendipitous Walks near New York City including a section for Birders*. The new book is titled: *Serendipitous Outings near New York City: On Foot in New Jersey, Long Island, the Hudson Valley, Connecticut and Pennsylvania*.

The new subtitle lists every geographical area that will be covered by name, rather than the vague "near New York City". This gives the search engines five more points of interest than the first subtitle did. When customers go to their computers looking for information, you never know exactly how they will key in the words. Will they type in "Walks in Connecticut?" or "Outings in the Hudson Valley?" The more keywords that exist in the title, the more possibilities this book will surface when the casual reader types in a particular word.

Series Names: Many of the best known imprints are named after their originators: whether that is Arthur Frommer or Thomas Cook, the tour company founder. But finding a new series name has turned the publishing world into a jousting field. Publishers rush to trademark anything that sounds like it could possibly take off as a series. 60 Hikes, 50 Hikes, the Campus Guides, Off the Beaten Path, Great Destinations, Cheap Eats, Cheap Sleeps, The Unofficial Guide, the Irreverent Guide, the Hotel Detective, ad infinitum.

The Copyright Page

This page is most important to you the author and the publisher. The copyright page goes on the verso (or other side) of the title page. It contains, among other things, the copyright citation. It usually also contains a disclaimer. It may also contain permission notes about photographs, trademarks and anything else of a legal nature.

The copyright citation: You can simply copy the wording of someone else's copyright page, e.g.: Copyright: 2007, Joe Doaks. All rights reserved. No part of this book can be reproduced or transmitted in any form or by any means, electronic or mechanical, including photocopying, recording or any other information storage or retrieval system without permission in writing from the publisher. (Some publishers add: with the exception of short paragraphs for the purpose of reviewing)

The CIP: If you are publishing with an established publishing house they will probably get a CIP or cataloging in publication "card" which is an electronic version of the old fashioned catalog card. The CIP card gives the Library of Congress classification for the book. Self-publishers who cannot get a CIP block may obtain a LCCN number. The LCCN number is usually put down at the bottom below or above the ISBN number.

The Disclaimer: Many authors and/or publishers put a disclaimer in the front of the book. This is basically a legal notice letting all readers be aware that the author is not responsible for any mishaps that may occur while visiting any of the places that were mentioned within the text. In other words, if a reader breaks his neck diving off a cliff in Acapulco, or gets mugged while visiting an offbeat art gallery, don't blame the author because he thought these were great fun. Here's an example:

All recreational activities include a certain amount of risk. The publisher and author disclaim any responsibility and any liability for any injury, harm or illness that may occur through or by use of any information in this book.

The trademark disclaimer: Many venues you cover are trademarked. Disney World, Air France, Celebrity Cruises and Holiday Inn are among the many names you may have reason to include in your book. Rather than add the trademark notation every time you mention the name, it is customary to make a blanket trademark disclaimer on the copyright page.

The Advisory Note: This is not so much a legal statement as simple advice that you are not responsible if the customer shows up at a museum which is either closed or charging twice as much as it did last month. It states the following: **Note**: Although every attempt is made to keep the information contained in this book as up-to-date as possible, prices, hours and availability of any of the destinations mentioned may change at any given time.

Credits and permissions: If you have the space, you might put such things as photo credits here. If not, put them in the back in the appendix. **Permissions**: If your book contains chapters by another author, or quotes that need permissions, or notations that some of this material appeared previously in magazines, newspapers or other books, here is where it goes.

The publisher's address: While the title page gives the publishers name and city, a more detailed address is usually put on the copyright page along with a website address. Optional: A note letting customers know that bulk sales are available at discount.

At the bottom: The ISBN number. (This number also appears on the back cover as part of the barcode. It identifies the particular book by code so that the computerized register can ring it up correctly). At the very bottom of the page: Printed in the USA (if it is).

The Foreword and the Preface

Very few travel books sport a foreword nowadays, unless it's a how-to-do-it book and the foreword is written by head of an airline or a well-known travel guru. The Foreword, written by an established expert, is used to give credibility to the work. (The author has to run out and find the expert himself.) The Preface is written by the author as a way of explaining the format of the book and/or the reason the author chose to write the guide in the first place. It may contain some biographical information and general comments.

Both the Foreword and the Preface are often replaced by an introductory chapter which covers both the author's intent and explains the manner in which the book is laid out. The Author's Biography may appear either in the front or back matter. It covers both personal information and background credentials, and may not be necessary if there is a preface.

Dedication and Acknowledgements

The Dedication goes on its own page. Here is where you thank your wife, husband, children or mother for their patience and support. Not necessary, but often inserted when there is room. Acknowledgements can run one or two pages depending on how many people you want to include. Editors, researchers, agents and anyone who offered photographs, advice, and excerpts are included in the acknowledgements. Sometimes the acknowledgements are combined with the dedication, or are incorporated into the preface.

The Table of Contents

When it comes to destination guides, the main question is: how much is covered and how much detailed information is given about each site. Here, for instance, is the Table of Contents of a typical destination book:

- Orientation
- History and Culture

- Hotels
- Restaurants
- Sights to See
- Museums
- Night Life
- Shopping
- Theaters and Sports Arenas
- Parks and Recreation
- What to Do with Kids
- Emergencies and other important facts
- Glossary of foreign terms
- Appendix
- Index

Whether it's a tiny press or Fodor's, any table of contents should give the reader an idea of what will be covered. The number of pages devoted to each section will identify the depth of coverage. So if one guide allows sixty pages for hotel listings and fifty pages for restaurants along with ten pages of general background and culture, while another spends eighty pages giving you the history, background and culture of the place, you know there is a different emphasis.

How-to-do-it books vary slightly. Here's the Table of Contents for *The Traveling Woman: Great Tips for Safe and Healthy Trips.*

Appendix:
1. Authors' biographies
2. Travel resources
3. Index

As you can see, the chapters are in order, but, as with many advice books, the progression from one topic to another is often a matter of personal choice. There is no exact order as there would be in a book about constructing a house. Here the packing could have come before the staying healthy chapter, Chapter 2 and Chapter 3 could have been interchanged, and Chapter 6 might have been placed practically anywhere.

Details of the Chapter: Because your table of contents (TOC) will be used as an outline for your book as well as a selling point to a potential publisher, the more details, the better. It will also be used as an enticement to a prospective buyer who glances at it in a bookstore, or when utilizing Amazon's "Search Inside the Book" feature. Therefore, your TOC should be clear as to what it covering and as specific as possible without overloading the page. Here are the sub-heads of one chapter in *The Packing Book* by Judith Gilford. (I have shortened some of them).

Chapter Four – The Carry on Wardrobe
    How Much to Take.......
    Clothing Guidelines.......
    Wardrobe Color Planner......
    Recommended Fabrics for Travel Wardrobe
    Layering — adjusting for climate......
    Clothing Care on the Road.....
    Shoes......
    Accessories......
    Making Your Packing List...
    Itinerary wardrobe planner....
    Daily Activity Planner...
    Women's Packing List...
    Men's Packing List...
    Tips to Lighten the Load
    Plan Ahead

All this before telling us how to pack the suitcase! As you can see, the TOC not only lets the potential reader understand how your book is set up, it also reveals the extent of your coverage. Therefore, he knows immediately that your book about Los Angeles will also cover a side trip to Disneyland, or your book about suitcase packing will also cover such topics as safety, wardrobe planning and business tips.

Chapter 12

Back Matter

Back matter is considered all those pages that appear after the chapters are over. This includes the following:

- The Glossary (if you have one)
- The Index
- The appendix which can include

- Bibliography
- List of Resources
- Author's Biography
- Short calendar listings of festivals and special events
- Other books by the same publisher or author
- Acknowledgements that were not covered elsewhere
- Feedback forms for readers
- Coupons for discount tickets or other advertisements

The Glossary

The glossary is basically a dictionary. Here you define words and phrases that were used throughout the book. Traditionally the glossary appears at the end of the book as one of the many appendixes. However in books geared to foreign tourists it is not unusual to find a short glossary at the beginning of each chapter in addition to the full one in the back.

There are other uses for a glossary besides foreign translations.

A how-to-do-it book that employs abbreviations, code words or specialized jargon will often sport a glossary of these terms at the end of the book. For example, in *The Pennypincher's Guide to Luxury Travel*, author Joel Widzer offers a ten-page glossary filled with travel jargon that is primarily terminology used by airlines and hotels. Some of these are familiar terms such as *blackout dates* and *overbooking*, others are codes like *Open Jaw*.

Glossaries are also used in destination guides to English-speaking countries where certain phraseology is different from the country of origin. Australia, England and Scotland all sport variations of the mother tongue. Even books devoted to the American South will often throw in a few vernacular phrases, known only to the local population, for the edification of the outsider. Books about a specific topic such as the rain forests of Central America (where you might need a glossary of flora and fauna) or Native American sacred places (where there may be names that have to be spelled out) are also examples of such lists.

Whatever the language, books geared toward the food and wine markets traditionally have a glossary where such terms as "brix" and "au beurre" are translated for the neophyte reader. Although most travel books put the glossary at the back of the book, there are some publishers that prefer to put it in the front matter.

The Appendix/Bibliography/Resource List

Traditionally, the appendix is not indexed. And because it is not indexed, it can be expanded or shortened easily with no worry about pagination. Within the last twenty years, the bibliography in non-fiction books has morphed into something called a List of Resources. These have ballooned to become larger than some chapters and they include random information for the reader as well as a bibliography of sources used.

In some books you will find Appendix A, Appendix B, and Appendix C rather than the old-fashioned Bibliography, Appendix, and Acknowledgements. Appendix A might include books and websites; Appendix B, all movies and fiction that have a connection with the destination; Appendix C, a biography of the author; and Appendix D, the glossary.

While the more common approach is to put the really important information in the first chapter or as a boxed page in the front matter, (and the lesser facts in the back), a few travel books put all the important information in the back, as an appendix. This includes the names of airlines (with telephone numbers and websites), railroads, police, health, embassies and consulates, the official websites of the countries, cities, provinces and states. By putting all these facts into the Appendix position, it creates a handy area where the customer can find this information immediately. Of course this must be noted in the Table of Contents, so people know where to find these most important numbers!

Here is an example:

Appendix 1: Consulates, airports, police stations, hospitals, Tourist Information Stations, Railroad Stations, banks, emergency telephone numbers.

Appendix 2: Other Resources; Here you can list all those websites for Chambers of Commerce, Tourist agencies, other books on the general subject matter, and anything else.

Other Resources: Let's say you are writing a travel guide to Switzerland. Although you undoubtedly will have lots of information imbedded within the text, a Guide to Other Resources at the end of the book might include the names, addresses, telephone numbers and websites of the country of Switzerland, the Swiss Airline, The Swiss Consulate, the Swiss Railroad, websites for specific cities like Zurich, Geneva, Bern, and websites for specific attractions within the country such as the Alps plus a list of international travel organizations.

You could also list other books about Switzerland, particularly non-competitive ones such as a restaurant guide, a hiking/mountain climbing guide, a language dictionary and so forth. It is also common to throw in a few history books on the subject. Both *Lonely Planet* and *Rough Guides* offer such additional morsels as novels and movies that use the resident country as a backdrop. This fashion has been picked up by other guides as well, but there is no overriding need to include such extras.

In the case of a book geared toward a specific audience such as theater lovers, gays, and handicapped travelers, the resource list could include general books on the topic and websites of organizations that cater to, or assist those customers. It's always good to add these to the appendix.

Format for the Bibliography: Here is the standard bibliographic format: Name of author first, then title, then city of publication, then publisher, then date. Using this format, the author's last name goes first. For example:

Hudgins, Barbara and Sarver, Patrick, New Jersey Day Trips, 10th edition, New Brunswick, NJ, Rutgers Univ. Press, 2004

But many resource lists change things around a bit, with the title first, then the author, then the publisher (with or without the city) and the date. Sometimes the date is left off.

New Jersey Day Trips, 10th ed. Barbara Hudgins & Patrick Sarver. Rutgers Univ. Press, 2004.

Bibliographic references to magazine articles, online articles, newspaper citations and other media all have their own formats. It is best to check a style manual on these.

But there is no law that says all bibliographic references must go at the end of the book. Many books include recommended readings at the end of the relevant chapter.

The Author's Biography

Traditionally in hard cover books, the inside back flap of the dust jacket is where we learned about the author. This was usually a mix of credentials and personal information so we would find out that Jane Doe received her B.A. from Snooty College, that she lived in Massachusetts with her husband and two dogs (or children) and that this was her second book. If she is a novelist we would then get a recitation of well-known literary journals where her work had appeared.

Very few travel books, except for travel pictorials and memoirs, are published in hardcover. The trade paperback is the format of choice, even at 400 pages. The author's full biography (usually a page) is often relegated to the back of the book although it is also found in the front matter. Of course, the most important credentials of the author (if he is President of the Travel Agents Association or the host of Travel Talk Radio) would be included in the back cover copy and the introduction.

The author's biography includes such facts as where he or she was born, grew up, and traveled and the body of work. Marital status, awards and honors, and perhaps a short quote from the best review or endorsement the author received are also standard fare. A well-posed picture, preferably by a professional photographer, is usually posted. This entire page can be transferred to the author's website and offered as a free download to any journalist who wants background information to go with an interview. The website www.ricksteves.com offers a good example of the author's biography.

Other Appendix Possibilities

Some publishers will put a short calendar of events in the appendix rather than treating it as a separate chapter. That way, changes can be made in future editions without throwing off the pagination. Acknowledgements to anyone who helped create the book plus photo credits are often found either here or on an acknowledgement page in the Front Matter.

A feedback form on the next to last page (after the index) or advertisements for other books in a series are other common extras tacked onto the back of the book.

The Index

Except for memoirs and directories, most guidebooks require an index. And there's a reason for that. Readers want to be able to look up the name of an attraction in a second and the alphabetical index will lead them to it immediately. What if they forgot the name of the restaurant? That's when it's helpful to have a separate index for restaurants.

How you set up your index depends on how you set up your book. If you were writing a book about New York City and

dividing it into geographical sections (midtown, Upper East Side, Broadway, West Side, etc.) you would use the standard alphabetical index. In the index, the Metropolitan Museum of Art appears under M (since articles such as "A" and "The" are routinely ignored). You also might have a heading in the index called "Museums" under which you list all the museums and include the Metropolitan in the indented style. This would be in addition to the regular alphabetical listing. Thus:
Museums,
    American Museum of Natural History, p. 34
    Jewish Museum, p. 95
    Metropolitan Museum of Art, p. 85-86
    Museum of Modern Art, p. 76-77
    Museum of the American Indian p. 13
    Museum of the City of New York, p.99
    Solomon R. Guggenheim Museum, pp. 8, 98

If you were dividing the chapters under subject headings instead of geographical regions, you would have a chapter called "Museums". In this case, you might choose to create several sub-chapters, one for Art Museums, one for Science and natural history museums, and one for ethnic museums. You would still list the Metropolitan Museum of Art alphabetically in the index, but a subject head of "Museums" would be unwieldy since you would be listing so many of them. It would be easier to format the list this way:

Museums, Art p. 56-78
Museums, Film p. 83-84
Museums, Natural History & Science p. 45-52
Museums, Ethnic p. 87-92

If you're writing a book called "New York City's Museums for Kids" you might construct the book alphabetically and use the index (or several indices) for more fanciful designations such as: midtown, uptown, downtown, and Brooklyn for one index (geographical) and the type of collection within the museum (dolls, interactive science, pre-school) for another.

Or you might divide the book into "children's museums" (those devoted completely to children) "natural science museums" (the book would cover only the children's and school-age sections of these) science and technology museums, and so forth. Here you would have a standard alphabetical index at the back so that readers looking for the American Museum of Natural History could find it quickly. You could also add an extra index for those museums suited to school kids, pre-school kids and teens.

Many publishing houses require in the contract that the author create an index. If he is incapable of this, he may have to pay to have someone else do it. A writer with some clout might be able to give that job to a professional and have the publisher pick up the tab. One agent suggests that you negotiate this clause so that it's fifty/fifty between you and the publisher.

There are many software indexing programs available, but even with them you have to make the major decisions as to what to include and what to consolidate. Those self-publishers who design their own books using Adobe's InDesign have the index software as part of the package. Some programs simply pick up every name (personal or institutional) in the text and automatically paginate each one. The author then has to go through the index and throw out those names not needed.

Some Indexing Decisions to Consider

Names: Do you want to index only destinations or do you want to include all the names in your historical and cultural descriptions? A lot depends on the depth and width of your book. If a man called Samuel Fuller built an interesting Victorian mansion, do you put the name Samuel Fuller in the index as well as the Fuller House? Probably not. If James Joyce happened to frequent a café in Zurich and you mention that as an aside, do you put James Joyce into the index? Probably yes, because a famous name creates interest.

What about Foreign Names? Things get trickier when you're doing a book on a foreign country or city. Let's take Paris for example. In *Rick Steves' Paris,* he calls the Musee D'orsay the Orsay Museum. Okay, he's anglicized everything and that museum is going to be found under O in the index. In *The Food Lovers Guide to Paris*, author Patricia Wells calls it the Musee d'Orsay. So it's going to be found under M in the index. The index should be consistent with the entry.

Alphabetization: This varies, and it is best to use a standard reference such as the Chicago Manual of Style for your alphabetization. The telephone directory may use one concept and your manual of style may use another. You can use either as long as you are consistent. Here is one style:

New Hampshire
New Jersey
New York
New York Botanical Gardens
Newark
Newton

Cross-reference: Cross references may appear in the index, especially where there is a confusion of names, such as: Sandy Hook: see Gateway National Park. You may also need a cross-reference where a section of town (Hollywood, Beverly Hills) needs distinction from the larger entity of Los Angeles. In cases where a suburb is overshadowed by its neighbor, there would be the cross-reference "**See**": such as: Silver Springs: see Ocala.

Consistency in indexing: When you do construct an index it should follow certain rules and they should be consistent. If you called him Louis IX in the text that's the way he should appear in the index. Most authors follow the name as it appears on official documents, so it's the Solomon R. Guggenheim Museum, The Tate Museum, the Franklin Institute, The Mark Twain House, Nelson Lakes National Park and Crazy Horse Monument.

Last name or first name? Most of the time it's last name first, then first name, unless it's the name of a place like Ruth Chris' Steakhouse or an event such as the Bob Hope Golf Classic.

In *Frommer's Irreverent Guide to Las Vegas*, 4th edition, the author mentions the names of several long-term performers at the top hotels throughout the book. In the general index they appear haphazardly or not at all. Rudner, Rita and Dion, Celine are given the last name treatment while Danny Gans and David Brenner go head first. Wolfgang Puck doesn't show up at all although his restaurants are mentioned in bold type. Liberace had the good sense to go by a single name so he goes under "L". On the other hand, Lance Burton, a master magician, is cited four times in the text (in bold) and shows up in the index under "L" but his name is italicized. This is an example of index sloppiness (or maybe a computer program gone wild).

Do reviewers look at the index? They certainly do. One reviewer praised a book on coastal Maine but quibbled that although the index included shops, hotels and restaurants, it did not include individual towns and cities by name. So you see that a user-friendly index that covers the data from several angles will always impress a reviewer!

Multiple Indexes

Specialized indexes will go after the general index. While the general index always indicates the page number, smaller specialized indexes do not. Therefore, if you have a special index called "Hot Spots" where you list all the clubs and late-night bars in the city you are covering, you simply list them alphabetically and the reader then has to check the regular index to find the page number. *The Zagat Restaurant Survey* probably takes the award for the greatest number of specialized indexes, but many other guides have followed their lead.

The Front and Back Cover

But wait — what about the cover and the back cover? These are decided by the publisher; sometimes with input from the author, sometimes not. Aside from the title and the series imprint if there is one, the front cover usually features one of the following:

- A photograph of the destination showing
  a definitive scene or activity.
- A collage of images, either photos or drawings,
  symbolic of the theme or destination of the book.
- Bold lettering with perhaps a single symbol of the

subject matter — used primarily in how-to-do-it books.

The back cover may feature additional photographs to make a point. The back cover also includes the basic blurb for the book and a quoted review or testimonial if one is available. The category (such as Travel or Travel/South America) may appear on the upper right or left hand corner, along with the price. At the bottom, an EAN barcode (which includes the ISBN number) is placed to make it easy for the computerized cash register to scan the title and price of the book for the retail customer. The back cover acts as an advertisement for the whole work and all the salient points should be listed. Many publishers use the same wording on the back cover as they do for their catalog write-up of the book.

What's Next?

Now that you have the framework and the format details covered, it's time to look at what goes inside the framework. The next section is devoted to the words and pictures that will make your travel guide a compelling read as well as a useful one.

Part Three
Words and Pictures

Chapter 13

Travel Writing 101

What skills should the travel writer bring to the table? What would an editor look for in the sample clippings sent in with a book proposal?

1. <u>An ability to observe. Close observation</u> will allow you to pinpoint the salient features of the destination or attraction you are covering.

2. <u>An ability to write physical description.</u> This may sound strange, especially when there are hundreds of writing teachers who tell you to show, not tell. Certainly you do not want to go in for overly florid descriptions, but some writers think they should eschew description altogether and just use factual presentation. Your descriptions should include:

- Color: Is the sea blue, azure, gray, turquoise, green with algae or almost as brown as the sand?
- Light: Whether it's the neon lights of a casino or the morning light on desert sand, light plays a part in the physical description of things.
- Texture: Rough concrete, burnished wood, silk fabrics in a clothing shop, the brass rail of a ship are all textures that bring the experience home to the reader.
- Smell: Fresh bread in bakeries, the salt sea

air, and diesel fumes on highways are part
and parcel of the travel experience.

- Sound: Did the ferryman blow a whistle?
  Do monkeys shriek or gabble? Even in a
  short piece, you can mention the clink of
  coins in a casino or seagulls squabbling
  over a piece of bread on the beach.
- Taste: Of course food and wine guides abound
  in descriptions that cater to this sense. But
  almost all guidebooks should include this
  sense, whether it's the dollop of real whipped
  cream in a Vienna coffee house or the pungent
  tingle of a special sauce in Thailand.
- The view: I know one writer who mentions
  the view quite often, but doesn't mention
  what it is he is viewing. If you are deep
  in a forest and come to a clearing, please
  remember to mention what it is you see.

3. An ability to write narration. A surprising percentage of travel
guide verbiage is given over to narration. Whether this means
pages of history, little anecdotes about famous people or places,
or even a day in the life of a soul-searching traveler, narration
comes in more often than you might expect. Look at the guidebooks in your house. How many include long sections on history
or background? Guidebook writers should be able to suffuse the
facts with a sense of drama so that the reader becomes involved
in the history and culture of the place.

4. A particular point of view and/or an opinion. Even if you don't
voice a strong opinion, your point of view will show some bias.
If you like quiet bars over noisy ones, if you prefer art museums
over science museums, if you like French pastry over Italian
pastry it will show in your descriptions.

How much of your opinion should you add? That depends
on the style of guidebook you are writing. Most popular travel
guides include the opinion of the author in some form or other
throughout the book. The reading audience wants to know your
reactions. After all, they can get effusive hype for free.

5. <u>A sense of fairness</u>. Maybe you hate festivals and open-air markets where people mill about and there's no place to sit down. Still in all, scads of people like them and it's your job to describe the action. This is the time to interview a flea-market addict, or observe the family at the hot-air balloon festival. Use their reactions instead of your own to give a fair assessment of the place.

7. <u>An ability to sum up</u> — especially in guidebooks where writers cannot take the leisurely route around Cairo souvenir shops, they must be able to sum up the exotic shopping experience in a paragraph or two. Getting the sense of the place to the reader in a few short sentences is an absolute necessity. You will often have to create a succinct write-up of 100, 150 or 200 words to convey the essence of the destination.

8. A willingness to check facts — or hire a fact checker! The publisher won't do it for you (except in a few specialized cases). The editor won't do it for you! If you place a museum or a park in the wrong city, or the wrong section of the right city, you'll hear from an annoyed customer pretty quickly! Read the comments on Amazon! Readers really get angry when the hotel you said was on Grand Street is really on Grand Avenue, over on the seedy side of town.

9. Grammar and spelling count. Maybe not as much as they once did, but editors, who are hired by publishers to go over your manuscript with a red pencil, will make you toe the line when it comes to grammar. If you are self-publishing, get someone with grammatical skills to go over your work — before it is typeset, not after!

But also note that a casual or folksy guidebook does not have to hew to the strictest guidelines of grammar. <u>Many readers prefer the casual tone since it makes them feel as if a good friend were giving them the inside facts on a vacation destination.</u>

Here are a few examples of the aspects of travel writing mentioned above:

Concise description: This summation of El Farol, a restaurant and lounge in Santa Fe, gives you the feel of the place quickly and adroitly:

"You're sitting at the bar when a stranger walks through the door, blinks at the dark low-ceiling room and plops down to tell you someone in Paris or London suggested he or she go to El Farol. It's that kind of place — the latest in Santa Fe's legendary succession of eccentric havens. Owner David Salazar says parts of the thick-walled adobe building date back to the 1830s; poets, prophets and punks have walked through its rustic doors.

(Courtesy: *The Santa Fe and Taos Book; A complete Guide, 4th edition*)

As you can see, this succinct paragraph (77 words) includes some description (the dark, low-ceilinged room, the thick-walled adobe building, rustic doors) some action (a stranger walks in and plops down beside you) a quotable authority (owner David Salazar) some history (the building dates back to the 1830s) and a general statement of opinion; this is one of Santa Fe's legendary eccentric havens that has catered to poets, prophets and punks and is known in international circles.

And all this before offering any details on the food, the drinks or the dance band that takes over late at night! A second paragraph fills you in on that information. Concise description comes into play most often in those round-up chapters found in almost every guidebook.

Voicing Your Opinion: Opinions are not necessarily relegated to one's view of the food or hospitality in a foreign country: one's outlook on life and one's political opinions are often thrown into the mix. Books that come through the independent press have more freedom of speech than those from larger publishers, but opinion pieces show up in a variety of guides. Here is an excerpt from *Explore the Virgin Islands*, 6th edition by Harry Pariser that shows a decided political attitude. This was a sidebar about one of the icons of British exploration. I have cut down the excerpt for length and added ellipses to indicate missing sentences.

Sir Francis Drake

"The world throughout history has been governed by prelates, officials, and brigands. There has regularly been a considerable confusion of roles between these three occupations. Even today, in the contemporary "First World," many brigands are lionized rather than jailed. So it should come as no surprise that a coarse and lowly pirate might have become a "Sir" in 16th-century Britain.

Born in Tavistock, England to a Protestant family, Francis Drake and his family were driven out of Devon early in his childhood following a Catholic uprising.....His first opportunity to hit the high seas came after a slaver hired him. He became acquainted with the lay of the land of the Spanish Main....

Having witnessed firsthand the weakness of the Spanish Empire, Drake had found his niche and continued activities that today might be characterized as international terrorism covertly funded by foreign governments. Some of his expeditions were paid by Queen Elizabeth (who reaped a portion of the financial rewards)."

(If you are wondering why Sir Francis appears in a book about the Virgin Islands it is because Drake docked at Virgin Gorda just before an attempt to surprise to Spanish fleet in San Juan harbor.)

"In the end, his adventuring proved to be the historical catalyst leading to Britain's empire and part of the reason one may visit the British Virgin Islands today. It is on such men that the existence of present-day 'Western democracies' has been based and it is the rationale for his virtual deification."

The author here is able to give a bit of historical background to the sunny islands he covers and throw in some meat for political discourse at the same time. Opinions on politics, ecotourism, tourist behavior and other topics are commonly found in guidebooks. The reader is probably more interested in your opinions on lodgings, food safety, street dangers, bargains and undiscovered nooks than on your personal take on the state of the world. However, many travel writers manage to sneak in an opinion on the world somewhere in the text.

What about a Hook? While magazine and newspaper editors require a hook and a lead paragraph, the guidebook author is not under the same pressure to grab the reader by the throat to interest him. In fact, most guidebook readers do not read the book from front to back at all, but will gravitate to the section that holds the most interest for them. This may be art museums, skiing, or how to find a good restaurant in a foreign city, so it is important to have balanced sections to the book.

A good lead sentence always helps. You'll find that in many guidebooks the first paragraph of each chapter is a summing up of what is to come. Because casual readers flip through the book looking for salient topics, put your best efforts into those first few paragraphs.

The long travel piece, so beloved of magazine editors, is rarely found in guidebooks. The longest section of a guidebook is often the narration of history and culture, and that is the closest one comes to a story with a beginning, middle and end. And frankly, that is the section the casual reader is most likely to skip, or to read intermittently on the flight over. Often an author will sneak a long personality piece or travel essay into a guidebook, under the guise of an "insider's look" at the destination.

Opening paragraphs

How do you begin your chapters? A common approach is the general statement (either about the area, the activity involved, historical facts or the writer's view), which could run one two or three paragraphs long. Then there is the strict descriptive view which morphs into a fuller exposition of facts and figures. Using "contrast and compare", personal statements and anecdotes are other standard ways of starting your text. Here are some examples:

The General Statement: "One thing you learn about Santa Fe (or any semi-arid or desert region) is that the difference in 24-hour temperature is the difference between night and day. The sun can beat down mercilessly on an 80-degree day but by nightfall you will need a sweater to protect your skin against the sharp chill of Santa Fe's 7000-feet high atmosphere."

The Historical Opening: Almost all destination guides have a chapter on the history of the place along with historic material strewn throughout the other chapters. When it comes to the basic history, the tendency is to start at the very beginning and then very quickly segue into fairly modern times. Naturally, when you're dealing with countries known for their ancient cultures, you would concentrate on that. The more typical entry starts like this:

"For thousands of years prior to the arrival of Europeans the aboriginal people of the Bay Area lived healthily and apparently peacefully on the naturally abundant land." (The Rough Guide to San Francisco).

The Straight Descriptive Approach: Often used in the first chapter in a destination guide as a way to introduce the pleasures of the place before going into details. This is where the writer goes to pains to produce a verbal picture that is unique and compelling. This description was written by John Muir during his sojourn in Cuba back in 1912, and it still brings forth a vibrant picture of the Caribbean.

"I climbed to the housetop to get a view of another of the fine sunsets of this land of flowers. The landscape was a strip of clear Gulf water, a strip of sylvan coast, a tranquil company of shell and coral keys, and a gloriously colored sky without a threatening cloud. All the winds were hushed and the calm of the heavens was as profound as that of the palmy islands and their encircling waters."

The Anecdotal Approach: A one-paragraph anecdote that then moves into a general description is often used both in travel articles and compilations. In one edition of *Fodor's Caribbean,* each one of the twenty-one covered islands begins either with an anecdote or a lush descriptive passage followed immediately by a few paragraphs full of facts and statistics and history. The anecdotes vary from a scene of native women sorting spices, to a tourist waiting for his fresh-caught lobster, to a visitor caught up in the rhythms of the beach-side steel drum band. Each one is supposed to synthesize the ambience of a specific Caribbean island.

If you can tell a story about a crusty fisherman, an exuberant foreign guide, a funny incident aboard a barge trip, or a haggle over a wooden sculpture in Haiti, you have your anecdotal opening.

The Compare and contrast approach: Many authors use this technique when they need a transition from one chapter to another. It is also used to differentiate one entry from another in a round-up chapter of museums or historic houses. For example: "Hiking along the rolling farmlands of southern Virginia is quite a different experience than traversing the mountainous region near Charlottesville," or "The quiet classic lines of the Roosevelt country home at Hyde Park are in stark contrast to the conspicuous elegance of the Vanderbilt Mansion four miles away."

The Personal Statement: When writing a personal memoir or a guidebook based on your taste or eccentricities, the general statement might be transformed into a personal statement that, in turn, becomes the springboard for subtexts.

> "I love cafes and bistros and during our six-month drive along the coast of Italy and into the southern provinces of France, I sipped coffee, tea and vino, munched dozens of bruschetta and brioche, and ate breakfast, lunch and dinner at more than one hundred of these enchanting venues."

The middle of the action approach: While this is used more often in travel articles than in travel guidebooks, it is one way to get the reader into the pulse of things immediately. It is most often used with the first person voice.

> "As the seaplane lurched toward the frozen glacier ahead, I forgot about the salmon buffet that awaited us and simply prayed that we would make a safe landing."

The explanatory opening: If you are composing a how-do-do-it book, you will need plenty of explanations and you will undoubtedly begin at the beginning.

"Why pay for first class tickets when with a few simple tricks you can get upgrades from your much cheaper business class ticket? In the following pages, I will show you exactly how to achieve this happy state of flying."

What to Avoid

Clichés and second hand prose. See the chapter on copyright.

Accurate but misleading statements: Open any travel brochure or read any travel publicity and you will find descriptions that are accurate but misleading. I call that Adspeak. It's the tendency for advertising copywriters to glide over reality to create a pretty picture for the public. Tourist Boards often sub-contract the state booklet and website to advertising agencies. These agencies then fill the pages with puffery. What ensues is a potpourri of impressions that may include some half-baked utterance from an employee or a rewrite from a previous article. Here, for instance, is an entry from the 2003 New Jersey State Tourism website. It comes right after a description of Barnegat Lighthouse State Park as part of a daytrip offered to visitors to the Jersey shore.

"Just beyond the awesome presence of "Old Barney" lies Island Beach State Park, a protected and undeveloped slice of beach lover's heaven. Far more lively are the boardwalks of Seaside Heights."

Nice writing. The only trouble is that this paragraph is completely misleading to a newcomer who has no knowledge of the state's topography or peculiar road system. A traveler would expect, from reading the above paragraph, that he could walk, bike, or at least drive from the Barnegat Lighthouse (commonly known as "Old Barney") to Island Beach State Park. He would also assume that Island Beach State Park would be a rather rustic, unruly section of sand dunes with no asphalt parking lots.

But in reality, Island Beach State Park is on a separate

peninsula just across an inlet from Barnegat Lighthouse State Park. And although the beach is clearly visible from the Barnegat Lighthouse jetties, unless you have a boat, you cannot get over there. Not only that, because the ocean currents are particularly dangerous at this point, you dare not try to swim over either.

As for Island Beach State Park, on the other side of the swirling waters, yes it is "protected and undeveloped" and it is also a beach lover's heaven. But not at the same time! Or rather, I should say, not at the same place. The beach lovers have asphalt parking lots, changing rooms, concession stands and lifeguard-protected areas of sand at several points along this five mile long beach. The protected and undeveloped area has limited access for humans — especially when the plovers are nesting — and is in a separate section.

Yes, Seaside Heights is a small town just north of Island Beach State Park, and it does have plenty of amusements and nightclub action. But it is also much less accessible from Barnegat Lighthouse than the quoted paragraph would lead you to believe. Only if you live in New Jersey would you realize that if you start out at the base of "Old Barney" you must drive nine miles south down Long Beach Island to reach the only bridge that crosses to Toms River on the mainland, then drive another fifteen minutes north to get to Manahawkin, then drive over yet another bridge to get onto another island, then turn right and find Seaside Heights. And finally, Island Beach State Park, a few miles south of Seaside Heights, charges an $8 entrance fee for cars and by this time probably has all its parking spaces filled up if it is a hot summer weekend!

I call the quoted paragraph "PR mish-mash", and you can find this type of description in every official communication from every state in the Union and probably many foreign countries as well. It should be the job of the travel guide author to clear up all the ambiguities and cut through the cotton-candy descriptions so that the beleaguered traveler can gauge his time and distance if he actually wants to visit the handsome Old Barney lighthouse and get in some beach time on the same day.

Brochure phrasing: I remember when I first read about the Duke Gardens in New Jersey. These are indoor gardens that were developed by Doris Duke on her estate in Somerville. All the guidebooks described them as "eleven miniature gardens under glass" each done in a different international style. When I finally visited the place, I noticed that this phrase came right out of the brochure.

But when I took the tour I was surprised to discover that these were interlinked greenhouses, each one the size of a large room or two, with distinct gardens and statuary of different countries within each setting. I had fully expected to find miniature gardens under glass covers, looking something like a bunch of miniature bonsai trees. The "under glass" description did not give a true sense of what the visitor would encounter and yet it was used in every guidebook because it was in the brochure.

Of course it's not only brochure writers and PR companies who do this. On a well-known private travel website one of the staff writers mentions Atlantic City as a one-day side trip from Philadelphia. Here is a quote:

> "The main attractions on the Boardwalk are the casinos, and it's well worth wandering into several before choosing a spot to hedge your bets. The newest kid on the block is the elegant, Italian style Borgata, featuring a landscaped pool and garden"

The author goes on to describe two or three of the well-known casinos on the boardwalk such as the Trump Taj Mahal and Caesar's. All fine and well and written in brisk, professional style. The only problem in the quote is the positioning of the Borgata. One would assume from the description that it is on the Boardwalk along with the other named casinos. But in reality, the Borgata is on the inlet side of town and because of the convoluted roads that lead up to that glassy, classy, "new kid on the block" it is no easy task to get there from the Boardwalk. It's several miles away and first you must hop into a car or cab or wait twenty minutes for the jitney to make the run. And then you have to navigate a particularly vexing knot of roads to arrive at the narrow entrance which is always overcrowded. So here again what seems on the surface to be an easy amble over from one point to another is actually much more complicated and time consuming than one would expect.

In reading reviews of travel books on Internet travel forums, I am amazed at how many customers fume at this type of writing. People constantly complain that directions are misleading or that the author forgot to mention some important piece of information which made the foray into a certain area more difficult, more dangerous or simply more time-consuming than he led them to believe. The examples above concern New Jersey because I know the territory intimately and can spot the misleading phrase a thousand yards away. But you'll find instances of them everywhere. So be careful when using the slick, quick description.

Don't overdo the personal point of view

A veteran travel writer can get away with a little egotism, because he knows how to make the travel essay or personality piece interesting. What the neophyte writer has to beware is the journal that becomes too detailed or too personal. No one really wants to know what he and his companion had for breakfast. And readers certainly don't want to know that he brushed his teeth afterwards (unless there was a particular problem with the color of the water).

What they do want to know is what type of breakfast is served and how it is served. Is there a buffet with pitchers of orange and grapefruit juice, cold cereal, cold milk, and a bowl of bananas set up on a table where the guests help themselves? Is breakfast offered cafeteria style with hot sausages, scrambled eggs, and pancakes set out on steam tables while the patrons pass by with trays? Is it served restaurant style by waiters who come with a carafe of coffee and then return fifteen minutes later to take your order? Are there still pensiones where the maid comes to your room in the morning with a tray of café au lait and croissants? Or is there no breakfast service at all, but just a sign in the lobby that steers you to the Starbucks across the street? Journaling is fine, but editing down the journal to get the salient details is paramount.

Now the literary travel book is another matter. There, presumably, the author can muse over a breakfast muffin for three pages, for the muffin will undoubtedly lead to larger thoughts or some insight into the environment or the culture that produced it. For the guidebook writer, the most important thing about the muffin is whether or not it is available and whether or not it is tasty!

Writing Exercises

Exercise One: Taming the "I" factor. Write at least two paragraphs on a local restaurant that you have visited. Include a description of the place (the décor, the type of seating, the friendliness of the staff and/or owner, perhaps a hint of the kind of clientele on hand) and a description of the food, although you do not have to go through the menu course by course. End up with an anecdote either about you, the owner, the waiter, or the place. Do this from the first person point of view. Then rewrite it using the third person.

Exercise Two: Transitions: Go from New York to L.A. by any means of travel without mentioning the name of either city. You can do this in one sentence or one paragraph. You can use any mode of transportation — airplane, car, RV, oxcart of whatever. If you live on another continent, choose two well-known cities and make the same sort of journey — in prose.

Exercise Three: Narration. Using basic research from the public domain or from brochure materials, write a page on the history and culture of any place you have ever visited. See if you can create your own lead paragraph, and rewrite the basic narration so that it sounds as if it is coming from your own voice, and not from an encyclopedia.

Exercise Four: Action. Run along the beach, fly a kite over the hill, skateboard along the cement boardwalk or do anything else that requires preliminary steps, the action, and a description of the world that surrounds the action and then the aftermath of the action. Then write it up.

Exercise Five: General statement — country and culture. Make a general statement about the people, architecture, or culture of some country you have visited recently. Use that as your opening paragraph.

Exercise Six: Do a write-up of a single place either from your travels or from your neighborhood. Write it as you would for the audience you imagine would be reading your book: either general, a family with kids, or special interest. Include the name, address, website, location, admission price, directions and anything else of importance. Word maximum: 400 words including all the above basic facts. Word minimum: 250 words.

After you have finished, look up the same place in at least one guidebook currently on the shelves and carefully analyze that entry.

1. How many of the 400 words (minus maybe 20 or 30 for basic info) did you spend on general description? How much did the other guidebook?
2. How much on history?
3. How much on details?
4. How much on advice or tips?
5. Did you rate the place or use an icon system? Did they?
6. What directions were given if any?

Recommended Reading:

There are a few books out on travel writing, and several hundred books out on the general art of writing. However, the bulk of books on writing concentrate on fiction and there are relatively few in the realm of non-fiction. The books and courses on travel writing usually emphasize writing for magazines, newspaper feature sections, and, more recently, the Internet. Some of them simply teach you ploys for getting free rides or stays at hotels with a few hints on the craft of creating the piece.

Still in all, it is worth reading books that deal specifically with travel writing, especially if you have no background whatsoever in the field. Most travel-writing books and courses hardly mention guidebooks since they are aimed at the article market. However, their summation of what constitutes good writing is certainly useful for any format.

These travel-writing books also go over the basics of the trade. That means the business end of keeping records for tax purposes; the practical end of taking notes and photographs and recording interviews; and of course endless tips on how to impress editors, write good query letters and garner article assignments. Here are the best known:

The Travel Writers Handbook/ by Louise Zobel. This classic book covers many areas of travel writing including the business side of keeping notes, keeping business records, how to interest travel editors in your story, the different types of travel pieces and so forth. Written primarily for free-lancers looking for assignments from magazine and newspaper (and now Internet) editors, this is still a great book both for newcomers as well as veterans.

Travel Writing: A Guide to Research, Writing and Selling. L. Peat O'Neil. An excellent book for the beginner as it is chock full of exercises for the travel writer to hone his or her skills. The author promotes journal-writing as a way to get your thoughts down and then cautions you to pare down your prose afterwards.

Lonely Planet Guide to Travel Writing. Don George. This one reminds me of a class in fiction writing. George uses many examples of what he considers the best in travel literature (or literary travel as he calls it). The book is geared to the literary end of travel writing. However there are chapters on getting assignments, how to research, and other basic topics. The one chapter devoted to guidebooks is written by a guest author, who emphasizes the importance of credentials and how to get them in order to impress editors at the big-name guidebook publishers.

There are also a number of courses given at the Learning Annex in major cities as well as online courses that promise you fame, fortune and free passage to anywhere in the world when you enter the exciting field of travel writing. Since I've never taken any of these courses, I can't vouch for them. However, the teacher usually has solid credentials, and considering how many would-be writers don't have a clue about how to get started, it probably doesn't hurt to take any of these courses as long as the price isn't ridiculous.

General Books on Writing

There are hundreds of books about writing with a few titles on creative non-fiction and a trip to the library to find them will work to your advantage, especially if you are a beginning author. The preliminary articles in such annuals as *The Writer's Market* and the *Writer's Handbook* also contain a cornucopia of wisdom. Check the Appendix for a list of such books.

Chapter 14

What Goes In and What Stays Out?

Choice of Details

There is probably no other factor that distinguishes one guidebook from another than the choice of details. I talked about boundaries in the Part One of this book, where you establish the basic limits for your book. But when it comes down to the actual writing of each individual entry, you now have to make another decision: which details do you include?

If you visit a zoo, are you most intrigued by the camels, the elephants or the lions? One writer might spend his greatest literary efforts on a monkey house and launch into a whole essay of the relationship of man to higher apes. Another might be intrigued by the reptile house. Still another might rhapsodize on the new penguin feeding area because that was the highlight of the press release.

For most travel books, the selection of details is part and parcel of the value of the book. You would expect a book called "Europe's Best Bargain Hotels" to have a good choice of bargain hotels that are low in cost but are not flea-bitten rat traps. Details about the breakfast one gets in the hotel, how large the room is, whether the neighborhood is safe and other basics are to be expected. Whether the author wants to throw in material about places to see in the area, the history of the hotel or personal stories about the hotel keepers and their wives depends on the concept of the book and the tone of the writing. But the important questions the book must answer are: Is it safe? Is it cheap? Is it convenient? How clean is it? And maybe — do they speak English? The audience for this book is looking primarily for value and it is the author's job to discover the best bargains for his readers.

Obviously, if there is something that catches your eye, you will want to note it down immediately. Some people keep small notebooks, others write details right on the brochures. One simple way of remembering the moment is to take a picture and with a digital camera that's easy enough. A close-up of a scenic waterfall or a bustling marketplace or the wallpaper and furnishings of a historic house can be used later for description.

There are also the things you did not see. The ads for most Alaskan cruise lines show a magnificent whale breaching out of the foam. But if you took an Alaskan cruise, did you actually spot any whales? And of those that you did see, were you close enough to get a good look? These are the details the reader wants to know.

Does that three-star hotel in Paris include a telephone? A hair dryer? Does the all-inclusive tour include drinks and tips? How much should you tip the day tour guide? Do you tip the sommelier at the fancy hotel if you only ordered iced tea?

The most popular guidebooks include not only details of description, but details that the reader needs for his trip. If you are writing a guidebook for a specific audience, such as families with young children or adventurous backpackers you will target your details and insights toward that audience. Parents of young children want to know the "boring" factor of any destination. Backpackers are interested in nuts and bolts details and also where to find other backpackers and reasonable lodgings.

Therefore, the audience for your book and your own interests helps determine which details you pick out. If your expertise is in gourmet cooking, you will undoubtedly describe the food and the ambience of each restaurant with great excitement. Perhaps you will even interview the chef and throw in his prized recipe.

If your audience is composed of senior citizens and/or handicapped people you will probably go over the parking facilities,
the bathrooms and the price of entrees in the same restaurant.

For example, in my write-up of the Bronx Zoo in the 10th
edition of *New Jersey Day Trips*, I spent a few sentences on the
overall view of the zoo as an open environment for animals. I
gave a few basic facts and scant history. I did, however, give
pretty detailed descriptions of the popular Gorilla exhibit, the
children's zoo, Jungle World, the World of Darkness, the World
of Birds, plus the Bengali Express and the tramcar as a means
of seeing the animals without walking. I also mentioned two
eateries. Since my audience consists primarily of families from
New Jersey, I concentrated on those exhibits most popular with
that group.

I also included the following bits of advice: the tramcar only
takes you halfway around the zoo (at which point you must get
off and get on line for the trip back), picnicking is allowed at
tables near the cafeteria, the children's zoo charges an extra fee
but is worth it, and the souvenir drink cup at the food stands is
highly overpriced. I gave driving directions from New Jersey only
and I used the directions from the website. I gave no mass transit
directions.

On the other hand, *Fodor's NYC Gold Guide 2006* edition gives
a slightly different view of the same place. It is a shorter entry
than mine and spends more time on the history of the zoo from
its beginnings to its more enlightened animal protective stance
nowadays. Basic facts as to number of animals and acreage are
included. There is a general overview of the way the place is
set up with moats for animals but only one specific exhibit (the
Gorilla Forest) is mentioned. Eating places are not mentioned
although there are icons underneath the entry signifying food,
restrooms and such.

Special advice offered: don't try to see the zoo in one day,
and line up early for the Gorilla Forest tickets. Directions were for
mass transit only (subway and bus stops) and no driving directions were given.

Of course Fodor's also runs a series for Kids and undoubtedly the Bronx Zoo would get fuller coverage within that series.

However, I mention this to show that any write-up is influenced by a number of criteria. First and foremost is the allowed space (particularly if you are writing for a series publisher), second is your audience and third is your own taste and predilections (that is, what you choose to look at or to remember).

Some guidebook authors deem it their job to simply list as much as possible with hardly any commentary. There are so many different exhibits at the Bronx Zoo that one could easily fill up five full paragraphs simply listing all the different animal enclosures and where they are, the eateries, the square mileage and details on driving and parking. But it is in the choosing of the particular details, the decision to include or exclude background stories or anecdotes, history or sociology, that an author stakes his ground in the guidebook wilderness, as it were. Anyone can collect information. It is the choice of ingredients and the shaping of them into a coherent and interesting whole that makes a guidebook and creates a loyal audience.

Why writers choose to emphasize one thing and not another has to do with their own background, their perceived audience, whether their information is first or second hand and the bias of the editor, if there is one. As a guidebook writer you always have the choice of leaving something out if you think it is unnecessary. Leaving something out because you didn't notice it is something else. Leaving it out because you think the audience is "too sophisticated" for that sort of information is a judgment call.

Look over the reader's comments on Amazon.com and other online travel forums. Many of these travelers take their guidebooks as seriously as amateur film critics take their movies. One complaint that comes up again and again is that the author left out some important piece of information.

> "He didn't mention the cross-street and I took three hours trying to find the place"
>
> "Nobody told us that this wonderful restaurant was closed on Sundays — just the day we happened to be in town."

Sometimes, it is obvious what you omitted and you may have

omitted it on purpose. For instance, some books only emphasize recommended sites, hotels and restaurants. Series such as the best hotels or the best Bed and Breakfasts will do this. The fact that something is omitted means they did not feel the particular attraction was worthy of inclusion. Some authors will omit attractions or hotels that are located in dangerous areas.

Sometimes it's a question of omitting something the author thought was clearly evident. For instance, I used to write up the prices in my book as: Admission fee: Adults: $10.00; Children 6 to 12: $5.00; Seniors: $7.50. (Seniors in this case refers to senior citizens). A friend with a four-year-old son told me I should point out that children who were five and under were free. I thought the fact that children 6 to 12 had to pay implied that fact. She didn't realize that, so in later editions, I changed it. Obviously for a family with small children, this can make a big difference, money-wise. And by writing it out rather than implying it, I made it easier for the reader to note those places that accommodate young kids.

Is It Worth Seeing? Here's a conundrum for the travel writer: is the place worth visiting? And if it isn't, should you just ignore it, or include it along with a warning to your readers that it is a waste of time? Rick Steves is known for his practical advice. In the book *"France, Belgium & the Netherlands"*, his write-up of the French capital includes a list called "Disappointments de Paris". Among the disappointments are The Madeleine (an imposing looking church built in the classical style with little of interest inside) and the Pantheon (a resting place for famous Frenchmen). This seems a wonderful way to face the problem. Mention the venue, but tell people it may be of interest from the outside but don't bother going in.

When it comes to just plain dangerous areas, there's a divergence of opinion. Guidebooks that specialize in "rougher" places include possibly dangerous hostels and city sections but warn you openly of the dangers. On the other hand, the authors of *The Unofficial Guide to Washington D.C.* (c1998) inform you directly that they are not including certain jazz clubs that are quite worthwhile, but are located in districts they consider unsafe for tourists.

Some guidebook authors will sidestep the problem by warning that you should only visit a particular spot if you take a taxi both ways. And it doesn't matter whether they are talking about a nightclub in the Caribbean, a restaurant in Thailand, or a religious shrine in India — the reader is supposed to understand that walking or driving your own car is an invitation to thieves and muggers.

Name every name? Just as hospitals name their wings after major donors, museums and gardens name every collection they inherit after the patron who donated it. These names appear in all the literature the place publishes, so you'll find the Johnson collection of medieval art and the Swan collection of Revolutionary muskets in every PR release. Is all this name-calling necessary? Obviously, the museum director wants reporters to include all their benefactors in every write-up. It is in their interest to publicize their patrons. But does the travel writer have to go along with it? Names take up valuable space and unless the collection is famous, they add very little value.

In one guidebook, the author mentioned an art museum that contains the George Rogoff collection of Russian painting, the Bennett collection of Soviet poster art and the Seymour Lansky collection of Japanese prints, among others. In fact, the only name the writer didn't include was the Sara Lee collection of Danish pastry in the museum café!

So you must make a choice. Do you want to please the attraction you are covering or please your reading public? Much depends on your audience. If you are writing a heavy tome on the collections of famous art museums, you might be more inclined to "name names" than if you are writing a general guide.

Discretion is the better part of History: Sometimes, docents are told not to discuss certain issues. In fact, many tour guides are trained to steer away from certain questions that come up, particularly if they refer to a scandal. I have visited Kykuit, the Rockefeller Mansion in Tarrytown, several times and have taken the group tour through this handsomely appointed house. The last full resident was one-time Governor of New York and Vice President of the U.S., Nelson Rockefeller. On every tour, a member of the group asked a question about the somewhat embarrassing circumstances of Nelson Rockefeller's death. The docents knew how to sidestep that question with a quiet "we don't talk about that" and then veer the talk toward Nelson's many philanthropies. Almost every "grand house" has a slight scandal attached to it. Docents tend to keep away from these, although it's easier to relate gossip about a long-dead San Francisco eccentric or a European king than about a prominent family whose trust fund is paying for the upkeep of the mansion.

As a travel writer, you are under no restrictions to limit yourself. Let's face it; backstage stories about the rich and famous always stir up interest and it would be a pity to forgo a juicy story on the basis of propriety. Whether you want to include anecdotes about mistresses, family quarrels, and hidden staircases really depends on the type of book you are writing. Historic sites have added cachet if there was a duel or two out in the garden and many a Bed and Breakfast boasts that the building was once a brothel!

Personal vignettes: In or out?

Besides the selection of details, there is the question of how much of your personal viewpoint will get into the piece. Will you include vignettes? How many? How far will they extend? Are you going to include vignettes of your husband, your children, and your dog? Will the story of your personal trainer's two-week stay at an Irish inn be included?

Choosing the personal vignette is of prime importance. The personal vignette is more acceptable today than it once was. This does not mean the audience is dying to hear the particulars of every minute of your trip. I have read articles in which the author mentions that she ordered a salad and her companion ordered a steak. Unless her companion is Brad Pitt, is there any reason to mention him? I personally resent traveling companions of unknown relationship to the author, who appear on the page simply to order the red wine when the author orders the white.

Now if there's a traveling companion who is klutzy (the suitcase on the upper rack falls on her head) or adventurous (she goes out running with the bulls, or deep-sea fishing for marlin

while the author sits on the beach) or outgoing (she meets every
student and artist on the Left Bank) then that's different. The
companion becomes a conduit for the reader, and her adventures
or predicaments become the educational vignettes of the book.
Instead of warning the reader of the perils of losing his passport,
you tell the funny story of how Sally got her pocketbook filched
in the student cafeteria at Trinity College in Dublin and everything she had to go through to get a new passport. But if Sally is
in your story simply because Sally accompanied you on the trip,
the less seen of her, the better.

Obsolete Material

Nothing earmarks a guide as being "old hat" as the appearance
of scores of outdated references. The obsolescence curse can also
strike the best of guidebooks, especially if their later, revised
editions have not been minutely researched.

I remember several years ago when a friend wanted to arrange
an outing to South Street Seaport in New York City. She suggested
that after lunch we board the excursion paddle-wheeler, the
DeWitt Clinton. Since South Street Seaport was included in my
book, I had recently checked for updating and discovered that
one of paddle-wheelers had been scuttled and the other one sold
down the river to New Orleans. I suggested we take the sloop
instead.

"Oh, no, they have the paddle-wheelers" my friend assured
me. "I found the information in the Michelin Guide. And they're
always right!"

"Check the copyright date on your Michelin" I said.

Sure enough it was three years old and sure enough the paddle-
wheelers had left New York harbor some time before. So much
for Michelin guides as the epitome of correctness. No travel guide
can keep up with the vagaries of the tourist trade, weather and
politics, even if they update every year (which most do not). So
even if you are doing a first edition, go over all the facts you have
collected and anything you have used in travel articles in the last
few years.

How do you check obsolescence? How many times have you come across a delicious new restaurant, a new ski lodge, or any attraction that seems perfect for a travel column? Two or three years later, when you're collecting everything for a book, you can't seem to find any trace of the place. Did it close? Was the name changed? Did they change the area code number?

This is a major problem facing travel writers: the restaurant that closes, the amusement pier that burns down, the historic house that caves in, the nature refuge that is placed off limits — you never receive an announcement. These places may have sent out scads of press releases when they opened, but now everything is hush-hush.

If a tsunami sweeps away a resort island, if floods, hurricanes or wars make tourism impossible, you will hear about it. But news of the demise of a minor attraction will only show up in the local paper — if it shows up at all. Sometimes the website still has the old information up, but no one answers the telephone. Other times the website disappears from sight and Google searches for the name only bring up references that are several years old.

If you think it's hard to track down that little hideaway you heard about, it's twice as difficult to find out about the one that went out of business. Nobody leaves a calling card. Sometimes you can find a news notice on the Internet if you research a name through the top-notch search engines. Sometimes, you just stumble onto it in a newspaper article or on the Internet. Many travel writers subscribe to newsletters and e-zines that track the variables of the travel scene in order to keep up-to-date.

Sometimes, some kindly soul takes it upon himself to list defunct and/or derelict attractions. For instance, I found a website called, "Defunct Jersey Amusement Parks" when I was following a news mention that the Dracula Castle and roller coaster at Nickel's Midway Pier in Wildwood had burned down. Good thing too. Here are a few things to look out for when researching whether a place still exists:

Was it in a war, flood or volcano zone? Of course those are the most obvious ones. How long-lasting are the effects? The major tsunami in Southeast Asia destroyed so much — and yet the tourist industry there wants the public to come back. Every place has to be checked out.

One-man wonders: The bane of travel writers is the one-man wonder that fizzles when the one man who put it up is no longer around. He might have died, gone bankrupt or just left town. It doesn't matter if we're talking topiaries, windmills, or a snorkeling shop — there's always some one-man wonder in a guidebook and chances are that it may have closed down.

Trends that change: Keep an eye out for the possible demise of ski slopes if the weather keeps getting warmer, racetracks in a state that allows casino gambling, anything that is politically incorrect and any place that is dependent on a clientele that is dying out for one reason or another.

Places that may no longer be on the map — or on the site, such as childhood homes of famous people (unless they have been saved by a committee). Some countries, notably England and Scotland, do put up historic plaques to note that Arthur Conan Doyle or Sir Walter Scott once resided in this dilapidated tenement. Most other countries don't even bother.

Places that exist but are not open to the public: Very often brochures for walking tours will include buildings and even parks that can be seen from the outside but are not open to the public. It is important that you make this clear to your reader. Nothing seems to tick off travelers more than to discover that a house or museum is closed to the public after they have spent three hours finding the place. Homes of the famous that now belong to someone else are part of this category. The occupants resent having strangers ring their doorbells and they really resent it when guidebooks print their addresses without adding that it is a private residence and not open to the public.

This also goes for wildlife refuges or natural areas that do not allow hiking or entrance of any kind. Sometimes this prohibition is only during breeding season, and sometimes it is year-round, but at any rate readers should be warned beforehand.

Restaurants: Restaurants have the highest quotient of deaths per capita which is one reason so many guidebooks stick to the staid and boring eateries or the super expensive ones that have lasted more than five years. Trendy places get trampled beneath the boots of the trend-setters and that's why clubs and "inside" nooks appear more often in magazines and newsletters than in guidebooks. (Top restaurant guides come out every year).

Out-of-date details to look for:

- ✓ Hours and prices, of course — most likely to change.
- ✓ Telephone numbers — especially area codes.
- ✓ Airport policies. You spent a chapter showing how to get all those lotions and cosmetics neatly into the carry-on and then the new airport restrictions prohibit them. Then they change the rules again, allowing some and not others.
- ✓ Name changes —Airports, ballparks, stadiums, even countries have changed their official name many times within the last ten years.
- ✓ Ownership changes — does that 4-star chef still own and operate that restaurant?
- ✓ Architectural changes — is the front door now where the side door used to be? That seems to happen every time they reconstruct a building.
- ✓ Closings? Did the place go out of business? Did a flood sweep away that pleasant park? Or has it been renamed and changed into an amusement park?
- ✓ Political changes. Whether it's an international venue or just a local town, a change of politicians or dictators can alter the status of a tourist destination in a hurry.
- ✓ Cultural changes. Is smoking now banned in all bars in New York City? Do women have to wear a head scarf in all Muslim countries? Do you tip in theaters in France but not in restaurants? There are always changes in customs and laws and it's up to the guidebook author to keep abreast of all of them.

Change of Status

What if the venue still exists, but is not as spiffy as it once was? The trendy bar that's not so trendy; the restaurant that has lost its top chef; the lake that was so popular with jet skiers now choking on algae — do you devalue these by giving them less stars or do you omit them altogether? This depends on your audience, and frankly, your own taste.

While some places die out altogether, others change direction, change management, lose their luster or their star attraction. Certainly one reason why there are second and third editions of guidebooks is that any of the facts may become obsolete at any time. There are a whole host of complications that can throw your beautifully crafted prose into the trash can. Here are the most common problems:

- The place revamps and tries for a different audience
- The place is closed for refurbishing at the time your guidebook comes out
- The place changes names but stays the same

The problem is often on a small scale. Let's say the famous chef at a restaurant quits or dies. Do you keep the restaurant in as a four-star, lower its rating or just warn everybody that the quality might still be high but the signature dishes of Chef Igor will be missing? I believe you should mention it. As for venues that are closed for refurbishing (which often takes two or three years) it's best to include the place in the book and mention the date for the planned re-opening.

Here are a few minor changes I had to contend with:

When I took my daughter and granddaughter to the Wild Safari at Six Flags Great Adventure, there seemed to be fewer animals on the road. Still in all, a camel stuck his head into the car for a forbidden apple and a few giraffes gave us the once over. My daughter kept telling her two-year-old, who was in the back seat: "Wait until we get to the monkeys — they're going to climb all over the car!"

Indeed, for years the baboons were allowed to traipse over the cars, although convertibles and soft topped cars had to take a bypass. My daughter was really looking forward to having the agile animals crawl all over the hood. We approached the monkey area and alas, they were all locked up behind a chain-link fence screeching at us like inmates at the recreation yard at Attica. I don't know if it was fear of lawsuits or what, but Six Flags had changed the rules. I cannot imagine writing up this place without warning folks that the monkeys won't be gamboling over the SUVs anymore. I get scads of press releases from Six Flags Great Adventure but not a word about this change.

Another case is the Forbes Magazine Galleries, a small free museum in downtown Manhattan. Here you could find thousands of toy soldiers in different uniforms set up for battle and toy sailboats of varying length and beauty. But the crown jewels of the collection were the fabulous bibelots that the house of Faberge had created for the Russian Czars. There were 130 pieces including twelve jeweled Easter eggs, tiaras and encrusted cigarette cases from the creative craftsman. They had been collected, along with Presidential papers, the toy armies and miniature sailboats by Malcolm Forbes the eccentric millionaire. The main part of this collection was kept on the ground floor of the Forbes Magazine building.

After Malcolm's death, many of the prize possessions of the Forbes Galleries were sold off. The Faberge collection went back to its home country thanks to some newly minted Russian billionaires. Other toys and trinkets have vanished from view. The Galleries are still open and still free to the public but are they as worthy of a visit now that the prize collection is gone?

Size Considerations: Cutting It down or Beefing It Up

Cutting It Down: Since many guidebook writers are also free-lancers who have a considerable stash of travel articles in their files and computers, they often find they have to pare down a previously written article to make it fit into a guidebook-size piece.

The typical travel article runs anywhere from six or seven hundred words to the all-encompassing 3000-word article that appears in the New York Times Travel section. An entry in a guidebook on the same subject may run anywhere from a simple 200-word description to a 1000-word article. In cutting down a previously written piece, you have to synthesize the main thrust of the article.

First, look for obsolete or irrelevant material. If you started with a seasonal approach such as: "Now that the darling buds of May are in bloom it's time to visit the Butchardt Gardens", clearly, that sentence has to go. The seasonal approach is obvious when it's an opening sentence, but further down in the article you might have made a reference to the fact that President's Day is a great time to visit Mount Vernon, or that the salmon are running in August. Since your guidebook may cover a span of two, three or four years, it is important to weed out any reference to specific events (for instance: now that Americans have invaded Iraq) or specific seasons (now that snow is on the ground).

Also look for statements such as "now that the Statue of Liberty is closed" or "now that the Statue of Liberty is open". The traveling exhibit of Van Gogh may have been great, but if it happened in 1999 the one-paragraph write-up you did that caught the essence of the painter so well, should be thrown into the delete pile.

There is also the "people" check. Let's say you interviewed the director of a museum or the spokesperson for an amusement park and quoted him or her in the article. Now, you'll probably want to recheck the facts anyway and talk to whomever is in charge at the point you are writing your guide, so it's best to leave people's names out of it since positions change all the time. Simply give the facts as they were stated.

Cutting the Fat: Even after throwing out all your seasonal and obsolete references, there's still plenty of cutting needed to trim 3000 words down to 450. You learn to look for the salient points. If there was a full paragraph lead into the subject, cut that down to a single sentence. An interview with a tourist can be tossed or put into a sidebar that can be placed somewhere else in the chapter.

Capsule reviews: When there are dozens of restaurants, bars, clubs to cover in a dozen different sections of town, the capsule review, familiar from city magazines and newspapers is used. In the following example, restaurants in and around San Francisco are chopped into districts (such as Mission, East Bay, Wine country) and further dissected by types of cuisine. That leaves room for about 20 to 25 words of text aside from the name, address and telephone number of the eatery, or about 35 words in all for each entry. Here is an example from *The Rough Guide to San Francisco* of a Mexican Restaurant in Marin County:

> "**Guaymas**, 5 Main St. Tiburon. 415/435-6300. Situated on a dock by the bay — meaning you get some remarkable views of the city to accompany some terrific Cal-Mex cuisine. Moderate."

When it comes time to edit your book, you may need to do even more pruning of your prose because of space limitations. But for now, keep an eye on the word count and make your decisions based on your content and your perceived audience.

Chapter 15

Basic Research

Most travel writers base their research on one or more of the following:

1. A personal visit to the place
2. Brochures, press releases and guides written by the Chamber of Commerce and by the specific locales themselves.
3. The website for basic information as well as updates and pictures.
4. Other Internet resources.
5. A telephone call or personal interview with the director of the place or the marketing or advertising director.
6. Anecdotes from other travelers.
7. Write-ups of the same place in other books, newspapers and magazines and the Internet (with attributed quotes if you are using verbatim material).
8. Photographs of the place, either taken by you (or a friend/relative) or slides, postcards, and pictures you bought when you visited.
9. A questionnaire.

Besides material on specific destinations, most non-fiction writers have the following in their library:
- An up-to-date almanac for facts and figures.

The World Almanac is still a great source for basic material about anyplace in the world.

- Online reference sources, such as Wikipedia, although these are not always foolproof.
- A major encyclopedia (either in hardcover or computer form).
- A geographical dictionary (Webster's has a good one)
- A biographical dictionary (Webster's among others)
- A standard dictionary (*Webster's Collegiate, Funk & Wagnall's* or *Random House*)
- Strunk & White, *The Elements of Style* (for consistent usage)
- *The Chicago Manual of Style*
- A thesaurus to find alternative words for overused ones

The importance of having good reference materials right at hand cannot be overstated. No matter how much homework you have done on your subject, no matter how many times you have visited the place, talked to the director and taken pictures, most of the little mistakes you make could have been easily verified in your own home using your own reference materials. Several errors that I have found in guidebooks could have been corrected easily by simply checking a standard reference book.

Authors of destination guidebooks to foreign countries (or even their own) usually spend a considerable amount of space on the history and background of the country including the biography of major figures in that history. This means a trip to the library and buying a few books on the history of Nepal or Mauritania or whatever territory your guide covers. Some histories go as far back as the original inhabitants of the site, and include a description of every upheaval and cultural change over a thousand years. In such cases, you need more than a cursory summary gleaned from a website.

The destination website should provide such information as passport requirements, health requirements (do you need certain shots?) and other necessities of travel. This means a check of the government's website. For those who specialize in outdoor travel, food and wine travel or how-to-travel, there are probably one or two standard texts in those fields that you should have on hand.

There are also a host of websites that specialize in a particular type of travel or outdoor activity such as www.gorp.com and www.away.com, (both connected to Orbitz). These and websites run by Travelocity and other travel portals all include information and articles. They are a source and also a possible market since they take material from free-lance writers. Www.johnnyjet.com combines personal travel stories with a portal to lots of travel information and travel articles in a variety of newspapers and magazines. Other Internet resources include: www.travellady.com, www.onthegopublishing.com, www.journeywoman .com, www.Gonomad.com, www.independenttraveler.com. and www.About.com .

Personal Sources of information

Local Research: Once you land at the destination, the first stop should be the Tourist Bureau which is almost always situated in the heart of town. Here you can find lists of hotels, walking maps, and brochures for local attractions. Railroad stations in many countries have a visitor's bureau where they can find you a place to stay or arrange for transportation to your next stop.

If you are staying at a better class hotel there may be a concierge who can give you the lowdown on everything. Taking a local tour bus may seem hokey to some, but it gets you around town quickly and you see the most important sites. Later, you can explore the nooks and crannies yourself, but a bus will give you the feel for a city quickly. Naturally, if you know the language and have a handle on the money, taking a regular passenger bus to see the city is a preferred means of transit for many travel writers. They may have to find their way back to square one themselves, but that's part of the adventure.

Using an interview source: There is an unspoken rule by newspaper and magazine editors that travel articles should be upbeat. That does not mean that travel writers will smooth over the rough spots they encounter on their travels — after all, that is one reason they are being paid — to warn fellow travelers about bumps on the road. But newspaper reporters will often quote the director or spokesman or tour guide for a particular destination, rather than express their own opinions. So what you might find in a newspaper feature article is the following:

"According to Sam Smith, director of development, the new theater center has turned Gotham City into a cultural haven for both residents and out-of-towners. Incorporating an arcade of small restaurants and boutiques, the center plans to attract 150,000 people per year."

This way, the reporter can get the upbeat information across without attributing any of the enthusiasm to his own observations. He can always add as an aside: "However, the theater center is not expected to be fully operational until next year."

Now whether it's a theater center in Gotham City or a dell of daffodils in a botanical garden, the number of wolves in a wildlife preserve or a fancy new hotel that has just opened in Antibes, you will need to get the statistics from the director of the place or the Chamber of Commerce to give substance to the piece. Whether or not you should parrot the director's assessment of how thrilling or fascinating the attraction is another matter. Newspapers editors routinely strike out overly enthusiastic praise — especially when it comes in the form of a press release. Guidebook writers and editors should do the same

Pinning down the facts: Sometimes, it's like pulling hen's teeth to get specifics from a Public Relations director, although you can always get pages and pages of "material" from one. Some amateur public relations people think a press release should read like an ad. So they will give you paragraph after paragraph telling how patrons can "feel like royalty after a super salt scrub in the hotel's new spa" without offering any information on the size, availability or prices of the spa, where it is in relation to the hotel, or even telling you what a super salt scrub is.

Future Changes: One author spent an hour on the telephone with the director of a large historical village. He checked the spelling of the historical name, the description of the historical mansion, and wrote down the best-known anecdotes. He listened to the director praise the place. The one thing he did not find out was that the main historic mansion in the village, the one that appears in every brochure, was closed due to smoke damage and would be closed for the following year. The director simply omitted that fact.

One of the most difficult aspects of travel writing is dealing with changes that are not apparent at the time of your visit. It is always a good idea to ask if there are any new exhibits, new construction or additions that are planned. But what if you suspect that there is a bankruptcy looming? Unfortunately directors and PR people are always reluctant to tell you that a main attraction is closed, or the Vermeer painting you traveled to see is on loan, or that a herd of deer ate up the much-vaunted rose garden.

So always ask the obvious question: Is it open? Will it be open next year? If it is a gristmill, does the mill operate? How often? If it's a ferry, does it operate during off-season? If it's a forest are the trails clearly marked? If it's Chef Pierre's restaurant, is Chef Pierre still there?

Hotel research: Getting the basic facts about hotels is not difficult. If what you want is the number of rooms, whether there are laundry facilities or valet service, minibars or coffee machines in the room, continental breakfast, indoor or outdoor pools, parking and that sort of thing you can get lists off the Internet or by making a simple phone call.

If you have not actually seen the hotel, it is hard to do more than compile the basics. Some travel writers visit the hotel by looking at the lobby, picking up a brochure, checking out the dining room, talking to the manager and perhaps getting a peek at one of the rooms. Many countries have their own system of rating hotels. In France, for instance, hotels are rated one, two, three, four or five stars on the basis of the number of amenities. These ratings may not coincide with American standards but they can be used for comparative judgments.

What about the neighborhood? What about the clientele? There are other factors beside the amenities or cleanliness of a hotel that make the difference between an enjoyable vacation and a stint on Fear Factor. Years ago, I stayed at a small hotel in

Puerto Rico that had been recommended in a budget guidebook. What I remember was that the door to the room next to mine was kicked in by the enraged suitor of the woman who was staying there. More recently I stayed at a centrally located hotel in Philadelphia. A boisterous crowd of teenagers kept the noise level in the corridors at a high decibel throughout the night and the stained carpet in the hall gave testimony to many a beer-soaked night. So while the hotel had a well-known franchise name and a marvelous location in the historic area, my sojourn there was decidedly uncomfortable. You may not be able to sleep in every hotel in your book, but you should try to check them out for a one-hour visit to get a sense of the place.

A Questionnaire

When compiling a directory or a quick-fact section of your guidebook, it is simpler to compile a questionnaire for hotels or other attractions where you list all possible amenities and have the recipient check off all relevant data (number of rooms, room service, etc.) and leave a space for comments. These can then be mailed or e-mailed to your contacts and assembled and checked later.

Other People's Opinion

Let's face it, with hundreds of travel forums online and with every branded travel guide now sporting a feedback page we have all entered the age of Zagatization. Since the appearance of the first Zagat Survey, the idea of cumulative feedback rather than the assessment of a single knowledgeable critic has taken hold. And now the Internet has opened up the floodgates to a torrent of opinions from everybody on every aspect of life. Opinions on hotels, restaurants, rain forests, destinations, airlines and everything in between can be found in a myriad of places. Cyberspace is awash with helpful private websites and blogs that cover everything from a personal essay on "my trip to Thailand" to detailed maps, photographs and visiting hours for practically any destination in the world.

There are also the many forums on the Internet which are

very helpful. This includes AOL and Yahoo communities (among them, travel, seniors and parenting) where people exchange information on their experiences at hotels, restaurants, airports, theme parks, aquariums, and such. There are also forums run by many of the top travel publishers. Now if you discover that five or six people say that a much-touted beer hall in Munich is over-priced, or that a famous tropical paradise had so many bullfrogs croaking all night that it was impossible to sleep, you can make note of it.

Many travelers like to make their comments known as a way to enter the travel-writing field. Others just like to get a gripe off their chest. Some people join the forums to ask questions — others join to answer them. Either way, this is a way of discovering other people's opinion without having to go through the embarrassment of asking a stranger how he liked the hi-speed train or the ferry crossing.

If you are working for a publisher who puts out a "branded" series, you may have access to their database of opinions, since the copyright for those opinions belongs to the publisher who owns the website. For instance, in the *2006 Unofficial Guide to Walt Disney World*, the tips from people who sent in the feed-back form in the back of the book were often the best advice in the entire book. Several people complained about the rental strollers — that they were too big for toddlers and that they had no storage space. At any rate, a friend made the decision to take her 18-month-old's stroller along on the plane, after she read these comments.

But what do you do when you are writing for a small publisher or self-publishing and don't have access to a handy database? Here are some places to check:

1. www.epinions.com. This website covers everything, not only travel. You can find anything from a short sentence to a three-paragraph diary of one's stay at a hotel.

2. www.amazon.com. Yes, the ubiquitous Amazon. In reading reviews of travel guides you will often pick up a great deal of personal information about specific trips. A reader might complain that the raved-about hotel had

rude desk clerks, lumpy beds and no hot water.

3. General travel forums. You'll find them under yahoo. com. You can also check out forums on the websites of all the major publishers in the travel guide field. But be very careful not to lift anything verbatim from these forums — they are copyrighted by the publishers who feature them. Also check popular sites such as www. familytravel.com, www.smarttravel.net , www.away. com and countless others.

4. Specific forums such as Parent Soup on AOL or gatherings of people with special interests such as senior citizens (they travel a lot), honeymooners (found on wedding sites like the Knot.com) and any specific interest group such as hikers, kayaker and wine-tasters.

5. The Letters to the Editor section in any travel magazine will often feature opinions, personal stories or corrections to a previously published article.

6. Google a particular destination or travel site. It's amazing how many people put their honeymoon trips, class reunions, group trips or adventurous travels up on websites and blogs for no other reason than they want to share them with the world. These Internet tourists make no bones about their feelings concerning the long lines, the weather, the waiters and anything else that irks them.

7. Travel blogs. You may find one that covers your area. You can ask permission for a quote if needs be.

8. Don't forget about first hand opinions! Whether it's your sixty-year-old neighbors who came back from a Panama Canal cruise and complained that everybody on board was "too old", the lady sitting next to you at a café in Nice who clues you in to the best hotel, or a twelve-year-old who boasts that he rode the Cyclone roller coaster and it "ruled", you can always use that information.

Talk to bellboys, talk to taxi drivers, talk to other travelers of all ages and income brackets. And be an eavesdropper. If you're standing in a hotel lobby and guests keep coming to the desk with various complaints, listen to what they are saying. Are the ice machines keeping them up all night? Make a note.

Checking the Facts

Telephone numbers and hours: The most basic fact in any travel guidebook is the telephone number and next comes the address, the town, the directions and the website. So check it once and check it twice. Then re-check any numbers that look like they might have problems. For instance if you notice a New York area code for a resort in the Bahamas, check it out. There may be a rational reason for it, or it might be a mistake. The only way to be absolutely positive is to dial it yourself.

While museum directors get steamed when you call a Post-Impressionist painting an Impressionist, there is only one topic that really angers the reader and that is incorrect information about prices, hours and addresses. No matter that you put an advisory at the beginning of the book stating that prices and hours change all the time — someone with a five-year-old copy of your guidebook will complain to the museum director that the place is supposed to be free because the author said so!

Certain factual details change so often that guidebook authors should try to avoid putting down exact numbers. Ferry times, for instance. The ferry between the Liberty State Park terminal and the Statue of Liberty changed its schedule so often that I stopped putting down actual times. Instead I wrote: "Hours: Generally between 9:30 a.m. and 4:30 p.m., once an hour during high season. Expands and contracts with the season."

Those Little Mistakes: In visiting or researching you take a lot of notes from tour guides, taxi drivers, museum directors, historic village docents and park rangers, so stories and anecdotes about historic figures, town incidents, famous storms and shipwrecks abound, but they may not be true. Sometimes the author will reach into his lifetime memory of assorted facts and get a few things twisted.

Names are the easiest things to get mixed up, whether you typed in Grant Street instead of Grant Avenue, or James Middleton instead of John Middleton, or black and red snapper instead of blackened red snapper. First, check your facts with the people in charge. Then check the website. And lastly, if there seems anything queasy about these "facts", check them against some outside source, such as a dictionary or encyclopedia. Here are a few mistakes I noticed simply by perusing travel guides about my local area:

1. Lonely Planet puts out a series on various states. Their book on the New York/New Jersey/Pennsylvania region mentions that the Great Swamp in Morris County allows camping. Now, New Jersey always gets short shrift when it's jammed between those other states, but since this series is beloved of backpackers, declaring that a wildlife refuge allows camping when it doesn't (and I live nearby, so I know) may throw off someone's travel plans.

2. Here's a quote from a travel guide to American Revolutionary War sites, published by a prestigious press: "Benjamin Franklin is an enduring figure from the early days of American independence, the only nonpresident on our currency." Wait a second — isn't Alexander Hamilton on the ten dollar bill? This is easy enough to check. Most people won't care, but if you are setting yourself up as an expert on history, be extra careful with those throwaway facts.

3. This one came from a general travel guide: "Columbus discovered the United States in 1492." Hmmm. He is popularly deemed to have discovered America (or at least an island near the continent) in 1492. The United States wasn't formed until 1776.

The Press Release Foul-up: Say you get a press release about a new addition to a hotel. The free-lance PR person who sent the press release has his name and telephone number at the top of the page. When typing up (or downloading) the material you want, you inadvertently use the PR firm's number as the contact telephone rather than the hotel's number. Somehow this telephone number appears in your book. You have to wait for a new printing and sometimes a whole new edition to fix up this mistake. Always check the top and bottom of the press release and make sure you didn't pick up the wrong number.

The Internet Foul-up: A website declares that there are 500,000 daffodil bulbs in the 27-acre garden. There are also rhododendrons, irises, a bridge, and a house on the acreage and 500,000 bulbs seems a bit much. I need the correct information so I call up. The lady in charge doesn't know; she has to check with the botanist in charge. He gets back to me two weeks later. Oh yes, he says, the typist made a mistake. It's not 500,000, it's supposed to be 50,000 and they will change it on the website. I change it to 50,000 daffodils in my book. They never change the website.

E-mail translations: I once did an article about a neighbor who had used the Earthwatch work/vacation program. He e-mailed me about 1400 words about his experience. When I rewrote the piece, I inadvertently changed an important detail in his copy. It seems he had studied honey ants and koala bear tracks in Australia. Somehow it came out as koala bears and honeybees. The article read pretty well, but of course the only thing the man noticed was that I had changed honey ants into honeybees. So it's always good to check with your original source before you go to press.

Website translations: A tricky business because one errant letter or number can throw the whole thing off. Also website owners often change names or service providers. How detailed should a website address be in a guidebook? Authors and publishers vary on this. Technology publishers almost always use a long, detailed address with lots of slashes. For a guidebook, I prefer a short address, so when I wrote up Franklin D. Roosevelt's home in Hyde Park, I simply put www.nps.gov as the website address.

You'll have one last chance to re-check the facts when you enter the editing stage. And remember — an outside editor will not check facts for you — that's your job! Or you can hire someone just to check the facts and statistics

Chapter 16

Plagiarism, Copyright Infringement and Second Hand Prose

I'm going to define plagiarism, copyright infringement and just plain old fashioned "second hand prose". Disclaimer: I am not a lawyer and the following is not meant as legal advice.

Plagiarism: When you use material from another source without permission and without notation as to where it came from and pass it off as your own, it is called plagiarism. While high school and college teachers fume when their students do this, it is practiced in the real world all the time. Whether intentionally or subconsciously, travel writers often lift a phrase or two from other authors. While factual material may be copied (i.e. the Cheops pyramid is 564 feet high) it is duplicating the unique wording about the facts that is deemed plagiarism.

Copyright infringement is a legal term. Your copyright protects your right to derive profits from your published material. Even if you published a poem on the Internet it belongs to you, unless there is some agreement made between you and the site owner.

In the world of book publishing, the copyright belongs to the author, unless it is given to the publisher. Most publishing contracts hammer out the details of exactly who owns what. When the writer hands in a work-for-hire, the publisher pays him and owns all rights.

However, as is often the case in travel writing, the author revises the material he researched and uses it again for other articles and books. Let's say a travel writer is given the assignment of checking out the nightlife in Budapest. He is one of perhaps five writers who are contributing to the book, and he is paid a lump sum for his work. He can use the knowledge he gained of Budapest in several other articles.

One author I know wrote a book about odd eating-places for one publisher and a book about odd architecture for another. Now since there's a pancake house in the odd shape of a shoe, it shows up on the pages of both books. And although most publishers' contracts include a no-conflict clause which states that the author cannot write a competing book for another publisher, what happens is that the author uses a different slant on the same material.

But what if someone else hijacks your incredible insights and polished prose? If you see your idea or your title show up somewhere else, you can assume that a.) It's a coincidence, or b.) They stole it from you. But since neither titles nor ideas can be copyrighted, there is not much you can do about it. It is the unique expression that counts! If the wording of the pancake-shoe house copy in someone else's book is so close to yours that you recognize your "voice", then you may have grounds for a lawsuit.

A Case of Copyright Infringement

The fact that everybody uses the same basic research material is not a sufficient excuse in cases of obvious copyright infringement. Several years ago, I had to sue a fairly well-known publisher because one of their authors had simply taken twenty-five pages of my book, pared them down a bit, and called the finished product his own. The immediate reaction of my lawyer, and later the lawyers for the publisher, was that this might be mere coincidence since so many travel guides dip from the same well.

I had to slog through the offending book, page by page, and note where everything — from the paragraph construction to the use of specific expressions to personal reactions based on my own background and taste — were copied.

It's quite common for one author to pick up an idea or a particular destination from another. Certainly if you've ever thumbed through a competitor's book, you would have noticed a few gems he raved about that you had overlooked. And you think: "Why didn't I include that jumping nightclub or that secluded inn in my book?" But cribbing attractions from another book is quite different from copying the other author's words and style. It is the latter that is subject to a copyright infringement suit.

What are the identifying features? Note where the first paragraph begins in each entry; no two writers will approach the same subject in exactly same way. And unless it can be proved that both authors took the first paragraph from a third source, such as a press release or an encyclopedia, it stands to reason that one of them took the construction from the other.

Of course a single paragraph isn't enough to prove infringement unless it's a poem or a song where the expression of each word is of paramount importance. Many an author knows that another writer took an idea, a concept and rephrased it in his own words. There is nothing much to be done about that. However when you find whole chunks of your style and observations floating around in someone else's work, you can be sure they did not surface there by accident. If you think plagiarism has occurred, here are some things to look for:

- Note the entire construction. Do the paragraphs follow each other in a similar fashion? Is the factual material set up in a very familiar manner?
- Note particular expressions. When I first visited a children's museum, the 15,000-square-foot space, filled with hands-on exhibits, reminded me of a giant nursery school, although it sported such sophisticated toys as helicopters and backhoes. And so I

mentioned this analogy. Sure enough, the plagiarist copied my first paragraph, the total construction
of the piece and my reference to a giant nursery
school. Since most people nowadays would use the
expression "pre-school" the wording stood out.
- Note similar errors. Whether it's spelling errors or
an erroneous historical fact, nothing illustrates the
art of copying better than the mistakes the plagiarist
unwittingly repeats. Obsolete material that appeared
in an earlier edition of a competing book is another
dead giveaway that the material was filched.

Who gets sued? Most publishers' contracts include a clause that
makes the author responsible in case of a legal action in which
they are found liable for damages. In real life, however, it is the
publishing house that gets sued, and they all carry insurance.
If there is a large settlement they may turn around and sue the
author in order to regain their costs.

In some recent cases, plagiarism came to light through the
media before there was ever a court case. This happened because
a third party was the first to notice the theft of words. In noto-
rious cases a reader will notice the problem and bring it to the
attention of the Internet world, so that it becomes a *cause celebre*
even before the aggrieved party is aware of the problem. In a well-
publicized fiction case, a student newspaper uncovered copied
material in a "chick-lit" novel written by a college student.

Meanwhile there are probably hundreds of cases like mine,
where a suit is settled out of court for a minor sum, the book is
taken off the market and all parties sign a paper stating that they
will keep quiet. Even when the case reaches the public view, the
settlement amount is rarely given and the lawyers insist that the
defending publisher admit no liability.

What Is Outside of Copyright?

The Public Domain: anything in the public domain is fair game.
This is includes words, pictures, border designs, songs from the
past and so forth. There are several categories of public domain.
The most common ones are:

1. The Dead Poet's Society: Using a quote from a writer who is long dead and whose works are in the public domain is permissible. Works from authors who have been dead the required time can be used without any permission. It is considered polite to mention the source, but it is not necessary.

> "My heart's in the highlands, my heart is not here,
> My heart's in the Highlands a-chasing the deer"

I'll bet many an author has used Robert Burns to brighten up his prose when he wrote about Scotland. Feel like quoting Shakespeare in your book on the British countryside? How about Lord Byron on Greece? Go ahead — help yourself! You can even put the quotes into those cute little sidebars that clutter up every travel guide from here to the Himalayas. The only caveat: don't use a recent translation of Tolstoy or Homer — the translation might be under copyright protection.

2. Freebies from live authors: Sometimes, an author will give *carte blanche* permission to use his words without any monetary consideration as long as you give proper attribution. On his website, Dan Poynter, one of the most visible gurus of self-publishing, has a list of quotes that anyone can use. The zinger is that if the author forgets to give Dan the proper credit, Poynter will ask for $250!

3. The United States Government: One of the most prolific "authors" is the government printing office. They put out all sorts of pamphlets and brochures which are in the public domain. Government agencies also have scads of stuff online — and you can borrow anything you want. The National Park Service and the Geological Survey (for maps) are just a few of the many agencies that are cornucopias of copy for the hungry writer. For the travel writer there is plenty of meat. Here, for instance, is a download from the National Park Service page on a park in Hot Springs, Arkansas.

> "The area now known as 'Hot Springs National Park'
> first became United States territory in 1803 as part of
> the Louisiana Purchase. The first permanent settlers to
> reach the Hot Springs area in 1807 were quick to realize

the springs' potential as a health resort. By the 1830s,
log cabins and a store had been built to meet the needs
(albeit in a rudimentary way) of visitors to the springs."

What if you took that paragraph and simply inserted it into
your book about the Ozarks: would that be copyright infringement? No. What if someone else lifted that paragraph from your
book and served it up as his own — did he commit copyright
infringement? No. When you use public domain material you
cannot claim it as your own even if someone else finds it in your
book. As a matter of fact, there have been many cases where a
writer has simply taken the public domain material put out by
the government, whether it is a pamphlet on how to cook toma-
toes or an oral history of Ellis Island, put it into a new format,
given it a new title, and published it under the author's name.

Wikipedia: Everyone knows this is a great free resource for facts
and information but did you realize that you can also lift full
paragraphs from their articles without any copyright problems?
That's right! It's free for the taking — no permissions, no quota-
tion marks! A courtesy note is expected. Of course you'll probably
want to alter the prose to match your own style — after all this is
an encyclopedia, even if it is online and free. But if you're looking
for that last-minute sketch of King Tut, this is the place: www.
wikipedia.com.

Press Releases and Advertising copy: If the material is part of
advertising copy, press release or brochures where the information falls within general permission guidelines you're usually
okay. Many press kits contain a sentence saying that the addressee
may use all information and photographs contained within. How
else would you know that a certain restaurant seats 200 people
or that their vegetables are all freshly picked if you did not get it
from the press release? If you are uncertain, then call the agency
and ask.

Since the information is freely given, it can be taken freely.
I was always surprised that so many newspapers ran my press
releases about *New Jersey Day Trips* verbatim. They often edited
for size, or changed the headline, but otherwise, the straight

release was printed. So it is not an unusual practice for newspapers and even magazines to take press release material and simply reprint it with a new headline. But should you, as the author of a guidebook do it? That's another question entirely. Most writers restructure free material in order to create a new work.

Fair Use Doctrine: "Fair Use" is a limitation of copyright protection and an accepted principle. Some publishers will put it into their copyright declaration in this fashion:

> "All rights reserved. No portion of this book may be reproduced in any form or by any electronic or mechanical means — except in the case of brief quotations in critical articles or reviews — without the written permission of the publishers."

This is a standard understanding in the literary world. If you are reviewing someone's book for your local paper, or doing a critical paper on a certain author you are allowed a few quotes. The circumstances of Fair Use depend on the amount of the portion used, whether the work competes with the original work, whether it is used for educational purposes and a few other conditions. Lawyers will always caution to get permission anyway.

When it comes to song lyrics and poetry, quoting even a short phrase is considered copyright infringement, so you absolutely must get permission and/or pay a fee to use anything that is under copyright protection.

Synchronicity

Writers sometimes assume that someone filched a phrase or observation but it may be a case of synchronicity. In other words, two writers come to the same idea as a coincidence. I remember when I wrote an article on the newly opened Rockefeller Estate in Tarrytown called Kykuit, I began the article with this sentence: "You may never be as rich as Rockefeller but at least you'll be able to enter the marbled foyer of a Rockefeller mansion, now that the estate at Kykuit is finally open."

Sure enough, an article in a New York newspaper started in

a similar manner with a reference to "rich as Rockefeller". Since that line occurs in a popular song, it is natural that both of us might think of it. So when it comes to fairly common observations, you are in the clear legally.

The Commonplace Description

Here's another situation. What happens when you state the obvious, even without the help of brochures or press kits? It is practically impossible to prosecute for copyright infringement in such a case. The Grand Canyon is breathtaking? The pack mules that go down the trail are sure-footed even though it feels like you're about to go over the edge? You cannot copyright the obvious or the mundane.

Certain phrases are used over and again in travel writing. Think of "crystal clear waters" and "powdery white sand beaches", "breathtaking views" and "sinfully delicious chocolate cake". (Decadent and sinful are common adjectives for chocolate rather than vanilla — must be the calories). Banal expressions cannot be copyrighted. Neither can factual material that can only be described in a limited number of ways. Think, for instance, of descriptions of the Egyptian pyramids, the snow-capped Andes and the green-canopied rain forest.

Second Hand Facts

Now this is something that everybody does — newspaper reporters especially will pick up a story that has come over a wire service and rewrite it with some additional embellishments. No one ever checks the original source and if a fact is incorrect in the original wire story, it remains that way.

Most travel writers research a destination before they ever set out to do a story, and that means poring over guidebooks, websites, press kits, history books, encyclopedias, interviews with experts and so forth. Very often there will be variations to the facts as the story acquires mileage. And of course the original source may have gotten some details wrong in the first place. Some blogs have been excellent in uncovering misinformation, while others have just passed it along.

One only has to watch those cable news programs that cover crime stories to see how quickly an unsubstantiated story can get palmed off as fact and argued over by a panel of experts all of whom are relying on a few interviews gleaned by a single over-zealous reporter. Riots and even wars have started over a rumor of wrongdoing by some government.

So while travel writers come from all corners of the literate world, they should use journalistic standards when it comes to repeating facts they have picked up from outside sources — whether these be websites, press releases, wire stories or newscasts. I know from covering historic houses that anecdotes and "history lessons" about these places have been reiterated by interpreters and docents and then written down in guidebooks, only to be replaced a few years later by completely different stories that refute the original ones.

Revising history happens all the time in travel literature. For the writer it is best to say, "According to the tour guide, Henry the Eighth had a full breakfast and went on a hunt the morning of the Queen's execution." That way, the writer can relate the anecdote without wading through six biographies of the King just to make sure it was true.

Libel

Aside from the question of copyright infringement and permissions, there is another legal area where travel writers sometimes tread — the area of libel. It is possible that a hotel or restaurant owner or a Chamber of Commerce might take affront at something you say and try to seek redress in the courts.

Luckily, the freedom of the press that we enjoy in the United States allows quite a bit of latitude when it comes to review-style write-ups. So if you say, "the milkshake at Dowd's tastes like Milk of Magnesia", you might get a nasty letter from the owner but you will probably not get sued. You can also report a fact that you have observed. If you mention that "several of our party who feasted on the seafood buffet at our hotel were up all night doing toilet duty", you are, after all, simply stating an observation.

Another thing you can do is put the criticism in the mouth of another person. So if you quote a patron at a ski resort who complains that the lines are too long, the personnel rude and that the other skiers are amateur hotshots who tailgate the regulars, you are able to get the message across without saying it yourself. And you can always balance things out by quoting another patron who reports that the powder was fine and the prices reasonable.

When it comes to minor insults — remarks that the service at a restaurant was slow, that half of the rides at the theme park were closed, or that the "free entrance fee" to the gardens did not include entrance to the zoo — these are acceptable comments in any guidebook. One expects to get a few warnings about incompetence or sloppiness in a travel guide. But be absolutely sure all your other facts about the place are correct. This is not the time to absent-mindedly mention that the square footage is 1600 feet when it's 16,000 feet, or that the restaurant does its own baking when they bring the desserts in. Anytime a venue feels that you have "done them wrong" they will not dwell on your comments but on your inaccuracies, even if these consist of describing the hotelier as Linda instead of Lynda.

On the other side of the coin — are you, as the author, liable if you recommend a place as being safe and an accident occurs? Are you liable if you recommend a car-rental agency as being inexpensive and the owners jack up the price with hidden charges that leave a bewildered patron broke? Hardly, but anyone is free to sue anyone. That doesn't mean they will win, but lawyers cost money. Most publishers keep an umbrella insurance policy to cover all contingencies.

And then the perverse often happens — as soon as you write up a river tubing company as safe, a drowning occurs the next week. An 'out-of-the-way places' book thrills about a nightclub in Indonesia and three weeks later there is a deadly fire. On a smaller scale, the Bed and Breakfast you recommend as reasonably priced with a bountiful breakfast suddenly jacks up their price and starts serving hardtack. Although these are embarrassing, there is no way any reasonable person would sue a guidebook on the basis of misinformation. But the disclaimer mentioned in Section 2 covers these possibilities.

In summation, do read at least one book on legal matters whether it is about libel, privacy invasion or copyright infringement. Photographs and maps are also common subjects of infringement (see the section on illustrations) and legal books go over these quite thoroughly.

Permissions

You may need to obtain permission for a quote that is under copyright, in which case you have to track down the owner of the rights. You also may have to get permission to re-use a travel article you yourself wrote that appeared in a newspaper or magazine. Generally free-lancers sell first North American rights to the buyer and then the rights revert to them. But if you are a staffer on a newspaper or a TV show you should check with them to see if there is any problem in re-using the material. Also, if you are a contributing writer or columnist to a newspaper or magazine (online included) where a contract has been signed which gave rights to the publisher rather than to you, check with the original publisher and/or a lawyer.

Recommended books: The Copyright, Permission and Libel Handbook by Lloyd J. Jassin and Steven C. Schecter. 1998. John Wiley & Sons

Recommended websites: www.publaw.com: Website of publishing attorney Lloyd Rich; www.IvanHoffman.com: another lawyer who specializes in the field.

Chapter 17

Photos, Maps and Illustrations

Illustrations include photographs, slides, maps, cartoons, clip art, sketches, water colors and line drawings. These are most often the responsibility of the author (or co-author) if the illustrations are an important element in the book. Cover illustrations are commonly done by the publisher. However, everything is negotiable and if you have a photo that you took which reproduces well, the publisher might incorporate it into the cover design. In that case you would very often receive an extra fee for the shot. The publisher (assuming you are not self-publishing) will usually pay for a good stock photo for the cover.

As for inside illustrations, including photos, authors and co-authors usually supply these (unless this is a series where the publisher uses his own photographers, artists or cartoonists). If you are only doing one chapter of a book that a publisher is putting together, the editors will probably take care of the illustrations. They may already have a relationship with an artist or photographer who supplies the illustrated material.

Policies differ quite a bit from one publisher to another and this can make quite a difference to your pocketbook. For instance, in its guidelines for book proposals, a certain publisher makes it very clear that they supply the photos. They have a special division that creates photographs (which they also sell on their website). So for those travel writers who also take expert photographs, it is up to them to negotiate which pictures are used. There are also publishers, such as Countryman Press, that prohibit public domain pictures and expect the author to contribute his own photographs to the work. But such things as clip art, icons and small designs on the page are almost always supplied by the publisher.

Photographs

In my one experience with a publishing house, I found that I and my co-author were expected to supply all photographs, and maps. However the publishing house didn't care if the photos were my own or if they came from any of the agencies, public or private, that I covered in the book. The only thing they insisted on was that we have proper permission forms for all outside pictures.

If the photographs become the main focus of the books, or if this is a travel pictorial, then the photographer (if he is someone else than yourself) will get equal billing, and most often, equal royalties. If you yourself are proposing a photographic travel essay then of course your photographs are part and parcel of the publishing package and you would be expected to show examples of your photographs as well as your prose.

There are a number of travel guide series that do not use photographs at all — most Fodor's books do not. Some publishers use maps but no photos. Some use cartoons (such as the Dummies series). So if you are pitching an idea to one of those publishers, you do not have to worry about illustrations.

On the other hand, if you are expected to supply the pictures yourself, this does not mean you have to take all the pictures, but simply that you are responsible for finding those photographs that illustrate the text. If you are self-publishing, then of course the whole project is up to you. Whether you include photographs, maps, clip-art icons and professional book design depends on your pocketbook and your audience.

Getting Organized: From the very beginning, you should make a list of photos you have available to you. Consider how they will fit into the chapters. Sometimes you may have a carton full of pictures of nature (a sunset over the beach, a waterfall, trees in winter) and nothing whatsoever for the chapter about shopping or museums. That is when you have to start hustling to find something you can use. So first, let's list the photographs you might have available for a particular project.

1. Pictures you get from sources (press kits, attractions, brochures)
2. Photos you take yourself
3. Photos you get from friends
4. Stock photos/slides
5. Free clip art photos
6. Public domain pictures/maps

If you are submitting material to a publisher, you will receive guidelines as to the type of photograph they want. They will usually send you a set of permission forms for those pictures that you receive from attractions, PR sources and government sources.

Quality of photos: Even in this day and age, a black and white glossy photograph reproduces better than a color photo on a black and white page. On the other hand, color photos and slides reproduce very well on covers and on coated inside sheets. However, color is more expensive to reproduce than black and white, so interior color photos are usually reserved for the more expensive coffee-table books of scenery. Yes, many travel guides, such as Lonely Planet now have several pages of color photographs inside, but if you notice, their retail price has gone up to accommodate this particular splurge.

Where Do You Find Photographs? In the travel field, the author does not necessarily pay directly from his own pocket when it comes to photographs. There are many resources for free photos and illustrations, and even some maps. These may come from the press kits of travel destinations in the form of black and white photos, color slides, color photos, CD discs, brochures, and even the cardboard covers of press kits, which reproduce better than paper brochures. A good book designer with the proper technology can even scan the picture off of a travel brochure (although you should get permission from the publishers of the brochure and give proper credit).

If you have the press kit from a destination, you will find this is the path of least resistance, since it usually comes with a blanket permission that allows you to use the pictures for any publicity purpose. Compared to paying for stock photos or having to adhere to a list of bureaucratic demands from a museum, an upside down shot of a roller coaster from a popular theme park will add action and ease of procurement to your book.

This vertical shot was on a CD sent by the Atlantic City Convention Bureau.

What about the destination website? The place may be happy to let you have a picture, but the photo may not have a high enough resolution to be used in a book. Photos should be at least 300 dpi. Many newspapers download pictures from websites and the results are passable but not usually sharp. Pictures "grabbed" from CDs also reproduce with a somewhat muddy look. If the thrust of your book is informational rather than pictorial, you may choose to take the inferior free photo from the website or CD rather than to pay $200 each for some great travel photo. Of course there are online sellers such as www.istock.com where a slew of photographs are available for a reasonable price.

As it happens, many travel writers are also good photographers (or they have husbands or co-authors who are) and they very much want their own photographs to be used. This may also be true of the sketch artist who doubles as writer and wants to use his sketches to give an impression of the destination.

When You Take Your Own Pictures: The good news is that if you use your own pictures you almost always retain rights to them. Be sure that is in the contract. That way, in case one of the pictures comes out really well, you can also sell prints as framed copies, make posters out of it, and create a stock photo or whatever else you desire. The publisher usually retains rights to use the photographs for publicity purposes such as creating a poster for a book signing, or sending out postcards to bookstores. The contract may also prohibit you from using the same photo in a competing book.

This is not a book about photography. There are plenty of books that will tell you how to take the "right" picture, how to compose it, what type of film to use for action shots and such. Obviously, if you are concentrating on a pictorial travel book you are in a pretty professional class.

However, there are many "arty" photographers who do not take satisfactory pictures for a genuine guidebook. They tend to go for the landscape photograph of looming mountains or a baroque plaza. Try for variety. Remember, the ultimate customer of the guidebook is someone who wants to travel to the place and needs some practical advice about where to stay, what to eat, what to see, and how to meet others. If you look at different travel guides you will notice that books about outdoors, hiking, biking, adventure and such almost always have action shots of people doing something, with the geography in the background.

A picture of a fisherman mending his net can be of interest whether the book is about Ireland or the coast of Maine. But the typical guidebook will balance an arty picture of the fisherman with a practical shot of party fishing boats available to tourists or fresh fish being sold at the dockside. People and animals are important to balance the architectural and natural landscape photographs. Here's what I like to see in a guidebook:

- Include something living in your
  pictures: humans, horses or dogs.
- A long shot view may be beautiful but you
  don't want a book full of long-shot views.
  Vary your scenes with a close-up — even a
  section of a building such as a balcony.
- A crowd scene should be balanced by a solo shot.
- Unless your book is about architectural history,
  don't fill up the pages with a series of buildings.
- The same goes for nature scenes — especially shots of trees bordering a stream.
- Readers of guidebooks are more interested
  in information than in a perfectly composed
  picture — include the important landmarks.
- Close-ups of food, restaurants, pastry shops,
  cheeses and wines always add a little "I
  wish I was there" feel to a book.
- Take both vertical and horizontal shots — you don't
  know the layout of the book yet, and a vertical shot
  may fit in the page better than a horizontal one.

Unless you are involved in a travel pictorial (in which case you undoubtedly know how to take a great shot) or are writing for a publisher known for their photography books (in which case there may be a separate photographer assigned to the project) a good standard shot is adequate for most travel guidebooks.

When it comes to standard shots — the gardens or palaces of some foreign country — if you have a sunny day and a decent camera you can probably get an acceptable picture. Standard shots are used in guidebooks for identification and you don't have to be Ansel Adams for the photo to be used. With the digital camera and the capacity for editing photos online, most people can create a pretty good picture by themselves. But stay away from the touristy "Here I am standing in front of a famous place" photograph.

What if the photos come from a state, county or community agency? Usually all photos that come from state, county or community agencies have been given to them by attractions within their perimeters or have been taken by public employees for public use. We have all seen those free guides to Oregon or Massachusetts that are chock full of pictures of people bicycling on country roads, running on the beach or relaxing at a hotel. If the state or county has permission to give these photos to outside publishers they will usually ask that the credit line includes the photographer. Thus a picture of the Cape May Lighthouse would include the caption line: "Photograph courtesy of the Cape May County Board of Tourism/Victor Di Sarno photographer."

Historical Photographs and Postcards: You often have to get permission from the owners of the historical photograph. A travel book might contain scenes from Cape Cod in 1915. If the photo is owned by the historical society you may have to get permission. If it was handed down to you by way of your great-grandfather, it is your own property.

With historical photographs the permission is sought from the owner of the photograph. The subject of the photograph whether a person or a hotel, may have long been vanished from the earth. Of course there are other sources for historical photographs but these require a fee. The best known ones are The Bettman Archives and the New York Public Library, but there are many new sources that are available through the Internet

Permissions: Remember there are different rules for newspapers and books. Newspaper photographers have a much wider berth in that they are "informing the public" and can take shots of just about anybody and anything as long as they are not invading the person's privacy without permission.

Since many guidebook writers also have a life as a newspaper journalist or travel feature writer, they may assume that the rules for newspapers are the same for book publishing. Not really. Publicists and PR agencies have tons of pictures of everything from the local cereal bowl queen to residents who happened to take a cruise to Alaska and they inundate newspapers with them. It is natural that a writer who has done a story on an Alaskan cruise for his or her newspaper would want to use the same picture for a book about cruises to Alaska. Best to check again, and get a written permission from the agency — usually no problem. Newspapers are considered editorial use and therefore come under the Freedom of the Press Amendment, while books somehow get shoved into the commercial use pile. Actually, the guidelines are very unclear and any lawyer will tell you to get permission first just to be on the safe side. If that is not possible, then take pictures of people from the back or from a distance so they cannot be identified. Taking pictures of public monuments and architectural buildings have different rules (some were changed in the 1990s) so it's best to check with a lawyer or consult a book on the subject of copyright.

Substitutions: Don't substitute one thing for another. It's true that most New England Protestant churches look alike, but if you try to substitute the tall white-steepled church in Rhode Island for one in New Hampshire, somebody is bound to notice the difference and complain. A hot-air balloon festival in Colorado has a different backdrop from one in New Jersey. Don't try to exchange one for the other.

Stock Pictures: Prices can vary for these, and they can run up to two or three hundred dollars. However there are Internet companies that can supply very reasonable shots. The two top ones in this category are www.istock.com and www.photos.com. You want to buy the ones that have 300 dpi so they will reproduce with enough clarity. Yes, the same picture may appear somewhere else, but can the casual reader really tell the difference between an istock photo of the Eiffel Tower and any other?

Permissions if you take your own pictures: Most parks and gardens have rules about permission to take pictures to be used for commercial use. Now if you are writing up a feature about the beautiful Local Gardens, chances are they will be happy to have you take the picture at no cost. They may even give you permission to use a picture someone else took for them as long as you include the photographer's name in the credit line.

However, most public parks and gardens have rules about taking wedding pictures by professional photographers that use their garden as a backdrop. There is usually a nominal fee ($10 or $20) and commercial photographers must reserve a specific time. This includes photographs taken for weddings, commercial ads, and so forth. Of course anything that involves adding ingredients to the picture (such as props for a TV commercial) would have to go through the proper permission procedure.

The National Park Service also has stipulations about commercial photography but allows photographs, both personal and commercial, that are taken without a tripod to be used in any media unless there are particular prohibitions. Check www.nps. gov for rules and regulations. Similar rules pertain in most countries when it comes to natural landscapes.

What about permission for strangers in your photograph? I took a photo of a little girl sitting on a stone turtle at the Camden Children's Garden in New Jersey. The photo of the moppet was used in the 10th edition of New Jersey Day Trips, published by Rutgers University Press. The editors there, who are extremely careful about permissions, decided that the girl's face, which was in a downward position, was hidden enough that she could not be recognized.

In the case of taking a random shot of people, there are several ways to go:

- Get permission immediately on the off chance that you might use the picture. (But how many strangers are going to give you their name and home address? This might be a new gambit to rob them.)
- Take a crowd shot on a public street, or public beach.
- Take the shot from the back or from an angle where the face is not distinguishable.
- Do not include anything that would put someone in an embarrassing position

When it comes to foreign countries, many photographers simply take the picture and hope there will be no problem. In some countries people resent having their picture taken. In others, they may expect some remuneration (in which case give them a few dollars.) I remember a sprightly man at the Cliffs of Mohr in Ireland who posed with his dog for a small fee. He showed up whenever the tourist buses pulled in.

Photographs taken by friends and relatives: It is not uncommon for you to hear from friends and relatives that they have an unbelievable shot of the Yosemite waterfall or a Fiji sunset after they hear you are writing a book about that destination. By all means look at what they have. Many people will be happy to give you the picture just to have their name in a book. Let them know truthfully that they may not get the photo back, or they may get it back after it has been marked up considerably. You could always offer them a fee for the inconvenience: $25.00 is not unusual. Assure the person that they will get a proper credit line and check that you have their name spelled correctly! Also look at the picture and check what year it was taken. Are those thatched huts still on the beach on that island or did they disappear in last year's hurricane? You don't want obsolete material in your book.

People who work at attractions: Generally, people who work as costumed docents or lovable animals in theme parks have already signed a waiver giving the attraction the right to use their image in all publicity and promotion. So if you take the photograph of a colonial housewife cooking at a restored house you may only need an okay from the restoration foundation to use the picture in your guidebook. Most theme parks don't care if you show their roller coasters or their costumed characters in the media as long as it is not shown in a derogatory manner. When it comes to highly protected trademark figures such as Mickey Mouse and others, better get permission first and go by any rules they have. If fees are necessary, see what you can negotiate or content yourself with outside pictures of sculpted shrubs that have character shapes.

Museum and Sculpture Pictures: Most museums have strict rules about taking pictures. Even if they allow this it is usually with the proviso that the photo is for personal use. If you want to use a museum picture in a book, there are permission forms to be filled out, and a fee, along with restrictions on the number of times you can use the picture. The same may go for public sculpture (at least for recent public sculpture).

One way to get around the whole issue is to simply buy a stock photograph from a website. As an author you may not want to put out the money, but if you find a reasonably priced picture that is just right for the book, you could inform your publisher of its availability. Of course if you were self-publishing you would have to pay for stock photos yourself, whether you hunt them down or your book designer does.

Obsolescence: Photographs given to you by a state agency or Chamber of Commerce may be several years old and may no longer reflect the reality of the place. Even if it's a black and white photo, it may show a historic tree that has since blown down, a house that once was white but has now been repainted maroon, or a completely new annex on that state capitol you had planned to use in your fifth chapter. If you can't find a replacement, use some other picture.

The same is true of a photograph you took yourself. That picture of the ladies in front of the antique store may be great, but if you know perfectly well that the store is now a restaurant, don't use it. When considering an older photograph, it is better to turn it into a generic example of a certain activity than to place it into a specific destination.

What about Security? We live in an age of the Patriot Act and Homeland Security and a heightened sense of awareness about the vulnerability of the infrastructure of practically anything. So there you are, taking a picture of a picturesque bridge and suddenly two policemen surround you and ask what you are doing. And that's in the United States, where at least you can speak the language! Have something handy, such as a letter of confirmation from a publishing house, that you are writing a book on the bridges of Madison County. Or pull out clippings from newspapers or magazines that show you are indeed a travel writer and not a foreign terrorist. Remember bridges and railroad stations, ships at port and grand government buildings make for good travel photos, but these sites could also be construed as terrorist targets. Have whatever credentials you need with you at all times!

Clip Art

There are reams of clip art — much more than what the average person receives when he buys a computer. The clip art that is used most often in travel books would be icons for road signs, handicapped access, restrooms, restaurants, and physical activities such as skiing and biking. Icons for nature such as leaves, squirrels, horseback riding, and international symbols for food, airports, etc. can be found on many word programs or can be bought for a very small fee. If you create your own icon, you should put a copyright notice about it in the front.

Clip art designs are also used for borders and for random illustrations throughout the text. The book designer will make the decision as to which ones are used, if any are used at all. If you are self-publishing you can tell your typesetter or book designer you want a strip of squirrels between every section of your book on parks. If you are working with a traditional publisher you can make the suggestion but it is up to the publisher as to whether or not he wants to spend the extra money

Other Illustrations

Pen-and-ink drawings are often used to give a certain ambience to the guide. In the Karen Brown series on charming inns and small hotels, a distinct format is used. Each hotel is illustrated by a pen-and-ink drawing while the cover always boasts a watercolor of a typical hideaway.

If there is a co-author or illustrator who has been brought on to create drawings or watercolors to brighten your book, much depends on the contract arrangements. The publishing company may use their own person to do illustrations, especially if this is a series that utilizes a certain format. The Dummies Books, for instance, uses cartoons for the chapter title page in their travel series. This would be contracted separately and hopefully the cartoonist has read your text so that his cartoons relate to your words. In the case where you and a partner envision a book together, with words and pictures in tandem, this would be part of your original book proposal. When it comes to self-publishers, be sure a contract with your partner is ironed out.

Writing the Picture Captions

One of the last things the author does is write the picture captions! Why? Sometimes, the pictures aren't decided upon until months after the text has been handed in and the book is laid out. Or the permission request for a certain photo may be denied and you have to substitute a different picture at the last moment.

Remember, captions are needed for pen-and-ink and water-color illustrations as well as photographs. For drawings, a simple caption announcing what it depicts usually suffices. Photographs, on the other hand, often call for more meaningful captions .You may want to sum up a concept underneath a photograph. Here's one I used for a shot of waterslides at a popular park:

> **"Waterparks, waterparks, everywhere. There are fifteen of them within this small, densely packed state. Seen here: the snaking water slides of Wacky Waters."**

Captions are usually put in bold and use a slightly smaller font size than the regular text. The courtesy line, which is traditionally put in the right hand lower corner above the caption, is put in italics, (e.g.: *Photo courtesy Birmingham Chamber of Commerce*). Your choice of captions depends on how much space you are allowed, how much information you want to convey and how much you want to emphasize your style. Remember, when people browse through a book they look first at the pictures! Here are some for the most common choices for captions:

1. The caption can simply announce a straight fact:
This covered bridge is decorated with a blue cow.

2. Or it can enlighten the text a bit:
The Blue Cow Covered Bridge is the pride of Overton, and the main reason many tourists stop there.

3. Or it can be the subject of a comment:
Why would anyone paint a blue cow on a bridge in Overton, which is far from any dairy country?

4. Or a bit of cultural history:
Legend has it that a cheese company paid the town to paint a blue

cow on its covered bridge.

In short, the caption can be used to identify, to impart information or make a comment. In a text-heavy book it may be best to relegate the caption to mere identification, the way it is done in an encyclopedia. So a photograph of the most famous cathedral in Paris would simply read: Notre Dame Cathedral, Paris. If the photo is particularly beautiful because of the season or the time of day, the caption could emphasize the moment such as: The plaza in front of Notre Dame Cathedral is clear of tourists in the early dawn light.

Writers who work primarily for newspaper and magazines may become accustomed to having the editors do the captions. Some newspapers have a reputation for clever, succinct captions. However, there's no reason not to have a clever caption if the tone of the piece warrants it. In a few cases, the travel publisher contracts the pictures to a specific photographer and it is he who writes the captions rather than the author.

If you are using photographs sent from a PR agency or a Travel and Convention Bureau, they often come with preset captions. Unless you want to use their captions, be sure to remove them and substitute your own, or the commercial caption may work its way into the text before you realize it.

Personal memoirs, travel essays and literary travel pieces rarely use illustrations but when they do the author may want a clever caption or a narrative that complements the written text. These books may use pen-and-ink drawings or water-colors instead of photographs. Humorous tales of travelers will often use cartoonists hired especially for the occasion. In that case, the cartoons would follow the text and not necessarily have a caption underneath. Budget publishers use clip art cartoons.

When photographs are used on the front or back covers, the captions for these are often found on the inside page or the back cover. If the photo represents a very well-known scene, and if no courtesy line is needed (because the picture was taken by the author or is in the public domain) there may be no caption at all. However, interior pictures should always have captions, or some way of identifying them to the reader.

Maps

While finding photographs is not much of a problem because you probably have plenty of your own and there are always free ones available from PR departments, maps are another thing entirely. It is difficult to get a free map except for those in the public domain that one finds on the Internet.

Royalty Free maps: If you want to bypass the problem of drawing your own map, or trying to trace an existing map and changing it enough to be sure you are not stepping on anyone's copyright, you can always just buy one. There are plenty of places on the Internet that advertise "royalty-free Maps". These vary from $95.00 to $500 depending on the map. Just be sure you have all your rights down pat. Are you buying the map or buying a license to use it? Be sure you have every right you need, but don't buy what you don't need.

Once you have the right to use the map you can create your own overlays to pinpoint the particular places you want to emphasize. If you are adept at Adobe Illustrator you can learn to do this yourself. Check with: www.maps.com, www.hammond.com and www.randmcnally.com.

Royalty Maps: Sometimes, the publisher may make a royalty deal with mapmaker or cartographer if the maps are to be an important part of the book. Even a small publisher can create his own deal. There was the author of a road guide who interspersed his book with sections of a map created by a leading map-maker in Canada. By making a deal with the company, he was able to create a detailed, interesting book that was much more authoritative than it would have been if he had tried to wing it himself.

Hand Drawn Maps: Plenty of people still trace the outline of an existing map and scan it into their computer. For simple "you are here" destination maps, this can suffice.

Maps for hiking and biking books: These are more intricate. Here's what Sue Freeman, owner of Footprint Press, related how she and her husband produced the maps for their guidebook series to hiking in the Rochester, New York area:

"For our first hiking guidebook, Footprint Press (www. footprintpress.com) hired a government agency with map making software to produce our maps. It was a long, drawn out process with results that weren't totally satisfactory. We quickly decided we had to learn how to make our own maps, so we could control the process and the outcome.

To do this, we purchased two software products. The first was Adobe Illustrator. The second was an electronic set of topographical maps of New York State from MapTech (www.maptech.com). We verified with MapTech that it was permissible to use their product to produce maps for guidebooks. With these tools, and more recently with hand held GPS units, we have produced maps for 14 guidebooks.

I'll use a hiking trail as an example, but we've used this process for road routes as well as trails. When we set out to explore any area, we see if a map exists. Sometimes for trails, the government agency or organization managing the land has produced a map. If this is true, we take the map with us on location. If not, we print a map of the region, either from MapTech or from GoogleMaps (www.google. com). Then we hike, ride or drive the area and write on the map any changes we find in roads, road names, trail location, parking areas, etc. We set the GPS unit on tracking and electronically track the route we follow.

At the office, we upload the GPS data into the MapTech map and the trail shows up as a red line on the green topo map. This becomes the background map that then gets traced using Illustrator. We make any edits based on our field research and label things to our liking. Illustrator allows us to create layers so we have the base map as one layer and symbols we use for trails and markings on another layer.

We can review the map and make any changes in a timely manner, when the field research is still fresh in our minds. The final map gets saved as an EPS file and placed in QuarkXpress during book layout, along with the 70 or so other maps that comprise a guidebook."

As you can see, there is more than one way to approach your map-making needs, and much depends on the subject of your book. It is the publisher who has the last say on maps, whether that is an outside publisher or you own self-publishing company.

Chapter 18

Editing and ProoYng

At some point or other you will look at your book and wonder if it is finished. You feel you have covered your subject and now it is time to start the edit. But first comes the page and word count. Maybe you wrote a little more than you expected to or perhaps you're running a little short and don't have enough material to fill up your expected pages. What to do?

Beef It Up: The need to beef up occurs most often when the topic you have chosen to cover is not quite enough to fill a book. This is when you use fillers like crazy. If you have outlined your scope correctly from the very beginning you shouldn't have too much of a problem when it comes to thin material. However, if you find yourself short ten or twenty pages, here are the most common cures for the problem.

1. Handy Tips & Quotes: Some standard travel guides use the "handy tip" as a way of both filling up space and giving more value to their presentation. The Handy Tip in this case is a little sidebar or a drop-down box that reiterates some point already made within the text. They are also useful for filling up a page that is three-quarters empty. You can also throw in sidebar quotes from practically anybody when you are running short on words or you want to jazz up the look of the page by adding an extra box.

2. Photographs: Sometimes you will see a book with several pages of photos jammed right smack in the center, just where the spine would crack open if you bent the pages back. That is usually a sign that the publisher had several empty pages at the back of the book and rather than let them go to waste, added photographs to fill up the space.
3. Expand the Appendix: Resource lists, lists of websites, coupons, extended author's biographies — the back matter can run ten, twenty or even thirty pages, depending on how many extras you add.

Cut It Down: If you find that you've gone over your allotted word count, go over your text and see if you can snip a sentence or two from each entry. Also go over the criteria you set up for what is included in the book. Did you add some unneeded extras? Throw them out! Pictures, borders, clip art and extra sidebars can also go in the garbage. And you can always shrink your appendix by deft surgery to the resource list.

Editing and Rewriting

Now it's rewrite time. This is when you look over everything with a cold eye and see how it reads. You should also ask friends and colleagues to look over the text. Check the following:

Descriptive details: In fiction writing, the author often "add flesh to the bones" of their characters during the first rewrite. In non-fiction you want to add "character" to the places you are describing. Undoubtedly you already have some good descriptive passages, but now is the time to go over your manuscript and add all the specifics you didn't get to the first time around. See if you can add word-pictures to give your writing a sense of the place. On the other hand, if you go in for overly lush descriptions, you can use the first rewrite to tone down your style. Sometimes you may just want to add more sensory description. In the 10th edition of *New Jersey Day Trips*, I added the yearly St. Ann's Festival to the write-up of Hoboken, simply to sneak in a mention of the sizzling sausage and peppers that are a staple of that fair.

Check your paragraph progression: Do a number of paragraphs all start with the same words, such as, "This museum has an impressive collection of" or "As I entered the hotel lobby"? Does each entry begin with an historic note? Try to vary your approach. Did you call those Caribbean beaches "silky white" too many times? Look up a different adjective. Did you repeat the same anecdote about Captain Cook in two different chapters? Cut one out. When doing short round-up pages, look to the opening words. Are there a heap of sentences that all begin the same way? Mix up your opening salvos with each entry: vary verbs and nouns, adjectives and adverbs

If you are crafting a road trip book, it's okay to start every chapter with a new destination, but scramble your opening paragraphs a bit so they don't all start with a description of the place or of your state of mind. If the book is written from a personal point of view, how many times have you used the word "I"? Can you cut down that number?

Recheck telephone numbers: Incorrect area codes are in there, like bacteria eating away at your structure. Nobody knows how or why, but the wrong area codes and telephone numbers creep in as surely as a pair of socks turns into one sock in the washing machine. It helps to have a list of the area codes handy at your elbow

General fact checking: While paid copy-editors will check for errors in spelling, grammar, syntax, and will sometimes fix wordiness and awkward passages, they rarely check for facts, unless a gross misrepresentation hits them in the eye. So there should be another person besides the author involved in fact-checking. It's best to use a peer in the same field of interest. It is this person who is most likely to realize that the theater you so lovingly described went bankrupt last week, or that the ferry to the fjord is no longer running. A sharp-eyed friend might notice that you mixed up the cantons of Switzerland, or that your idea of how to discipline a child in a restaurant seems to be too harsh (or too permissive) for your intended readership.

Are there historical facts that sound a bit off? Now is the time mop up all those little inconsistencies. Go back and re-read the book one more time. Did you get certain facts right the first time? This is when it's good to return to those postcards, slides, brochures, and notes you took while you were traveling. Make a checklist for such questions as:

- ✓ Is the bedcover in the room Marie Antoinette slept in, red or blue?
- ✓ Is Benjamin Franklin really the only non-president on U.S. paper bills?
- ✓ When did May Day observations begin?
- ✓ Is that castle made of limestone or brownstone or sandstone?
- ✓ Did Michelangelo live in the 15th or 16th century?

Then check the manuscript for format, grammar and spelling:

1. Does the layout and abbreviations conform to the guidelines sent by the publishing house — or your own, if you are self-publishing?
2. Is your format consistent? Are all the colons and semicolons in the correct place? Any changes made after typesetting become very costly.
3. Are there misspellings and grammatical errors that you can spot at first glance?

Underlining for the Index

If you haven't already done this as you went along, then this is the time to go through the manuscript and either underline, make bold or code-in whatever words you want in the index. What you do depends on whether you are going to use a software program, give the work to a professional indexer, or simply do it yourself the old-fashioned way by underlining or using index cards. Some index programs simply pick up every proper noun in the text which you can then edit down afterwards.

Place your photographs after the first edit

After the first edit, you can decide exactly where the photographs should go. When you write the captions they can either reiterate something already in the text or add new information to the chapter. Favorite photographs may have to be jettisoned and less exciting ones kept because of the way the chapters fall or the need for a particular type of photo (vertical rather than horizontal, interior rather than exterior, human rather than architectural) for a particular chapter. The production staff has the last word on this.

The Second Edit

This is usually done by a professional editor if you are writing for a publisher. Many self-publishers also pay editors to go over their work. This is called a line edit and the primary purpose is to catch grammatical errors, change awkward phrases (or point them out and expect the author to change them) and find inaccurate spellings. The editor will also catch problems in agreement (his/theirs) and time (walking, walks, walked). An editor paid by the publisher will also adhere to the same manual of style that the publisher gave you.

It is important to understand that the line editor does not check facts for you! If you say Michelangelo lived in the 17th century she will not change it — she may put a question mark there if she is particularly astute, but don't count on it! Editors do not consider that part of their job. Hire a fact checker, if needs be.

In some cases, the publisher's editor also defines the format and decides such things as the headings, running heads, photo captions, and what should be put in larger type. The book designer or production manager decides on the type and font and placement of photographs (with input from the author) but based on the editor's guidelines. If you are self-publishing you do all of this yourself or hire a book designer to do it for you.

After the edited manuscript comes back to you, it is now your turn to rewrite and re-edit if necessary. If you have an editor who has made "suggestions" for rephrasing, you will have to rewrite those portions unless you feel they are unwarranted. The author usually accepts grammatical and spelling errors unless he feels the editor has changed the meaning of his prose. In one case, an editor changed "110 Bank Street" – the name of a restaurant — to "110 Bank St." because that's what the style manual dictated. Of course, it had to be changed back!

Re-read the title, the sub-title and the back cover copy plus the picture captions, before the book goes to press! Be sure that everything that should be capitalized is capitalized. Don't forget to check both the front and back of the book cover! Authors sometimes discover that their names were misspelled on the back cover copy or the first page of the book, because these were the only pages that had never been checked for accuracy!

Proofreading

Traditionally one person read the original text out loud while the other scrutinized the proofs to catch any changes, errors, words that were dropped out, or spelling errors. This is hardly necessary nowadays since the typeset text has been transmuted from the original CD, which has already been gone over by several readers and at least one editor. But proofing is still important to pick up little errors that you may have missed before. It is particularly important to go over the index to make sure that nothing has been left out (sometimes whole portions of the alphabet disappear) and that the page numbers in the index correspond to the page numbers in the text.

Pictures are often sent separately to be proofed, so here also, check that the caption reads the way you wrote it, and that the photo has not been put in upside down or facing the wrong direction. The back cover copy, the front cover and front pages are also places where book production people often fail to notice a problem because they are concentrating so much on color and configuration. The spine for instance: did they misspell your name on the spine, or crush the title letters together? This happens more often than you would imagine.

Proofing The Index: This is one time when you should proof against the typeset book. It's best to do it with two people, one calling out the name and page number, and the other checking against text. If a software program was used, there may be more entries than you want, so you'll need to do some pruning.

Standard Resources for editing: Besides a manual of style and the reference works mentioned earlier, a good editor should have a few books on usage and online resources. Here are a few:

- *The Elements of Style* by Strunk & White: (This book helps to define problematic words and phrasing).
- *The Elements of Grammar* by Margaret Shertzer: Includes such items as writing weights and measures and mileage (one-tenth or 1/10th?) and other details.
- Up-to-date maps (often on websites)
- Telephone books for area codes (or try http://decoder.American.com)
- ZIP book for zip codes
- Reliable online references for the 800 numbers of airlines, hotel chains and specific destinations.

Part Four

Publishing and Promoting Your Book

Chapter 19

The Paths to Publishing

For a writer to create a book and then have no concept of how to get it to market seems silly, and yet so many authors look no further than their last page. Thanks to modern technology, there are now a number of ways to get a book into the hands of a customer — although this may not necessarily include a bookstore as a middleman. So how does one turn a completed manuscript into a viable book with an attractive cover, an exciting back cover and several hundred pages of copy and illustrations in between?

- Traditional publishing
- Self-publishing
- Vanity publishing
- POD publishers
- Straight from the website

Traditional Publishers

The traditional publisher pays the author on the basis of royalties or on a work-for-hire basis once a manuscript is accepted. (Both methods are common among travel publishers.) These companies get hundreds of book proposals per month. Some of the larger traditional publishers will not accept a book proposal except through a literary agent. Others in the travel field will accept newcomers as writer/researchers or re-writers of second editions if their credentials are good enough. But there are many small, independent and university publishers who do not require agents. Here is a short rundown of the traditional publishing world. (Note: if the publisher asks the author to foot the bill for book design, printing, shipping or review copies, he is a subsidy publisher.)

Royalty Publishing

What is the typical royalty? It's hard to pin down "typical" because publishers are closed-mouth about what they give and authors rarely share their earnings unless they are high up on the royalty ladder. Royalties are a percentage or a commission given to the writer for creating the work. The percentage you get depends as much on the size of the publishing company as it does on your name as a writer. In the travel field there are a few giant companies that produce series like clockwork. Some of these companies do not pay royalties at all, but prefer a work-for-hire arrangement.

Generally, non-fiction authors who are represented by agents can get a percentage of the list (or retail) price of the book. If they get 10% of an 18.95 book they make $1.895 for each book sold. If 10,000 copies are sold during the run of the edition the author collects $1.895 x 10,000 minus book returns.

Often there is a stipulation in the contract that when the book has sold 7500 or 10,000 copies, the royalty rises to 12% and again to 15% at the 15,000-sale point. On the other hand, books sold to book clubs may only get 5% of the price and books sold at deep discount also severely diminish the author's take.

For many guide writers, however, especially those who contract to small or academic presses, the royalty is based on net, which is the sum that the publisher receives after the bookstore, wholesaler and distributor have each taken their cut of the list price. So if the book sells for $18.95 and the publisher sells it direct to a bookstore for a forty-percent discount, the publisher receives 60% of $18.95 or $11.37 and the author gets 10% of that sum ($1.137).

But it is more often the case that a small publisher sells through a wholesaler or a distributor. Sales through wholesalers are usually 50 to 55% of the list price. Sales through distributors (who in turn sell to wholesalers) can be anywhere from 62% to 70% of the list price. So 45% (the wholesaler price) of $18.95 is $8.527. If the author gets 10% of the net he then receives 85 cents for every book sold or $8500.00 for an edition that sells 10,000 copies. This may be over a period of two or three years. (However, a popular guide can achieve sales of thirty, forty or even fifty thousand for a single edition.)

Of course, not all copies are sold one way or the other; it is usually a combination of retail and wholesale options. There are also sales direct from the publisher's website which should earn the author more money, and sales to book clubs and organizations at a high discount that earn the author less.

How do you Contact a Publisher? Publishers employ editors, who sift through submitted manuscripts, choosing those that fit their general plan or niche. After some negotiation, they then sign a contract with the author. Although most mid-size and small publishers will look at a book proposal, major names usually insist the proposal come through a literary agent.

The author is responsible for all verification and liability of the work. Author and publisher may share responsibility for indexing and pictures. The author usually gets an advance (against royalties) to tide him over. The advance may vary from $500 from a small press to $20,000 and more from a large publishing house. The author submits the finished copy within the contracted period of time. It is then edited and proofread by the publisher. The process between the acceptance of the manuscript and the actual publication date may take up to two years.

The submission process consists of:
    a.   Query letter or book proposal
    b.   Negotiation & acceptance
    c.   Finished manuscript

What is an advance? One often reads in the newspapers of some famous author who will receive a four-million-dollar advance for his book. This is an advance against royalties and don't start dreaming — that is for celebrities and the numbers are often exaggerated.

Although this advance cannot be taken away even if the book sells only 700 copies, your royalties are reduced by the amount of the advance. And remember, you get no royalties on review copies, so if your publisher sends out 300 review copies and has printed 5000 books you only get royalties on 4700 (assuming that all 4700 are sold).

So for the average small publisher, an advance of 10% against the net profits from a book with a printing of 5000 copies is quite common. Surprisingly, some travel writers make as much from buying their books back from the publisher at 50% discount and selling them vigorously at lectures as they do from royalties, especially if they have to share their royalty with a co-author or photographer.

Publishing process: Once a contract is signed, the process begins. An editor takes over the reins and oversees the direction of the book. In some cases the editor may ask for additional material or rewrites. The editor also makes the decision about the number of illustrations that will be used. The publisher pays for the book to be copy-edited, designed and formatted. The author looks over the manuscript after it has been copyedited and may make minor changes, but the publisher will usually not pay for any major revisions. The copyright may go to the author or to the publisher depending on the contract but the publisher usually pays the copyright fee.

Before the book hits the bookstores, the publisher handles the early promotion (review copies, and insertion into the catalog). Closer to publication date, the publisher sends out press releases and may also arrange for book signings or talks in bookstores. But after the first month or two, the author is pretty much on his own, and must arrange and/or pay for his own publicity.

Large or small, publishers do expect their authors to make appearances at bookstore signings. Although individual book signings rarely result in large sales, the book signing circuit is considered essential for publicity, and it costs nothing to the publisher. Of course, talks at libraries and local organizations are more lucrative for the author, but he usually has to arrange for them himself. If the author already has a platform (a radio show, a travel column or a newsletter) he is expected to use his vantage point to create publicity for the book.

What further royalties? The advance on royalties is handed out in increments — for instance you might get half upon the signing of the contract and half when the final manuscript is handed in. The next time you see a penny from the publisher is after your royalties have "earned out" the advance. Many non-fiction authors who get decent advances (say $20,000) never see any more cash beyond that first payout. Their book may have sold just as many copies as the publisher predicted and the advance equals what their royalties would be if they were handed out coin by coin. Sometimes the book does not even earn enough to counter the advance. Luckily, the advance is sacrosanct, so that the author keeps it even if the publisher loses money on the venture.

The Work- for-Hire Publisher

Many well-known travel publishers pay on a work-for-hire basis. The editor for a series simply hires one, two or three travel writers to do a book on, say, Croatia. The editor assigns one person to do the restaurants and hotels and another to do the historic sites. Each person is paid as if he were doing a long travel article, so he may be getting a per-job rate (say two chapters) or a per-word rate. Photographs are negotiated separately, or the editor may find the photos himself from his own sources. Flat-fee is another way of saying "work for hire" and certain well-known travel publishers, such as Fodor's, pay primarily on a flat fee basis whether it's a single author or several who are doing the work. The copyright will belong to the publisher in this case.

Do You Need An Agent?

Many of the larger publishers no longer want their editors to wade through thousands of submissions. Therefore, they will only look at proposals submitted through literary agents.

What Does the Agent Do? The agent not only submits a manuscript to a publisher or several publishers at a time, he also negotiates the terms of the contract. Since most boilerplate contracts favor the publisher, it is up to the agent to get the best terms possible. He will get the best terms for your royalty percentage (particularly the advance) and protect your rights when it comes to ancillary and subsidiary rights. He will get the best deal for you in terms of foreign rights, the number of free copies, the cost of buyback copies and so forth. Since the check is sent to the agent who takes his cut and then sends the rest to you, the agent will also be on his toes when it comes to late payments from the publisher.

Where do you find a literary agent? The simplest way is to go to your local library's reference section and look at the lists in *Literary Market Place, Writer's Market* and other standard works. Always check for the specialty of the agent — you don't want to send your non-fiction piece to an agent who specializes in children's books. One suggestion is to look at the acknowledgement page of authors of other travel guides. There are usually profuse thanks to everybody, including the author's agent and his editor. These are two names that are worth knowing!

There are also several books on the subject. These are aimed at understanding the role of the agent in relation to the publisher and the author. Some may include lists of agents but these become outdated soon. The main virtue of a book about agents is to protect you against "fake" agents who scam unwary writers in a variety of ways. You will also learn exactly what an agent can and cannot do for you. While it's unlikely a sophisticated travel writer would be scammed by a fake agent, it is still a good idea to visit www.predatorsandeditors.com for their opinions on who is kosher and who is not.

For a simple list of agents you can go to www.aars.com. These members belong to a professional organization that upholds a certain amount of integrity. However, this list does not include telephone numbers (agents hate to be called) or the specialties of the listed members.

When you don't have an agent: When submitting to a small press, you will not need an agent. However, it is really important for travel writers to read at least one book about publishing. Even if you been selling articles to magazines for years and know every magazine and newspaper editor in town, the rules and regulations (even for legal matters such as photo permissions) are different in the book publishing world. If you have to negotiate for yourself, be prepared.

The Regional and Niche Press

There are plenty of small, regional and niche presses that do not require agents. Their author submission guidelines are right on their website, along with a sample of books they have already published.

A Regional press is one that concentrates on a particular region. It could be an area as small as Cape Cod or as large as New England, the Southeast or the Northwest. The typical regional press publishes histories, cookbooks, travel guides, biographies and occasionally fiction, poetry and children's books.

A Vermont regional press might have a catalog that includes Vermont Houses (a pictorial), A Guide to Vermont's historic sites, The Maple Sugar Cookbook, Foliage Tours of Vermont, The Best Inns of Vermont and New Hampshire, The Calvin Coolidge Quote Book, and so forth. These books would be found in gift shops and hotels as well as bookstores throughout the state and in neighboring areas.

The Niche Press as I mentioned in the rundown on categories, concentrates on a particular activity, or a particular type of traveler. Food and Wine publishers stay within that niche category and Outdoors and Recreation publisher keep to their subject. A typical niche catalog might include: Best Fishing Lakes in Vermont, Best Fishing Lakes in Minnesota, How to Tie Fishing Lures, 100 Best Fishing Stories, The Top Fishing Beaches on the East Coast, Where to Fish in Florida and Fresh Caught Fish Recipes.

In each case the publishing house keeps its focus on the region or the niche but is able to expand sideways into the various subjects of history, biography, travel, recreation, or cooking, when a particular title warrants it.

There is often a quota for each type of book, so the Vermont-based press might keep its travel titles to a maximum of five a year so that it has room for its cookbooks and biographies.

On the other hand, if a regional travel series becomes popular the press may go beyond its traditional boundaries and cover other territories. The Berkshire House Press for instance started out concentrating on the Berkshire Mountains in Massachusetts, but the format for their Great Destinations series sold so well that they branched out into *Great Destinations* for Napa Valley, Santa Fe, Savannah and other destinations. Berkshire House was bought out by W.W. Norton in 2003 and the editorial functions given to the Countryman Press of Vermont. Ironically, the Great Destinations Series name remains, while Berkshire House has disappeared from sight.

The positive side of regional presses is that they know their territory and usually have contacts with local stores and outlets. They may use a local jobber or regional wholesaler to distribute their books and thus bypass the problems associated with wholesalers like Ingram. Or they may be an independent subdivision of a larger publishing house.

The niche publisher can usually find non-bookstore outlets to handle its stock. A local author sells more of his "Gone Fishing" series in sporting goods stores than in bookstores. The Footprint Press based in Rochester sold their hiking series through outfitter clothing stores and newsstands as well as from their website.

There are also non-travel niche publishers that might include a travel title or two as it pertains to their niche. A publishing house devoted to parenting might accept a manuscript on how to travel with a toddler (or a teenager). A Gay/lesbian press might do a series on destination travel with their clientele in mind. So it is always possible to send a travel book proposal to a small publishing house if the audience for that book coincides with the audience built into that publishing house.

While small publishers offer the best possibilities for a new writer, be sure you retain the copyright to your work in case of death, dissolution, bankruptcy or takeover by a larger press. You will be expected to help promote your book in any case. But with small publishers you can sometimes work hand in hand and promote a relationship. (Note: the small, regional and niche publishers I refer to here operate in the traditional publisher mode: they pay for the book design, editing, printing and distribution of the book and give the author a royalty. Subsidy houses will be discussed later).

The University Press

Most state universities in the U.S. are heavily subsidized by their state legislatures. That includes the university press. While their first priority is to provide a venue for scholarly literature and to provide an outlet for their many studies programs (such as Women's Studies, Ethnic Studies and Urban Studies), they also may have a trade division which sells primarily through bookstores rather than through academic channels. The trade division is usually open to submissions of books about the state written by and for laymen. So while there may be a scholarly tome on the ethnic diversity of the state of Wisconsin, the trade division might come out with a guide to the lakes of Wisconsin or a cookbook based on ethnic recipes.

University presses vary widely in their policies for non-academic trade books. Private universities have different policies (and different pressures) than state universities so it is best to look at each website on an individual basis. If you see that they have published books in the popular mold rather than the academic (and you can tell this by reading a few excerpted pages), then it is worth trying them out with a book proposal. Be aware that submission guidelines are often set up for their academic books so just disregard the section that asks for the number of papers published in scholarly journals and offer your own credentials instead.

While University presses do not expect you to be represented by a literary agent and are open to submissions, they are also very frugal when it comes to royalties and promotion costs. In other words you'll be at the low end of the royalty scale and promotion will be limited to catalogs and perhaps some sales representatives. However, you don't have to worry about them going into bankruptcy and they generally can get their books onto the shelves of bookstores in their home state. They tend to be loyal to their writers and will publish their second, third and fourth efforts as well.

Recommended reading:

Damn! Why Didn't I Write That? How Ordinary People are Raking in $100,000 or more Writing Nonfiction Books & How You Can Too! Marc McCutcheon.

An author and literary agent, McCutcheon offers an overview of the publishing world. He emphasizes the importance of finding the right niche and getting in early on a new wave of interest.

The Everything Get Published Book. Peter Rubie.

The author maps out the process of writing, creating a book proposal, and editing. Although written for the novice, many an expert journalist who understands little of the bookselling process will find this guide useful. The best chapter is the one on the contract. The author, who is a literary agent, goes over it with a fine tooth comb.

Self-Publishing

First of all I'm not talking about subsidy publishing, vanity publishing or author mills. For that, see the next entry. I am talking about true self-publishing where the author arranges for the typesetting (or does it himself if he knows InDesign) and the printing, buys his own ISBN number in the name of his company, arranges for his own warehousing, or more often, stacks the cartons in the garage, and of course has to find a way to distribute the book, whether through the internet or through retail stores. One can also self-publish using POD technology but I'll get into that later.

This is not a quick or easy task, but the financial rewards can be happy, if not spectacular. Even a modestly successful travel title can bring in the equal of a modest salary in heartland America.

Because traditional printing requires volume to get the cost per unit down to a reasonable fee, the standard print run is a minimum of 3000 books, and more often, 5000. This means an investment of several thousand dollars and requires a place to stack all those cartons. There are people who will help you — book designers, cover designers, typesetters, website designers, book coaches, publicists, marketers but they all come at a price. The more you can do for yourself — whether you design the book yourself or find a neighbor who can make a collage out of your postcards for the cover — the less the initial cost of the print run.

Many travel titles are self-published (if you noticed, early on, I mentioned that Arthur Frommer, Rick Steves, Tony and Maureen Wheeler, and Tim and Nina Zagat all started out that way). Nowadays, a high percent of regional and niche titles still fall in that category. Books that cover a defined area and can easily be placed in local stores have the best chance of success. That is because the biggest problem for self-publishers is finding a distributor and that is getting more difficult all the time. However, local titles can be distributed by the publisher himself or by local "jobbers" who go into bookstores, newsstands and shops. Books that cater to a distinct niche audience (such as handicapped people, or single woman travelers) can also be successfully marketed by using specialty shops, the Internet, and newsletters catering to those markets.

Like all authors, the self-publisher is expected to market his book by making appearances at stores and signings. He also has the extra task of trying to get his book accepted by bookstores, including the chain stores, whose portals are guarded by fire-breathing guard-dogs known as buyers. Actually it isn't that bad, and many self-published books used to be accepted by Barnes & Noble, Books A Million, and Borders. But because of the flood of books coming in from POD purveyors like Xlibris and iuniverse, the chain stores have raised the drawbridge to their castles. Not only are many POD books banned by some chains, but true self-published authors have suffered by association with the POD "self-publishing providers" and find it more difficult to breach the walls of the citadel than before.

Internet stores such as Amazon will take any published book as long as it has an ISBN number, a cover, and adheres to whatever rules of taste the online bookstore maintains. Some adventurous guidebook authors have bypassed ISBN numbers and brick and mortar stores altogether, opting to sell fewer books at no discount through their websites. Many others contain their efforts to Amazon by selling direct through the Amazon Advantage program. In other words, full speed into the Internet and damn everybody else. (Of course such self-publishers also use book fairs and library talks as a way to sell direct to their audience). **Note:** An ISBN number, which Americans have to buy from the R.R. Bowker Company (about $240 for a set of ten), identifies the book and the publisher. It is put on a code on the back of the book and scans into any cash register. Amazon uses an ASIN number for product identification, which in the case of books, is the ISBN number.

A Word about Distribution: For the self-publisher who opts for bookstores, the real problem becomes distribution. You can find book designers or if you're of the technical persuasion you can learn to lay out the book yourself. You can find editors, or if in dire straits, bring in a school teacher friend to go over the manuscript for you. You can hire a book coach who does some of those tasks for you at an additional cost and offers added peace of mind. But finding a distributor? That's not so easy.

Let me explain. Ingram and Baker & Taylor are the largest wholesalers. They take from 50% to 55% of the cut. However, Ingram, the wholesaler most bookstores depend on (because they use the Ingram database as a way of finding which books are stocked), kicked out the micro publishers a few years ago. Today you must be selling $20,000 or $25,000 (the number varies) worth of stock through Ingram to be taken on by them. Otherwise you must go through a "distributor" who takes an additional cut. (The backdoor to the Ingram database is to use Lightning Source, which is a subsidiary of the company as your Print-on-Demand printer. But that has its problems also. See below). As for Baker & Taylor you can register with them, but to get stocked is also a problem.

When I first started out in self-publishing back in the mid-1980s things were a little different. If you had a self-published book that people wanted, bookstore owners were more likely to give you a chance. And there were certainly more independent bookstores back then. There were also a number of regional wholesalers who did a great job of getting the smaller and regional publishers into the stores. Pacific Pipeline and Bookpeople on the West

Coast, Koen distributors and Bookazine on the East Coast, and Sunbelt in the Southwest were a few, but many of these are no longer around.

My main wholesalers were Baker & Taylor and Koen Distributors. They got the book into most of the bookstores in New Jersey, including the chains. However, it was only when my book was finally carried by Ingram that the title appeared on the main database of most stores. Getting into that database is of prime importance; otherwise some teen-aged clerk will inform you that your book does not exist.

There are few distributors who work with one-title publishers nowadays. However there are other options that travel self-publishers can explore. One is the non-bookstore area, such as outdoor outfitting stores for recreational activities, cookbook stores for travel/food titles and so on. There is an independent wholesaler named Quality Books that will distribute to libraries, Eastern National handles retail distribution to many national parks, and Event Network oversees the stores at several botanical gardens, zoos and aquariums. Some publishers aim all their marketing at such stores where returns are not a problem.

There is also the possibility of piggy-backing onto another publisher. Many micro-publishers distribute their books through small, medium and even large publishers. Luckily, there are still ways of getting into the market although it may be more difficult today than it once was.

As for the self-publisher — he has to learn to create a business identity, print out invoices, collect sales tax (in some states) and of course, accept returns if he sells to bookstores. He also has to buy a string of ISBN numbers from R.R. Bowker, get a Library of Congress card number, (getting a CIP number is quite a hassle and not really necessary) and learn to announce his book by making out an Advance Title form. After the book is printed, the author should fill out a copyright form (available on the Internet at www.libcong.us.) and send it, along with two copies of the book and $45 to the Copyright Office of the Library of Congress. He should also send a copy to the Cataloging Division if he has used a LCCN.

Returns: One major problem for any publisher, including the self-publisher, is book returns. A word about "returns" for those who do not understand the concept. Back in the Depression days, publishers worked out an agreement with bookstores that unsold books could be returned to the publisher for the full cost (minus shipping). In those days an unsold book was one was that never sold and stayed on the shelf and therefore would be in pretty good shape. Nowadays, returns are sent in any shape and form: banged up, coffee-stained or obviously thumbed through. What's worse, a bookstore will return a whole batch of travel books in January and February, only to re-order the self-same title in March.

Returns are not only a problem for self-publishers. If your travel guide is accepted by a royalty publisher and the book sells 7000 copies in a year but 400 of those are returned, you only get paid for 6600 copies. In other words, you do not get paid for the returns. What's more, most publishers subtract 20% against future returns when they pay out their royalties to their authors. (That means that if the publisher owes you $3000 he pays you $2400.) There is no way of knowing whether the book will sell hundreds of thousands or will be shipped back by the carton-load in a few months. For this reason publishers like to stick with a known quantity, and authors try to get the best advance possible.

While the royalty author makes no money on returns, the self-published author can recycle some of his returned books by selling them at book fairs, garage sales and on Amazon Market-place. If he paid $2.50 a unit for his initial run of typesetting and printing, he may at least get his cost back. Self-publishing is no piece of cake, but it does offer the writer two things: independence of viewpoint and a chance to make a decent return on one's investment.

There is no way I can cover such a large topic as self-publishing completely in these pages. Anyone contemplating a plunge into the waters of true self-publishing should consult at least one book on the subject. You should also join at least one small publisher's association and join the group lists you can find at yahoo.com. The best known associations are: PMA- Publishers

Marketing Association. www.pma-online.org and SPAN (www. spannet.org).

Recommended Reading:

The Self-Publishing Manual by Dan Poynter. Latest edition. Poynter is considered the top guru of self-publishing, but it's important to realize that not all of his suggestions necessarily relate to your particular field.

The Complete Guide Self-Publishing, 4th ed. by Marilyn & Tom Ross. Writers Digest Books. Another classic that goes over the process from A to Z with lots of attention to detail and suggestions for promotion.

Subsidy/Vanity Publishing

You've probably heard the word Vanity publishing but what does it mean? It is simply a common term for subsidy publishing. Vanity publishers openly advertise for writers. When the author submits a manuscript it is "accepted". But the reality is that vanity publishers accept just about everything they get. However, the editors flatter the writer and make him feel he has passed several hurdles to be part of the publishing pantheon; hence the term "vanity".

In the old days, the vanity publisher printed hundreds of copies and charged the author for the cost of editing, book design, and printing. The quality was not high, but the price for the services was. The cost ran into the thousands of dollars because the author had to bear the brunt of everything plus the shipping of hundreds of books. The publisher did hardly any marketing and most booksellers would not stock titles with known vanity imprints. Therefore, the author ended up selling the books to friends and relatives and to any traffic he could drum up.

Nowadays the subsidy market is dominated by large, well-funded corporations who use the print-on-demand process to manufacture the books. This lowers the cost of producing each book and has resulted in thousands of subsidy books flooding the market.

What is POD?

Basically Print-on-Demand (or POD) is a method of printing that differs from traditional printing. Traditional offset or web sheet printing is based on volume, so that a print run of 5000 copies costs less than a run of 500 copies per copy — but of course the total cost may be seven or eight thousand dollars. POD printing is done with a large press that prints, collates and binds the book in one operation. In other words a complete book is produced in about 5 minutes.

Because each print run consists of one book, there is no savings in printing 3000 or 5000 copies. The author saves by writing a shorter book because aside from the set-up fee, the charge is per page. So if it costs .015 cents to print one page (plus 90 cents for the cover), a book that is 150 pages long will be cheaper than a book that consists of 200 pages.

Obviously, the total cost is more expensive *per unit* than offset. But since print-on- demand means that only one book is printed at a time (after a setup fee) the total cost is cheaper than offset printing if you decide to print only a few copies. Fifty to 100 is common for a first "printing". If you went direct to a POD printer (such as Lightning Source) the cost for a 240-page book might be around $4.50 per book including setup fee. You also save the cost of warehousing 5000 books.

If you print through Lightning Source (LSI), you must establish yourself as a publisher, buy ISBN numbers from Bowker, and go through the same red-tape that traditional self-publishers do, so there are other costs involved. However you have the savings and convenience of no overhead. There is no warehousing and no inventory insurance. There may be a shipping fee to you, but as of now, LSI will ship to Ingram at no cost.

POD Purveyors or Publishers

I am calling them POD Purveyors and some people call them POD publishers, but they call themselves "Self-Publishers". Whatever you call them, they have managed to muddy the waters so well that the majority of people lump all self-publishers into this one pool. The best known ones are Xlibris, iuniverse, Author House,

Trafford, Lulu, Booksurge and Infinity although new ones and variations on the theme are popping up all the time.

These companies openly advertise for authors on the Internet and in writing magazines. Although they call themselves "self-publishers", they are really subsidy publishing companies that use the new technique of Print-on-Demand. However they do nothing in terms of editing or proofreading (unless you pay extra for these services). They show you how to set up the book using Microsoft's Word program. If you want anything extra such as pictures or maps, you have to pay for them yourself. You can also pay to produce your own cover if you hate the ones they offer.

What does it cost? It varies, because the POD purveyors also sell you book-marketing tools, and extras like bookmarks and postcards. The same book that would cost you $4.50 if sent direct to a POD printer like Lightning Source will cost up to eleven dollars (depending on the page count) with a POD "publisher".

There are also all the many services you buy. For instance, one company charges $150 to register your book with the Copyright Office. If you did that yourself it would cost you $45 plus the cost of the two books, plus cost of mailing. So you see there is a markup on everything as well as the printing cost. POD purveyors make much more money selling services to authors than they do in selling the author's books to the public. One POD Purveyor offers to get you an LCCN number for $75.00! LCCN numbers are absolutely free to the publisher. Of course you are not really the publisher — they are!

Even though most POD publishers refer to their clients as "self publishers" that is not really the case. Their advertising stamps them with the dread stigma of the Vanity Press and bookstores and distributors resist stocking them. However, the general public and many newspapers have accepted them as "self-publishers". Because POD publishers will accept any manuscript of any quality, they are considered suspect. This is a pity, because there are many quality works buried within the mass and there are some POD publishers who maintain standards of acceptance.

Most authors buy copies of their book direct from the POD publisher (at something like 35% off) and then re-sell them to friends and relatives or at talks. This may work if the author's

234 Crafting the Travel Guidebook

intent is to let his friends and relatives read his memoirs, travel or otherwise. It also works for self-empowerment or business authors who sell primarily through lectures. Since they sell their works at $79 or $89 a pop, the high price per unit for the book is not a problem. And POD publishers do take a lot of the self-publishing grunt work off your hands. But for novelists who have dreams of glory, it is a hard road. (Yes, there are exceptions. If you manage to sell 5000 copies of your POD book by dint of heavy publicity, you might get noticed by traditional publishers.) For travel writers there is very little advantage.

To sum up, POD publishers present these problems to the travel guide author:

1. The physical quality is not as high as traditional offset printing. The editing is up to the author. Misspellings, questionable grammar, inconsistencies in use of icons and other such problems stamp the book as amateurish. (You can solve this problem by hiring a professional editor).

2. The book covers are often cheesy. (Authors most comfortable with POD publishers have commissioned their own covers.)

3. The POD publisher retains the ISBN number. This means that they are the publisher, not you. This only becomes a problem if your book starts selling well and you want to take over the reins yourself or interest a "real" publisher in your work. It is important to understand whether or not you can get out of your contract.

4. Although many of them tell you they can get you into bookstores, what they really mean is that they use Lightning Source as their actual POD printer. Since Lightning Source is owned by the same company that owns Ingram (the largest book wholesaler in the USA) your book automatically goes into Ingram's database. But that is all it does. The bookstores have the ability to order from Ingram, but that does not guarantee that they will. This is why so many "self-publishers" are chagrined to discover that their book is absent from

the shelves. The fact is, bookstore managers don't
like to stock books from POD publishers. At best,
they will order a single copy if a customer asks.

6. The POD publisher puts the price on the book. It is
    almost always too high in relation to competing titles
    in the field. The cost to profit ratio is skewed. Even if a
    bookstore does order your book, your take is very small.

7. The traditional reviewing community (Publishers
    Weekly, Library Journal, and The NY Times)
    will not bother with a POD publisher. However,
    many newspapers and magazines will do feature
    stories on authors if they like the angle or fit, or
    if the author is a local person. Some large dailies
    don't notice the difference anyway, and Internet
    reviewers tend to accept books from all corners.

To see more discussion of the difference between POD
purveyors, POD printing and self-publishing go to the following
websites:

www.creativemindspress.com;
www.predatorsandeditors.com; and
www.absolutewrite.com.

If you are determined to use a POD purveyor anyway because
you don't want the bother of setting up as a publishing company,
buying ISBN numbers and all that jazz, please pick and choose
carefully among the companies out there. Some are better than
others and new outfits popping up all the time. Whatever you do,
look over their contracts very carefully. And remember, whether
you self-publish the old fashioned way or use a subsidy press,
the marketing of the book falls on your shoulders. The best book
to cover this subject is called *The Fine Print of Self-Publishing* by
Mark Levine. Levine is a lawyer who has analyzed the contracts
of many POD publishers and rates them according to his scale.
So what's the good news about POD Publishers? There are certain
seductive factors:

1. You don't have to write a fancy book proposal because

they don't care. They'll take just about anyone.
2. Your initial cost isn't too high. Most people spend between $1500 and $2500.
3. You don't have to buy any ISBN numbers.
4. Certain titles will succeed anyway. (The author then has to start all over again by becoming a "real" self-publisher.)
5. Once in a while a novel or memoir is picked by a mainstream publisher.

So if you are selling tours to Spain and want a quick and snappy book to offer to clients, or if you get paid to give lectures on the gardens of Ireland and want to make a few extra bucks with back-of-the-room sales, this is not a bad way to go. Just realize that because of the pricing structure, bookstore sales do not fit this particular model. And check Mark Levine's book for contract information. You do not want to get stuck for the next seven years with a company you hate.

Selling Online with Lightning Source

What is Lightning Source? Lightning Source (LSI for short) is not a POD provider, it is a POD printer. (It is also a distributor). In fact, many of the online publishers who boast that they can get you into the Ingram database are actually sending the books out to Lightning Source to be printed and shipped. This is because Lightning Source is owned by Ingram.

Most bookstores in America depend on the Ingram database. In other words, if you walk into a bookstore and ask for a particular title, the clerk will look at his computer screen. He will tell you where it is in the store, or that it is not carried but he can order it for you — or he will tell you the book doesn't "exist". Of course it exists — it simply is not on the Ingram database!

Thus, any LSI book can be ordered by bookstores. But since bookstores resist POD titles, you can bypass the stores by selling direct from your website or from online bookstores. Since the per unit cost of a POD book is higher than a book produced by offset, The POD method makes sense for true self-publishers in the following cases, particularly for online sales:

- Where you have a short book — say 115 pages — which would look paltry on a bookshelf — but contains all the information you need to impart. In the travel field, the most likely candidate would be the how-to-it book on a subject like suitcase packing or getting through airports.
- Where you have a niche audience book such as a guide to handicapped travel, where the customer would prefer to order the book online.
- Where you have a book that you esti-mate will sell less than 800 copies a year but might sell consistently year after year.
- Where you are traveling so often that you want a system that basically takes care of itself and you don't have to worry about warehouses, insurance and bookstores.

You can do this because LSI not only prints the book it also distributes it through Ingram to online stores such as Amazon. com. LSI can also distribute single copies to customers (in other words, fulfill your orders) for an extra fee.

Recommended Reading

Print-On-Demand by Morris Rosenthal: A clear and concise manual on using Lightning Source for direct sales to customers. He explains Google Adwords.

Aiming for Amazon by Aaron Shepard. Very clear instructions on selling online and how to translate WORD into PDF files.

What about E-books?

There was a great buzz about e-books a few years ago. That has died down but there are still e-books that sell well. If you look at Amazon's e-book bestsellers they tend to be computer books, business books and (ahem) sex books. For the travel writer, an e-book version of his travel book might be a good way for someone in Australia or India to access the content for a much lower price than buying a bound book and then paying for slow and expensive shipping.

There are a few writers who have simply created basic e-book versions of their guide and sell them from their websites. For the author who is able to build up traffic to his website and has the right type of book for the e-book customer (usually short and highly informative) this is a viable way to bypass the whole cumbersome publishing process and sell direct to the customer. Much of the retail price of a physical book is eaten up by the costs of printing and shipping, and the cuts taken by distributors, wholesalers and retailers. With an e-book the only cost is the setup and the commission you pay to the website shopping cart service that you use to process the e-book sale to the customer.

Your printed books can also be offered as an e-book. The website www.hadami.com specializes in PDF e-book versions of travel books. This is a simple site that takes 50% of the price and puts your title up for sale as an e-book. E-books are usually sold at a lower price than their printed counterparts.

The ability to sell an e-book from a website, or produce one book at a time using POD technology, means that a whole new world is opening up — particularly for self-publishers. We'll see what happens ten years from now

Chapter 20

Book Proposals

What Is a Book Proposal?

Assuming you are trying to sell to a traditional publisher, you must now prepare a book proposal. Basically, a book proposal boils down to a few elements, and if you have those elements and you find a publishing house that is interested in your area, you have a good chance of getting a book contract. If you are self-publishing, then a book marketing plan covers much of the same elements.

And now, what are the elements of your book proposal that count? These are going to sound familiar:

- Does this book have an audience — and where can this audience be found?
- What is this book about — and how narrowly or widely does it cover its subject? How does it differ from other books on the same subject?
- What are the author's credentials to write this book?
- Are there clippings available? (Most publishers want a sample of published work)
- Is the author willing to promote the book at book signings and lectures? Does he have a platform such as a newspaper column, radio show or popular website which he can use to publicize the work?

Of the five elements, the actual book proposal comprises the first two. Your credentials go on a separate page (although you'd mention them in the cover letter) and your clippings are attached to the back of the proposal. Your proposal should consist of several pages and should include:

A. The Overview

1. The concept. Statistics can help here: e.g. every year over 300,000 weddings take place at a romantic destination. This book will outline how to create a destination wedding!

2. The scope. Show the geographical boundaries of your book.

3. The assumed audience — and how your book is slanted to that audience. If you have an established platform, how you can use it to reach that audience.

4. The competition for the audience (or lack thereof). Here, a list of competitive books on the subject, by name, is usually required. So if you want to do a book on Mexico City, you had better see how many others there are presently on the marketplace. Is the city just a chapter in book about Mexico, or are there five or ten books just on the city itself. How are they arranged? What do they cover? How would your book be different? Are they published by English, American or Mexican publishers? How old are they?

5. Why you are the person to write this book /your background. This is where you trot out your credentials (and your following, if you have one). Did you write travel articles for your college newspaper? Did your color pictures appear in National Geographic? Are you the food editor for the Sacramento Bee? Are you the travel editor for the Bergen Record? Are you the editor of a newsletter for a bicycle club with 1200 members? Are you a contributing travel writer for a local newspaper, a woman's monthly, or a travel website?

6. The approximate length of the book (e.g. 70,000 words

plus 10 photographs)

7. Any extras you can add — your own maps, photographs, etc.

8. Your position and how it can help you promote the book (e.g. travel editor, TV travel expert, famous hotelier, owner of a popular travel website, or travel columnist). You can also mention contacts you have. One woman who wrote a book about regional restaurants asked her friend, a well-known food critic, to write the foreword. His name was put on the front cover!

9. If you have none of these, flaunt whatever you do have. If you belong to clubs or organizations where you could give lectures on the topic be sure to mention this.

10. Other venues besides bookstores where the book might sell well.

B. The Table of Contents:

This should be precise and clear since the table of contents will act as an outline for the book. Your basic format and organization of material will be evident.

C. Sample chapter or two

(follow the publisher's guidelines here — they vary)

D. Author biography.

This should be short and sweet. Your background, your other published works, where you live and your marital details. A head shot is usually put in one corner of the bio.

E. Clippings.

(If you have several books to your credit, you do not need clippings.) These should be articles published in newspapers, magazines, online magazines or newsletters. Be sure the name of the publication and the date are noted somewhere.

For more specifics on non-fiction book proposals, check out articles in The Writer's Digest or on the Internet, and chapters in books on publishing. Certain admonitions come up all the time:

1. Your cover letter should contain your name, address, phone number and e-mail address
2. Succeeding pages of your proposal should be numbered and include your last name and the book title in the upper right hand corner.
3. Run everything through spellchecker and then check yourself for spelling and grammatical errors.
4. Do not make threats or limitations: e.g. "I've already copyrighted this material so don't try to steal it".
5. If you are sending to a particular editor, check his name the day before you mail the proposal. Editors play musical chairs with publishing houses and publishing houses are in a constant state of flux themselves.
6. If you are sending the proposal to a literary agent, find one who specializes in non-fiction, particularly travel books.
7. Enclose a self-addressed stamped envelope if you want a reply.

Note: Authors of How-To-Do-It travel books should carefully follow instructions for book proposals as they are shown for non-fiction books. While it is comparatively easy to create chapters for a destination guide, a book about how to exchange houses for vacations, or how to fly like a VIP has to be worked up in a logical manner so that one step follows the other.

Remember, half of the battle for book acceptance is to find the right publisher for your project. Do not send out blind submissions. Check the websites of any publisher you are considering. Do they specialize in travel shopping guides or is their catalog strictly food and wine? Do they seem geared to the adventurous traveler? Are they a general publishing house that takes random travel titles of any ilk? If it's a small house, are all their titles written by the same author? (This suggests that this is a one or two-person operation.) Are they in transition? (This means they have either been bought out by a bigger house, are changing their marketing direction or are facing financial difficulties.)

Marketing Plan — Emphasize Other Venues

In creating a book proposal, either for an outside publisher or for your own small press, you should be able to tally up the venues where you think the book might have a good chance of being snapped up. Since many travel titles are impulse buys, having a presence in an airport gift shop, a winery, or gourmet cooking stores may trigger a sale.

On the other hand, many people will go to bike stores, outdoor outfitters and of course, regular book stores, precisely because they are looking for a book on hiking the Adirondacks. So it is important that the salespeople in the store are aware of your guide.

If customers have access to the Internet they might also look there. When placing your book on Amazon, be sure that the online retailer has it listed in as many categories as possible. In other words, a book on backpacking through Turkey should be found under the headings: Turkey, Adventure travel, backpacking, Middle East travel, and so forth.

Publishers (if you are an author) and Distributors (if you are a self-publisher) expect you to have a marketing plan on hand when you present a manuscript. Part of the marketing plan is that you understand where your title might best be displayed. Another is the willingness to go on radio and TV talk shows, attend bookstore signings and give speeches to local interest groups to promote the title

Multi-authored Books

Remember — you do not have to have a book proposal to write for a travel guide publisher. Many publishers accept writer/ researchers who submit their credentials and areas of expertise. If you have compiled a directory of all the museums in Melbourne, Australia or even all the hospitals and health clinics, they may want you to cover that area in a chapter on Melbourne that someone else is writing. If you are a photojournalist who follows all the NASCAR races, they may need such coverage for a book called the Sports Fan Traveler. Food editors from regional newspapers are often plucked to cover the restaurants in a certain city or state. One of the best ways for a newcomer to gain credentials is to have been a contributing writer to some well-known travel series.

Author's Guidelines

Specific guidelines for submission of ideas/manuscripts, queries and book proposals are usually found in the "About Us" section of the publisher's website. This section tells you how many books they publish per year (5 or 50 — it makes a big difference in their ability to add new titles) and how they pay (work-for-hire or royalty).

Traditional publishers that only look at manuscripts submitted by agents will post a notice to that effect on their website and in such books as *Writer's Digest* and *Literary Marketplace*. They may say "no unsolicited manuscripts" or "agent submission only" but their intent is clear. They are not going to waste their time, effort, or the possibility of a lawsuit on an unsolicited work.

Some top guidebook publishers have listings on their website when they are looking for local authors for particular destinations. One publisher may be looking for expatriates in Southeast Asia for a series aimed at long-term visitors; another for a local writer to cover clubs in Atlanta. Always check the website for all possibilities!

Recommended Reading:

The Writers Market/ Latest edition.
Every writer should have a copy of this. Since it comes out every year, get the most recent edition. Besides the lists of magazine markets and a list of general publishers, there are articles that go beyond the usual "writer's block" filler.

Literary Market Place
It's expensive and many authors go to their local library to check it out (almost every library is the country has one). This book lists publishers, agents and dozens of other participants of the literary world.

Chapter 21

The List of Publishers

The following list includes large, mid-size and small publishers (including a few British and Canadian houses) that carry travel titles. Many were once independent and are now owned by bigger entities, but still maintain editorial control. Others have been swallowed up by larger houses and have lost all editorial independence. Since the publishing landscape changes all the time, be sure to refer to updated websites to view the submissions policies for the various imprints.

For many large publishers that have travel divisions, the general policy of "no unsolicited manuscripts" prevails. For others, the editors of the travel division may accept resumes of your published works and areas of expertise for possible future assignments.

I have divided the list into four categories: Publishing houses that specialize in travel titles; general publishers that include travel series and titles in their catalogs; small, independent and niche publishers (U.S. only); and University publishers. For a full list of all publishers in the United States consult *Books In Print* at your local library. For detailed descriptions of specific publishers and specific editors check the annual editions of *Literary Market Place* and *Writer's Market*. The following list includes telephone numbers and websites where available.

Publishing Houses that specialize in travel titles

Avalon Travel Publishing.
1400 65th St., Suite 250
Emeryville, CA 94608
510-595-3664
www.travelmatters.com
www.moon.com
Publishes Moon Travel Guides, the Rick Steves series and others. Each
series has a very distinct format. Check guidelines. (Avalon is merging
into Perseus books but most series will continue).

Countryman Press
P.O. Box 748
Woodstock, VT, 05091
802-457-4826
www.countrymanpress.com

Specializes in New England but has branched out to all of USA and
Canada. Although it is a division of W.W. Norton (500 Fifth Ave., N.Y.,
NY 10110) editorial offices remain in Vermont. Its imprint **Backcountry
Press** specializes in biking and hiking books. The former Berkshire
House Press titles are now part of Countryman.

Fodor's Guides/ Editorial Director
1745 Broadway
New York, NY 10019
212-782-9000
Website: www.fodors.com
Although it is a division of Random House, Fodor's maintains its own
editorial identity. They pay either a flat fee or royalty depending on the
line. Fodor's covers practically everything geographically, but also has a
line of special interest books. They will accept writing samples for future
reference.

Footprint Handbooks
6 Riverside Court
Lower Bristol Road
Bath, BA2 3DZ
England
www.footprintbooks.com
British publisher that specializes in travel guides.

Frommer's Travel Guides.
Wiley Publishing, Inc.
111 River St., 5th Flr.

Hoboken, NJ 07030
www.frommers.com
Although it is now a division of Wiley Publishers, Frommer's Guides has
its own editors and will take author's resumes for future possible assignments. Check website.

Globe Pequot Press
246 Goose Lane
Guilford, CT 06437
203-458-4500
www.globe-pequot.com
A medium-sized travel-oriented press, Globe Pequot has its own travel
line with a heavy regional emphasis in the USA. They also own Falcon,
Insider & Lyons Press, which each specialize in different travel markets.
Check website for specific editors and submission guidelines.

Hippocrene Books
171 Madison Ave.
New York, NY 10016
212-685-4371
www.hippocrenebooks.com
Specializes in foreign language dictionaries, travel books, and ethnic
cookbooks.

Hunter Publishing
P.O. Box 746
Walpole, MA 02081
800-255-0343
www.hunterpublishing.com
Publishes several travel series and will accept queries, although their
website doesn't list submission guidelines.

Langenscheidt Publishers/Insight Guides
33-36 33rd St.
Long Island City, NY 11106
718-784-0055
www.langenscheidt.com
Langenscheidt, a German company, now owns mapmakers Hammond,
Hagstrom and American Maps as well as Berlitz (phrasebooks and
guides). Insight Guides, a subsidiary, maintains editorial offices in
London. Their address is:
Insight Guides
58 Borough High St.
London, SE1 1XF
www.insightguides.com

Let's Go Publishers
67 Mt. Auburn St.
Cambridge, MA 02138
617-495-9659
www.letsgo.com
Researchers/writers must be full-time Harvard University students.
Although St. Martin's Press is the official publisher, the series maintains
its own editorial control.

Lonely Planet
150 Linden St.
Oakland, CA 94607
510-893-8555
www.lonelyplanet.com
This independent company has offices in Australia, USA and the U.K.
You can find their specific guidelines on their website. They also list
destinations that they are currently considering, and want seasoned
travel writers to cover them. However they will take newcomers for
re-edits of older books. Send resume to:
Publishing Administrator
Lonely Planet Publications
Locked Bag 1
Foots Cray, Victoria 3011
Australia
Or e-mail: recruitingauthors@lonelyplanet.com

Rough Guides
80 Strand
London WC2R ORL
United Kingdom
www.roughguides.com
Although there is a New York office, editorial control remains in London.
They specialize in down-to-earth guides and are owned by the Penguin
publishers. Website has requirements for submissions.

Thomas Cook Publishers
PO Box 227
Peterborough PE 3 8SB
United Kingdom
+44 (0) 1733 416477
www.Thomascookpublishers.com
Publishes maps, short guides and Independent Traveler Series. Subsid-
iary of well-known travel company.

Traveler's Tales Inc.
853 Alma St.
Palo Alto, CA 94301
650-462-2110
www.travelerstales.com
Small independent company that publishes several anthology series
featuring literary and personal travel essays and humorous stories. They
take unsolicited submissions for short pieces. No book proposals.

Ulysses Travel Guides
4176 St. Denis
Montreal, Quebec, Canada
H2W 2M5
514-843-9447
www.ulyssesguides.com
This is Canada's only publisher devoted solely to travel titles. They take
submission queries.

General Trade Publishers that publish travel titles

Chronicle Books
Adult Trade Division
680 Second St., Sixth Floor
San Francisco, CA 94107
415-537-4200
Website: www.chroniclebooks.com
General non-fiction. Their travel books include both general and Cali-
fornia titles.

Dorling Kinderesly Publishers (DK)
(Owned by Penguin)
375 Hudson St.
New York, NY 10014
212-366-2000
www.dk.com
Does other books besides travel, and is known for their stunning
graphics. Editorial offices for the Eyewitness Travel Series are in London
at:
DK Publishing
80 Strand
London, WC2R ORL
020-7010 3000

Farrar, Straus & Giroux
19 Union Square West
New York, NY 10003
212-741-6900
www.fsgbooks.com
Some travel titles. Imprints include North Point Press. Owned by larger press but has independent editorial control.

Harper Collins
10 East 53rd St.
New York, NY 10022
212-207-7000
www.harpercollins.com
This merged company includes the William Morrow imprint among others. Owned by multi-media News Corporation. Publishes several travel titles, including the *Access* series. Agents only.

Random House
1745 Broadway
New York, NY 10019
212-572-8702
www.randomhouse.com
Aside from its Fodor's Guides (see above) Random House and its many divisions publish travel, literary travel and other titles in the general field. Divisions include: Crown Publishers (Crown Journeys are travel memoirs by well-known authors), Broadway Books, and others. Agents only.

Rizzoli/Universe Int. Publications
300 Park Ave. South, 3rd Floor
New York, NY 10010
www.rizzoliusa.com
212-387-3400
Known for their high quality picture books, Rizzoli does travel pictorials. Their Universe imprint does trade paperback travel guides. Accepts proposals.

Simon & Schuster
1230 Ave. of the Americas
New York, NY 10020
www.simonsays.com
Now part of CBS, this media giant owns the Free Press, Scribner, Fireside Press and other subsidiaries. Agents only.

St. Martin's Press
175 Fifth Ave.
New York, NY 10010
This general publisher, which is owned by larger German publisher,
includes a few travel titles. Agents only.

Ten Speed Press
P.O. Box 7123-S
Berkeley, CA 94707
510-559-1600
www.tenspeed.com
Well-known "small" press: includes careers, spirituality, and travel titles
in their adult division. Submissions accepted.

Wiley Publishers
111 River St.
Hoboken, NJ 07030
201-798-6088
www.wiley.com
This huge educational publisher owns several travel imprints including
The Unofficial Guides and the Dummies series. These divisions do not
take unsolicited manuscripts. However, their Frommer's division has its
own policy. See above.

Workman Publishing
225 Varick St.
New York, NY 10014
212-254-5900
www.workmanweb.com
This independent press publishes some travel titles along with other non-
fiction. Submissions accepted.

Regional and Niche Publishers (US only)

The following range from mid-size to tiny publishers and most
will accept book proposals from authors without agents. Read
website guidelines.

Appalachian Mountain Club Books
5 Joy ST.
Boston, MA 02108.
617-523-0655.
www.outdoors.org
Northeast outdoors: hiking, biking, kayaking, plus general nature books.

Camino Books
P.O. Box 59026
Philadelphia, PA 19102
Tel.: 215-413-1917
www.caminobooks.com
Emphasis on Philadelphia & Middle Atlantic states.

Down East Books
P.O. Box 679
Camden, ME 04843
207-594-9544
www.downeast.com
Mainly Maine, but some Canadian maritime provinces also. They also
publish Down East magazine.

Down the Shore Press
P.O. Box 3100
Harvey Cedars, NJ 08008
609-978-1233
www.down-the-shore.com
The Jersey shore area. Histories, calendars, some guidebooks.

Epicenter Press
P.O. Box 82368
Kenmore, WA 98028
425-485-6822
www.epicenterpress.com
Concentrates on Alaska history and culture. Some travel.

Fulcrum Publishers
4690 Table Mountain Parkway, Suite 100
Golden, CO 80403
303-277-1623
www.fulcrum-books.com
General non-fiction; includes armchair travel, outdoors & regional.

Golden West Publishers
4113 N. Longview
Phoenix, AZ 85014
602-265-4392
www.goldenwestpublishers.com
Southwest emphasis. Cookbooks, but does some hiking and trail titles.

Graphic Arts Center
3019 N. Yeon
Portland, OR 97210
800-452-3032
www.gacpc.com
Imprints include Westwinds Press, Alaska Northwest Books.
Photography books, histories, travel. Pacific Northwest concentration.
Recently reorganized.

Hastings House
P.O. Box 908
Winter Park FL 32790
407-339-3600
www.hastingshousebooks.com, www.daytripbooks.com
Day trip series among others.

Impact Publishers
9104-N Manassas Drive
Manassas Park, VA 220111-5211
703-361-7300
www.impactpublications.com
Primarily career & business but carries several travel titles.

Interlink Publishing Co.
46 Crosby St.
Northampton MA, 01060
800-238-LINK
www.interlinkbooks.com
Pictorials, cookbooks, world travel and politics.

The Intrepid Traveler
P.O. Box 531
Branford, CT 06405
203-469-0214
www.intrepidtraveler.com
The Intrepid Traveler owner Kelly Monaghan wrote "*How to Be a Home-Based Travel Agent*" but he also publishes other authors. Several Florida titles plus travel "how-to" and insider material.

John F. Blair Publisher
1406 Plaza Drive
Winston-Salem, NC 27103
336-768-1374
www.blairpub.com
Regional publisher with southeastern slant, particularly the Carolinas.

Johnson Books
3005 Center Green Drive, Suite 202
Boulder, CO 80301
303-443-9766
www.johnsonbooks.com
Colorado, Western and Native American interest.

Lake Claremont Press
P.O. Box 25291
Chicago, IL 60625
773-728-1600
www.Lakeclaremontpress.com
Chicago area — tour guides, histories, general interest.

Menasha Ridge Press
2204 First Ave. South, Suite 102
Birmingham, AL 35233
205-322-0439
www.menasharidge.com
Publishes "60 Hikes" series and other outdoor books. Southern
emphasis.

National Geographic Society
1145 17th St. NW
Washington, DC 20036-4688
202-857-7000
www.nationalgeographic.com
Guidelines for magazine writers/photographers only on website,
although books are published under NGS name. Also publishes literary
travel using well-known authors.

Open Road Publishing
P.O. Box 284
Cold Spring Harbor, NY 11724
631-692-7172
www.openroadguides.com
Small press with both local and destination series.

Peachtree Publishers
1700 Chattahoochee Ave.
Atlanta, GA 30318-2112
404-876-8761
www.peachtree-online.com
Good-sized press focuses on books for kids, YA, self-help and Southern
regional interest.

Pelican Press
1000 Burmaster St.
Gretna, LA 70053-2246
504-368-1175
www.pelicanpub.com
Louisiana regional, travel and other non-fiction titles.

Pineapple Press
P.O. Box 3889
Sarasota, FL 34230
941-739-2219
www.pineapplepress.com
Florida & southeastern interest, including travel

Plexus publishing, Inc.
143 Old Marlton Pike
Medford, NJ 08055
609-654-6500
www.plexuspublishing.com
New Jersey nature guidebooks, biology.

Ragged Mountain Press
P.O. Box 220
Camden, ME 04843-0220
207-236-4837
www.raggedmountainpress.com
A small division of McGraw Hill with independent editorial offices in
Maine. Outdoor recreational emphasis.

Sasquatch Books
119 S. Main St., Suite 400
Seattle, WA 98104
206-476-4300.
www.sasquatchbooks.com
Specializes in West Coast books — known for their Best Places series.

Seal Press
1400 65th St., Suite 250
Emeryville, CA 94608
510-595-3664
www.sealpress.com
This is a division of Avalon Publishing (Avalon Travel is a separate division) that concentrates on women's empowerment titles. Publishes
several travel titles from the female perspective, including anthologies.

Sierra Club Books
85 Second St.
San Francisco, CA 94105
415-977-5720
www.sierraclubbooks.org
Heavy environmental and ecological slant as befits this organization.

Stackpole Books
5067 Ritter Road
Mechanicsburg, PA 17055
717-796-0411
www.stackpolebooks.com
Includes outdoor books, such as fishing, nature series and adventure
travel along with history, military and Middle Atlantic state titles. Send
queries to specific editors on their website.

Sunbelt Publications
1256 Fayette St.
El Cajon, CA 92020
www.sunbeltpub.com
619-258-4911
Southern & Baja California: outdoors, guidebooks, histories. Also distributes for other area publishers.

Trails Books
923 Williamson St.
Madison, WI 53703
www.Trailsbooks.com
800-258-5830
Outdoor books on Wisconsin and Midwest. Prairie Oak Press is now a
division.

Tuttle Publishing
364 Innovation Drive
North Clarendon, VT 05759
www.tuttlepublishing.com
802-773-8930
Part of Periplus Publishers. Specializes in cultural books on Asia. Some
maps, guides and dictionaries.

Ulysses Press
P.O. Box 3440
Berkeley CA 94703
510-601-8301

www.ulyssespress.com
Hidden Hawaii and other Hidden series. Travel books plus alternative lifestyle books. Send proposals to Acquisitions Editor.

Voyageur Press
380 Jackson St..
St. Paul, MN 55101
651-430-2210
www.voyageurpress.com
Midwestern books, including travel. Now part of MBI books.

Whereabouts Press
1111 Eighth St., Suite D
Berkeley, CA 94710
www.whereaboutspress.com
510-527-8280
Primarily anthologies of well-known writers.

Wilderness Press
1200 5th St. Berkeley, CA 94710
510-558-1666
www.wildernesspress.com
Destination guidebooks for hiking, backpacking, kayaking, plus "how-to" wilderness guides.

Note: There are tiny regional and niche publishers that are basically one or two person ventures that are not included here. Although they may publish several titles, most are written by the owners of the press. These micro-publishers will occasionally take an outside author if the book is within their strict purview.

University Publishers

This is just a sampling of the many university presses in the United States both public and private: for a full list go to www.aaup.org.

Indiana University Press
601 N. Morton St.
Bloomington, IN 47404
812-855-8817
www.inpress.indiana.edu

Northwestern University Press
629 Noyes St.
Evanston, IL 60268-4210
847-491-2046

http://nupress.northwestern.edu

Ohio University Press
Scott Quadrangle
Athens, Ohio 45701
740-593-1155
www.ohiou.edu/oupress

Ohio State University Press
180 Pressey Hall
1070 Cormack Road
Columbus, OH 43210-1002
614-292-6930
www.ohiostatepress.org

Pennsylvania State University Press
820 North University Dr.
University Park, PA 16802-1003
814-865-1327
www.psupress.org

Rutgers University Press (NJ state university)
100 Joyce Kilmer Ave.
Piscataway, NJ 08854-8099
732-445-7762
www.rutgerspress.rutgers.edu

University of Arizona Press
355 South Euclid Ave.
Suite 103
Tucson, AZ 85719
520-621-1441
www.uapress.arizona.edu

University of California Press
2120 Berkeley Way
Berkeley, CA 94704-1012
510-642-4247
www.ucpress.edu

University of Georgia Press
330 Research Drive
Athens, GA, 30602-4901
706-369-6141
www.ugapress.uga.edu

University of Hawaii Press
2840 Kolowalu St.
Honolulu. HI 96822
808-956-8257
www.uhpress.hawaii.edu

University of Minnesota Press
Suite 290
111 Third Ave.
Minneapolis, MN 55401
612-627-1970
www.upress.umn.edu

University of Missouri Press
2910 Le Mone Blvd.
Columbia, MO 65201
573-882-7641
www.umsystem.edu/upress

University of Nebraska Press
1111 Lincoln Mall, suite 400
Lincoln, NE 68588-0630
402-472-3581
www.nebraskapress.unl.edu

University of Nevada Press
Morrill Hall, Mailstop 166
Reno, NV 89557-0076
775-784-6573
www.NVbooks.nevada.edu

University of New Mexico Press
7601 Randolph Road SE
Suite 200S
Albuquerque, NM 87106-4276
505-277-2346
www.unmpress.com

University of North Carolina Press
116 South Boundary St.
P.O. Box 2288
Chapel Hill, NC 27515-2288
www.uncpress.unc-edu

University of Oklahoma Press
1005 Asp Ave.
Norman, OK 73019
405-25-2000
www.uopress.com

University of Pittsburgh Press
Eureka Building, 4th Flr.
3400 Forbes Ave.
Pittsburgh, PA 15260
412-383-2456
www.pitt.edu/-press/

University of South Carolina Press
1600 Hampton St., 5th Floor
Columbia, SC 29208
803-777-5243
www.sc.edu/uscpress/

University Press of Colorado
5589 Arapahoe Ave. #206C
Boulder, CO 80303
919-966-3561
www.upcolorado.com

University Press of Florida
15 NW 15th St.
Gainesville, FL 32611
352-392-1351
www.upf.com

University Press of Kentucky
663 South Limestone St.
Lexington, KY 40508-4008
859-257-8150
www.kentuckypress.com

University Press of Mississippi
3825 Ridgewood Road
Jackson, MS 39211-6492
601-432-6205
www.upress.state.ms

University Press of New England
One Court St., Suite 250
Hanover, NH 03766-1358
603-448-1533
www.upne.com
This press acts as a consortium for Brandies, Dartmouth, The University
of New Hampshire, Tufts, The University of Vermont and Northeastern
University.

Website Based Publishers

This is one area where new publishers are actively looking for writers —
especially for short pieces to go into travel anthologies, but don't expect
much in the way of payment.

Europe from a Backpack
P.O. Box 70525
Seattle, WA 98127-0525
www.Europebackpack.com
Separate books called *Italy from a Backpack*, *Spain from a Backpack*, etc.
Personal travel stories from 800 to 2000 words. Aimed at budget, inde-
pendent and the college travel market.

Viva Travel Guides
124 Mt. Auburn St.
Suite 200N
Cambridge, MA 02138-5758
970-744-4244
www.vivatravelguides.com
Their emphasis is on South America. This entrepreneurial group sells
e-books from its site but have some printed books. They are looking for
travel writers with Spanish/English savvy.

Chapter 22

Publicity and Promotion

Now that you actually have a book published, you may think your work is finished. For most writers, the work of promoting and publicizing the book is just beginning!

Regardless of the entity publishing the book, whether it's a traditional publisher, a subsidy publisher or a self-publisher, the task of promoting the book falls most heavily on the shoulders of the author. If you publish through a traditional house, the publisher will send out review copies to the proper media and send out general press releases. Unless you are a high-powered name, they will not go to any lengths to get you radio or TV interviews. However, most presses will send your book to the pre-publication media. These are journals that require an advance copy of the book several months before it is officially published. These include:

- Library Journal
- Booklist
- Publisher's Weekly (has an issue devoted to travel books-more news than reviews)
- Large city papers such as the NY Times and the LA Times

Your book will also appear in the publisher's catalog that is sent to bookstores and libraries. Your publisher may also send out a separate mailing to travel booksellers and magazines, and send you out for signings at local bookstores. You, the author, will be asked to submit names of possible reviewers for your book.

Most local papers (both the daily and weekly variety) will accept the finished book for review. But it should be sent out immediately upon publication with the appropriate cover letter or press kit. Small, regional and niche publishers often know the reviewers and feature writers that cover their area and target them.

Endorsements

Endorsements are also a form of advertising that is also done before the book is published. The author or publisher gets a celebrity in the field or a well-respected writer or editor to post a few lines about the book. These are placed on the back cover and/or on pages before the title page.

How is this done? The publisher (or the author) sends out a galley to the potential endorser with a plea for a short blurb. The recipient, who is aware that his name will appear on the back cover of a book not his own, and therefore increase his visibility, may comply if he has the time. Here are some typical endorsements:

> "We appreciate this book which accentuates all the glorious mountains and rivers that make our state so attractive to both visitors and residents. Author Joe Doe has really done a fine job in pointing out all the many diversions that (fill in the name) has to offer."
> —Governor David Jones

> "No one knows the back streets of London better than Joan Doe who has been our correspondent for twenty years. Whether it's the newest club, the best seats at the theater, or the best time to walk through Kensington, she'll tell you about it. Is afternoon tea at Harrows really worth it? How do you negotiate the Underground? Joan has all the answers."
> —Benny Faux, Travel Editor, Boston Sun Times

Many books on publishing, and certainly those on self-publishing, make a big to-do about getting endorsements from well-known authorities in the field. And they certainly practice what they preach. The back cover, and front pages of such tomes have a litany of praise from dozens of other authors.

How important are endorsements? Does a travel writer need them? Let's put it this way — they are more important to some non-fiction books than others. If you are writing a book on how to avoid heart disease and you are not a doctor — or even a nurse — it certainly helps to get an endorsement from a doctor. If you are a novelist, getting an endorsement from a leading literary light certainly helps! If Stephen King says your book is so enthralling that he stayed up all night to finish it, you have it made.

Readers of travel guides are more interested in the author's credentials than what others say about him. Of course, once reviews come in, especially those from newspapers with well-known travel sections, they should be put on the back cover immediately. The how-to-do-it category of travel book usually does sport an endorsement. A book written by an airline pilot might have a blurb from the president of an airline assuring everyone that this guy really knows what he's talking about. A travel memoir could use the same help as a fiction book. But if you have a solid, well-researched travel book, an endorsement is not going to make you or break you.

On the other hand, when a possibility presents itself, take advantage. I watched Rachel Ray on the Food Channel when she was doing her "$40 a Day" series. In several key cities she used a guidebook. However, she rarely showed the cover or mentioned the name. Now that Rachel Ray is on network TV and all over the place, the publisher of that book would be well served to track down the segment. "As seen on Rachel Ray's *$40 A Day*" certainly helps. Her trip to Hawaii featured a prolonged on-camera shot of the Dummies guide to that state — so one publicist was awake to the possibilities of free exposure!

Book Reviews

When the book first comes out, it is traditional to get as many reviews as possible. Publishers routinely send the pre-pub copies to the above-mentioned journals. While most large and medium sized publishers still adhere to this traditional way of doing things, many small presses and self-publishers skip that step and concentrate on Internet announcements, direct mail, and press releases to travel editors once the book is actually printed.

Are book reviews really that important to a travel book? Yes and no. In reality, write-ups about a travel guide are often placed in feature articles in newspapers and magazines rather than the review section. Whenever you see an article about a travel advisor's "picks" for the ten most romantic hideaways, or the ten most secluded beaches, there will inevitably be a plug for a book or two that covers the subject. The trick is to figure out an article angle that will feature your book and present that angle to your press contact.

As for reviews, you have a much better chance of getting one, or at least a mention in a round-up review, if you send the book to the Feature Editor or the Travel Editor rather than the book editor. This goes for both newspapers and magazines. Getting lists of general book reviewers may sound great, but you have a better chance at coverage by getting a list of travel editors. A press release along with an e-mail address to the editor is sufficient — he can always ask for a review copy if he is interested.

However travel columnists who feature a "Travel Bookshelf" should receive a review copy as standard procedure. Here for instance, is the Travel Bookshelf of Toni Stroud (now Toni Salama) of the Chicago Tribune on a particular week. I have shortened and paraphrased her reviews to give you an idea of the various types and styles of the guidebooks that were covered. As you can see, this list includes a variety of subjects, formats and angles.

1. *Time Out: Cheap Eats in London* (Penguin)
Divides London into five districts then further divides it into neighborhoods. Maps locate the restaurants. The style is hip and studded with British slang and the reviews pull no punches. Some photos. Part of a series.

2. *The Antique & Flea Markets of Italy* (The Little Bookroom)
A straight list (in other words, the directory style) that is arranged by the day of the month in which the markets are held. Some

mention of the sort of items sold.

3. *My Paris Sketchbook* (Flammarion)
A hardcover picture book with watercolors and sketches that brings the city to life. Some text is included. This is considered a gift book.

4. *In Lincoln's Footsteps* (Trails Books)
Places relating to Lincoln's life that are open to the public are covered. Where he grew up, lived, worked, and was buried with explanations about their importance. 27 places in all are covered. Practical information includes hours, fees, etc. Sidebars include quotes from Lincoln.

5. *Isle Royale National Park Foot Trails and Water Routes* (Mountaineers Books)
The reviewer is very favorable to the style of author Jim DuFresne who adds beauty and wonderment to this guide, which also includes practical matter on trail maps, time and distance notes and launch location. Only misfire according to the reviewer: the plain green cover.

6. *Backroads Bicycling in Wisconsin* (Backcountry Guides)
This is a 2nd edition and part of the Backroads series. 28 bicycle tours are covered in detail, and are fronted by a chart that lists the distance, general terrain and points of interest for each.

In this particular round-up review column, a variety of styles, venues and publishers, small and large are covered. However, the last three books are set in the Chicago Tribune's backyard. A travel columnist in Los Angeles might favor books about California and the Southwest as well as general interest guides.

Suggest a roundup article yourself

This means having to include other titles, but travel writers and editors are always looking for "roundup" articles. So a roundup of recent books about Alaska, or a roundup of romantic hideaway books just before Valentine's Day (with your book topping the list) is an easy way to get a mention even if you have to mention a few others too.

Use the Travel Advice Columnists

You know the travel advice columnists; they appear in Sunday papers, on the Internet and elsewhere. Send a copy of your book to the travel columnist who seems most compatible with your subject, with a cover letter and press release. Then two weeks later have someone else send in a letter asking if there are any theater festivals in Canada because he just loves the theater and is planning a two week trip in a few months. Of course your book on the subject will be the one on top of the pile, so hopefully it will get the mention.

Use Specialty Columnists and Magazines

The author of a book about restaurant destinations contacted an acquaintance on the staff of the daily newspaper with the largest circulation in the state. Were they interested in an article on restaurant recipes from her new book? Since the acquaintance worked on the food page, of course they were intrigued. Although the book was published by a well-known press, it was the author who made the contact and created the article, which ran front-page in the feature section.

The author of a book about traveling with pets got a full write-up in the weekly pet column of the same newspaper. And using that article as a prop, she contacted other animal-targeted columnists in newspapers across the country.

A book about budget travel could go to a money columnist; a guide to RV traveling might merit a write-up in an RV magazine. There are hundreds of magazines devoted to pets, hobbies, ethnic groups, health, fitness and ecology that all could be targeted.

Use newsletters

Remember the anecdote I related about the book proposal from the bicyclists who wanted to do a guide to the best routes in northern New Jersey? The fact that they were the editors of a newsletter to the biggest bike association in the area gave them an immediate platform from which to sell the book. Nowadays, e-newsletters are all the rage and if you can get a mention in an appropriate one, it can trigger lots of sales.

Use the Internet

There are countless ways to use the Internet. Here are a few:

About.com: Start with About.com and track down individual guides to your subject area. There might be more than one, since a book about traveling with dogs can go to a pet column as well as a general travel column. How can the guide publicize your book? Why he can review it, or interview you, or mention it as part of a number of books that cover a certain topic.

Take, for instance, a column written by the Guide for Senior Travel. In it, he interviewed the author of a book about barrier-free travel. This is a book aimed primarily at people who use wheelchairs, walkers or canes and need easy access to wherever they are going. But a book about retired Baby Boomers who travel would work just as well.

If you can't wangle an interview, you can always try the viewer's comments section. Here you can sneak in a mention of your book if it is done in a subtle way. For instance, you can write: "I really enjoyed your write-up of the Taverna Athena on the isle of Mikos. While I was researching my book *18 days on the Greek Islands* I spent many a happy afternoon there, listening to anecdotes about the island's inhabitants." So check out all the About.com guides to Travel to see where your book might fit in, and don't forget all the other interest group guides — Literature, Parenting, Rock Hunting, and Photography — for possible mentions.

Amazon.com: One quick and easy way to promote your title is to disguise yourself as a reader and make a favorable comment in the space provided by Amazon and bn.com. The place where it says: "Be the first person to review this book" — that's the place you want to be.

Don't overdo it. Overly gushy reviews of your book by you and your friends will signal collusion. Just write a solid reasoned paragraph on why you liked the book and point out its value to other readers. Send e-mails to friends and relatives in other states with a pre-written "reviews" and ask them to send it in to Amazon as their own. Each time emphasize a different aspect of the book.

Of course there are other ways to milk Amazon. The best is the "Look Inside the Book" Feature. You definitely want that because it allows readers to see your Table of Contents, your index and a sample of your writing style. Amazon now allows authors to have a Plog (their variation of a blog) and to put pictures up.

What about reviewing other books in your field while pushing your own title? Many publicity gurus advocate this, while some authors deride it. I would say: choose carefully. Look for complementary books, and don't trash the competition. **Listmania** is another Amazon opportunity. Here you can create a list of travel books to a certain destination and put your own book at the top of the list!

AOL Interest Groups: These include such topics as Parenting, Seniors, Travel, and Dating. A friend of mine who is a PR specialist once got an author booked on the parenting group for a chat session. The book was a grandmother's memory scrapbook. The author had a full hour chat on the parenting website. Her book was highlighted on the page with a direct link to Amazon.com. Although the session only lasted an hour, it was heralded for weeks beforehand, and the book remained highlighted on the site for a month afterwards.

Internet Reviewers: The number of newspaper reviewers is dwindling. The number of online reviewers is growing. Whether it's www.midwestbookreview.com, www.heartlandreviews.com, www.readerviews.com or individual reviewers on Amazon who have amassed a following, this is a quick and easy way to get a review (although these places have guidelines too.) Search the Internet for travel columnists and reviewers who specialize in travel or outdoor topics. For instance, Norm Goldman has his own review site called www.bookpleasures.com but he also reviews travel titles for www.bootsnall.com a well-known travel community site. There are even travel bloggers who will review a book or two.

Travel Websites & Forums: There are dozens of websites that host reader's forums. Of course the most prominent of these are the websites of well-known travel publishers such as Lonely Planet, Fodor's and Frommer's. Can you get a mention of your book on these websites? Perhaps on the travel forums you can sneak in a mention of your title or at least your topic. Remember though, that all comments belong to the website owner. There are also travel interest groups on yahoo.com.

And you can always write up a short trip that connects to your book and try to place it on popular websites such as www. travelerstales.com, www.travellady.com, www.gonomad.com and others. Even though these sites pay little or nothing, they do have editorial standards equal to many top newspapers so that an appearance here enhances your credentials and your visibility.

Youtube.com, myspace.com and all imitators: If your audience is young, hip or both, here is where they congregate. All you need is a camera and some imagination to make your own version of a Travel Channel video.

E-books: An e-book version of your printed book on such websites as www.hadimi.com (which specializes in travel) works as an advertisement as well as a way to reach readers who live in far-off lands.

Book Signings

It may come as a blow to your self-esteem, but patrons do not storm the barricades to get a copy of your hot new title in their outstretched hands. The average book "event" at a Big Box bookstore may garner something between four and twelve people. In fact the bookstore CRM (Community Relations Manager) will urge you to bring along your own compadres to "fill up the seats" when you appear. In an independent bookstore, where people stream in and out, your little book-signing table might attract a few people. You may not get many sales but you'll get a story in the local paper.

The main reason for book signings is that it is a cheap way to get publicity. The bookstore sends out a list of "events" to the local paper. The big chains like Barnes and Noble also include book talks/signings in their monthly newsletter to patrons. Your best contact is the local CRM, who may book you alone or with complementary authors.

From the author's point of view, the best thing about the book signing is that you get to meet the public and answer a few questions (and also learn a thing or two, because people who go to these things are usually knowledgeable on the subject). You may discover that a mother with young children is more interested in having her kids visit a real farm than an exotic zoo, or that the small planetarium you thought was so cute, closed three months ago.

It is also a chance to meet the CRM. If you are lucky she will have sent out a killer press kit, which impresses local newspapers so much that they do a full-length article on your book. (Believe it or not, this actually happened to me. The CRM at the Princeton Marketfair B&N sent out such a good press kit that I received more publicity from that one appearance there than I did when the 10th edition of my book initially came out.)

Appearances at small venues also have unusual outcomes. When I did a book signing at a local AAA bookstore only three people showed up. But the manager had sold many copies the previous week and the article in the North Jersey AAA newsletter (with 175,000 customers) made my sales zoom elsewhere.

Now if you have an outgoing personality, know how to give a zinging presentation and promote your appearance at the bookstore on all the local radio stations and newspapers, you may actually attract a large crowd and sell lots of books. But don't despair if you only sell four or five. It's the ripple effect of book signing that counts, so keep on trying.

Other In-store Promotions

Publishers, whether large, small or micro (often meaning self-publishers) have found there are other paths to in-store promotions besides book signings. You can suggest to your local independent that a bevy of travel books would look great in the window with a banner proclaiming "Now that it's Spring, Let's Get Out of the House" or "Discover Your Own State" or" Road Trips for Everyone" depending on your title.

For the chain stores, getting your book on the *endcaps* (those slots at the end of each aisle) or the large *Point of Purchase* bins (sometimes called dumps) that are located at the front of the store sometimes depends on money. Chain stores do promotions on a theme (such as travel) all the time. Publishers pay to have their books featured in these prominent areas. The cost depends on how many stores are involved. A regional promotion will cost much less than a national promotion. And then there are the free promotions such as the one when employees pick their favorite titles.

Talks and Lectures

How would you like to give a slide talk in front of forty eager listeners at the local library or club function and get paid for your time? The answer is easy. What's more, you will sell more books at the library or club than at a bookstore signing because you have a captive audience that is interested in your subject.

When you contact the organization ask for a small stipend (most do pay for speakers, but some don't). The hosting group will take care of the publicity and you will be able to sell your books directly to the audience. So if you are with a traditional publisher, be sure your contract allows you to buy back your books — at 50% if possible! If you are self-publishing, here is where you make the most money — you don't have to pay intermediaries and you get the cash right away.

Clubs that would be interested in your travel title include Newcomer's groups (for local and regional books) photography groups (for outdoors & pictorial books) Sierra Club and similar groups (for outdoors and activity titles), women's clubs (for exotic destinations) and biking and hiking groups. Also, any organization devoted to the special audience I talked about in the Category chapter would be a perfect fit if you have a book of interest to that audience. Even memoirs and travel essays seem to go over well with the club and library crowd.

Radio and TV

Radio: Get on a radio program where you can call in from your home (actually they call you a few minutes before air time). It's free. Only make sure that books are available in the bookstores within the radio station's broadcast area, and of course at the online bookstores. If you can sneak in your own website, fine.

Certainly radio is the easiest form of publicity, since you can do it from the comfort of your own home in most cases and it's all over in a matter of five, ten or fifteen minutes. What's more, there are hundreds of small-watt radio stations all over the country that are happy to welcome a bona-fide author on their show. If you're a regional author so much the better.

Get a list of phone-in radio shows and see which ones fit your niche. You don't necessarily even have to go on the show. One chatty radio hostess mentioned my book because I sent it to her in the hopes that someone would ask a question about someplace in New Jersey. And I also once had a few minutes on the Alan Colmes show (yes, the same guy who is now the tramped-on liberal on Fox channel's Hannity and Colmes show). He had an early morning radio show in New York City some years ago. A copy of the book and a letter was all it took to get me on.

Nowadays, the podcast is another way of reaching the at-home audience. This is a basic radio style interview that is done through the Internet.

TV: Look to your local stations. See if you can snag a segment on your city or state TV news or feature programs. It's free and you can build up your communication skills by appearing on local stations. Almost all interviewers ask the same questions and after a while you will have a repertoire of answers. My dog-loving friend was on a cable station pushing her canine travel book, and I've been on a couple of local stations either as a member of a panel or as the subject of an interview.

In Summation

Naturally you should check out a few books to learn the basics of marketing. It's amazing how many authors are clueless when it comes to this necessity of the business. Here are the most common ways to attract attention to your title:

- Word of mouth. If you have the first or the best book on a destination or a really useful how-to-book on travel, word will get around. This includes "hand selling" by bookstores (where a clerk or owner recommends a book).
- Name Brand Recognition: One reason writers try to get assignments with the brand-name publishers is that the name alone will sell a certain number of copies and that means they are assured of a sound royalty.
- Good book reviews. There are plenty of travel editors out there who do monthly roundups of travel titles. If the Travel editor does not routinely do book reviews, then create a travel story with your book as the source material and send it out as a press release. And try the Internet reviewers.
- Amazon.com reader reviews wield some influence. Thankfully, they make no distinction between small presses, self-publishers and the better known names.
- TV exposure: Whether it's your local TV channel or a series on PBS, any television exposure helps. Forget about Oprah. Concentrate on shows where your particular audience will tune in.
- Make yourself an expert. By starting a website and/ or a blog, giving lectures at local adult schools and clubs, offering quotes to travel websites, or by acting as a guide on certain well-known websites, you can build up an audience.
- Allow excerpts to be published –in magazines if you can swing a deal where you actually get a fee — or for free on the many travel maga-zines and websites on the Internet.
- Write articles pertinent to your topic everywhere you can, and make sure the byline reads: "Joe Doaks, author of 50 Ways to Travel for Practically Nothing."

Selling from Your Website

You can publicize your book through Amazon and travel forums and blogs without having a website. But for self-publishers and those authors who want to push themselves as experts in the field, a website is a necessity.

Search engines: To sell from your website you need to get high on the search engines for your topic. This is called search engine optimization. The act of selling from your website requires that you have good up-to-date content and a way that potential customers can order from you. This is everyone's dream job: stay at home, collect the money, and mail out a few hundred copies to customers a month. Check out websites such as www.theweb-savvywriter.com and books such as *Plug Your Book* for tips on optimization as well as insider information about the Internet.

Of course, it costs money to maintain a website. If you are technically inclined and can do it yourself, great! If you are not, there are people who can design websites and others who can maintain them. It may not entail thousands of dollars but it will cost a certain amount. Many authors maintain websites just for exposure. Others simply go to free blogspots and get noticed that way.

Shopping Carts: If you plan to sell your books from your website you need some way of collecting money online. This usually involves working through PayPal, although there are other companies such as CCNow and Mel's Carts that have systems running.

Most contracts with publishers prohibit authors from selling directly from their website; publishers want the authors to link to their site or to online stores. If you are a self-publisher who sells through a wholesaler, there is no prohibition to selling direct since the wholesaler sells only to the trade. However with distributors there may be a clause in your contract about direct selling. Be sure to check it out and ask for the ability to sell direct both online and to non-book retailers.

What If you don't have a shopping Cart? There are plenty of websites that have no shopping carts and therefore the customer has no quick way to buy the item. Either the website owner uses an affiliate connection (such as Amazon) or he offers an address where the customer can send a check. The address is usually a P.O. Box because very few people want their home address on view on the Internet. However, most websites offer a shopping cart because customers are used to buying online with a credit card.

What's an Affiliate? If you feel that maintaining a shopping cart on your website is too much time or trouble, you can simply redirect sales to online bookstores that pay you a small commission by becoming an affiliate. The affiliate system, more or less invented by Amazon.com, lets you link your book from your website to the exact page at Amazon where your book appears. If someone clicks through from your website to theirs, and buys your book, you get a small commission. If someone clicks through and buys a different book you also get a commission. There are other companies besides Amazon that offer affiliate status and sometimes give as much as 15% commission. It's worth checking out.

What about e-books? You can write a short report on some subject related to your book and sell it from your website as an e-book or e-report. Many web-savvy writers make more money from their e-books than from their real ones!

Producing Extra Income

Having a guidebook with your name on it is like having a ham in the larder. You can always cut off slices to use in the future to provide extra income. Here are a few methods to augment your income and your visibility as an expert:

- Create new articles out of the basic research you did for the book. There are many trade and business magazines that pay well for travel articles that are slanted to their audience.
- Give talks and slide lectures. Most groups pay an honorarium and they also offer the opportunity for back-of-the-room sales.
- Sell photographs you took for the book, whether at an art fair or from your own website. If you

signed with a traditional publisher, make sure such
a contingency is put into the contract. If you self-
publish the photographs are yours anyway. And
there are always the pictures you took that didn't
make it into the book for one reason or another.

- Get a gig as a travel lecturer on a cruise ship. They
  don't pay you, but you get the cruise for free — and you
  can arrange to have your books sold at the ship's store.
- If you have a website, consider taking ads that are
  compatible with your content. And there are always
  affiliate programs with online book and video stores
  that will bring in a small percent of the sale price.
- Set up a tour of your specialty with yourself as the
  guide. I've known people who have given guided
  tours of the gardens of Ireland and the food markets of
  Marrakech for small groups of ten or twelve. It covers
  the cost of your travel and creates a circle of customers.
- Teach classes at your local adult school.
- As a specialist in your area you can now offer travel
  columns to newspapers and online websites.
- Create e-books out of your updates or extra
  material and sell them from your website.
- Get a producer to create a travel series based
  on your book. The Travel Channel, the Food
  channel and PBS have all shown dozens of travel
  series that have turned authors into TV stars.
- Become a spokesperson for a cruise line, a
  RV association or even a customer's travel
  group, based on your expertise.

Although the initial payment for a guidebook may not be
overwhelming, there is no end of possibilities for the future. You
may become the author of a best-selling series, or as a self-publisher, the founder of a small empire. Whether you simply write
one good book or many, you will always have the satisfaction of
being able to combine your love of traveling with your love of
writing and thus be able to reach people with your words — and
visit your favorite destinations at the same time!

Appendix

Travel Books

Here is a list of travel books that were referred to or quoted in the text. The original publisher of the particular edition is cited, although the present edition of the same book may have a different publisher through mergers or buyouts

25 Mountain Bike Tours in New Jersey. Peter Kick, Backcountry Publications/Countryman Press, 1997

52 Great Weekend Escapes: Northern California. Chris Becker, Globe Pequot, 2005

100 Best Cruise Vacations. Theodore Scull, Globe Pequot, 2003

100 Best U.S. Wedding Destinations. Kathryn Loving, Insider's Guide/ Globe Pequot, 2006.

1000 Places to See Before You Die. Patricia Schulz, Workman Publishing, 2005

Access Guide to Chicago.7th ed. Richard Warnum, Harper Collins, 2006

Along the Interstate 75. Dave Hunter, Mile Oak Publishing, 2004

The Chowhound's Guide to the San Francisco Bay Area. Jim Leff et al. Penguin, 2005

Day Walker: 32 Hikes in the New York Metropolitan Area. New York New Jersey Trail Conference, 2002

Discover America Diaries. Priscilla Rhodes, Postcard Café, 2003

Duncan Hines: The Man Behind the Cake Mix. Louis Hatchett, Mercer Univ. Press, 2001

Explore the Virgin Islands, 6th ed. Harry Pariser, Manatee Press, 2005

Fodor's NYC Gold Guide, 2006. Fodor/Random House

Food Lover's Guide to Paris, 4th ed. Patricia Wells, Workman Publishing, 1999

Free L.A. Troy Corley ed., Corley Publications, 2004

Free O. C. Robert Stock, Corley Publications, 2004

Frommer's Irreverent Guide to Las Vegas, 4th ed. Frommer Publishing. 2006

Great Destinations: The Santa Fe & Taos Book by Sharon Niederman & Brandt Morgan. Berkshire House publishers, 1998

Imagined London. Anna Quindlen. National Geographic Directions, 2004
Live Your Road Trip Dream. Carol & Phil White, RSI publishers, 2004
Lonely Planet Guide to Travel Writing. Don George, ed., Lonely Planet, 2005
Lonely Planet: Vietnam, 7th ed. Lonely Planet Publishers, 2003
Natural Wonders of Virginia. Deane and Garvey Winegar, Country Roads Press, 2000.
New Jersey Day Trips, 9th ed. Barbara Hudgins, Woodmont Press, 2000.
On the Road with Your Pet. Mobil Travel Guides, 1998.
The Packing Book. Judith Gilford, Ten Speed Press, 1996
The Penny Pincher's Passport to Luxury Travel. Joel Widzer, 2nd ed. Travelers' Tales, 2004
Rick Steves' France, Belgium & the Netherlands, 2002. Rick Steves & Steve Smith, Avalon Travel
Rick Steves' Germany & Austria 2005. Avalon Travel Publishers
Rick Steves' Paris. Latest edition. Avalon Travel
Rough Guide to San Francisco, 5th ed. Rough Guides/Penguin, 2000
Rough Guide to Vietnam. Rough Guides/Penguin. 2003
Rowing to Alaska. Wayne McLennan, Granta Books, 2005.
A Travel Guide to the Jewish Caribbean and South America. Ben G. Frank, Pelican Publishers, 2004.
Traveling Woman: Great Tips for Safe and Healthy Trips. Swain & Comer, Impact Publications, 2001
Tropical Family Vacations. Laura Sutherland, St. Martins/Griffin, 1999.
Trouble Free Travel with Children. Vicki Lanksy et al., MJF Books, 1996.
The Unofficial Guide to Washington D.C. 4th ed. Joe Surkiewicz, Bob Sehlinger & Eve Zibart, MacMillan Travel, 1998
The Unofficial Guide to Disney World 2006, Sehlinger et al.,Wiley & Co.
Walking Shakespeare's London. Nicholas Robins, Interlink Books, 2005.
Zagat Restaurant Survey. Zagat Publishers.

Other Resources

Some of these have been mentioned elsewhere in the text. Others mentioned in a particular context are not repeated here.

Books on Travel Writing

Lonely Planet Guide to Travel Writing. Don George, Lonely Planet, 2005
Travel Writer's Guide. Gordon Burgett, Communications Unlimited, 2002
The Travel Writer's Handbook, 5th ed. Louise Purwin Zobel, Surrey Books
Travel Writing, 2nd edition. Peit O'Neil, Writer's Digest Books

Books on Publishing and Self-Publishing

The Everything Publishing Book. Peter Rubie, Adams Publishers, 2000
The Self-Publishing Manual, latest edition. Dan Poynter, Para Publishing.
The Publishing Game: How to get Published in 30 Days. Fern Reiss, 2002
Damn, Why Didn't I Write That? Marc McCutcheon, Quill Driver Books,
    2001.
The Complete Idiots Guide to Publishing. Latest edition.
Print on Demand Publishing. Morris Rosenthal, Foner Books, 2004.
Aiming at Amazon. Aaron Shepard, Shepard Pub., 2006
The Fine Print of Self-Publishing. Mark Levine, Bascom Hall Pub., 2006
The Copyright, Libel & Permissions Handbook. Jassin & Schecter, Wiley,
    1998

Books on Marketing and Promotion

1001 Ways to Market your Book, 6th ed. John Kremer. Open Horizons,
    2006
Plug your Book. Steve Weber. Weberbooks, 2007.
From Book to Bestseller. Penny Sansevieri, Morgan James Pub. 2006
Complete Guide to Book Publicity. Jodee Blanco, Allworth Press, 2004
Publicize Your Book. Jacqueline Deval, Peregrine, 2003.

Organizations for Writers and Publishers

American Society of Journalists & Authors (ASJA). www.ASJA.org:
    Admission requirements, dues.
International Food, Wine & Travel Writers Association.
    www.IFW&TWA.org: Admission requirements, dues. Good website.
National Writer's Union. www.nwu.org.:for freelancers, some require-
    ments, dues.
Outdoor Writers Association of America. www.owar.org. Requirements,
    dues.
Publisher's Marking Association (PMA): Small publishers.
    www.pma-online.org
Small Publisher's Association of North America (SPAN): Small and self-
    publishers. www.spannet.org
Small Publishers, Writers and Artist's Network (SPAWN). Dues. No
    restrictions.
Society of American Travel Writers .www.satw.org. Admission require-
    ments, dues
Travel Media Association of Canada.www.travelmedia.ca. Canadians
    only. Admission requirements, dues
Travel Publishers Association: Co-op book fairs.

Websites, Blogs & Newsletters

For research:
www.expedia.com
www.travelocity.com
www.orbitz.com
www.away.com
www.johnnyjet.com
www.transitionsabroad.com
www.copyright.gov

For tips/markets for your work:
www.journeywoman.com
www.bootsnall.com
www.gonomad.com
www.goworldtravel.com
www.travelblog.com
www.travelblog.org
www.travellady.com
www.travelwriters.com
www.worldhum.com

On writing & publishing in general
www.absolutewrite.com
www.bookwire.com
www.shelfawareness.com
www.writing.com
www.writerswrite.com

On marketing and publicity:
www.bookmarket.com
www.ebookmarketing.com
www.publicityhound.com
www.web-savvywriter.com
www.para-pub.com
www.bookbuzz.com
www.frugalmarketer.com

Distributors for non-bookstore outlets
Eastern National
470 Maryland Dr., Suite 1
Fort Washington, PA 19034
215-283-6900
www.easternnational.org

Buys for eastern national parks of U.S.

Western National Parks
Association
12880 North Vistoso Village Dr.
Tuscon, AZ, 85755
520-622-1999
www.wnpa.org
Buys for western national parks of U.S.

Peregrine Outfitter
25 Omega Drive
P.O. Box 1500
Williston, VT. 05495
800-222-3088
www.peregrineoutfitter.com
Buys for outdoor outfitters stores.

Event Network
Purchasing Dept.
1010 Turquoise St., Suite 325
San Diego, CA 92109
503-635-1299/ 858-488-7507
www.eventnetwork.com
Handles gift shops in zoos, aquariums & gardens.

Quality Distributors
1003 West Pines Road
Oregon, IL 61061
800-323-4241
www.quality-books.com
Distributes directly to libraries.

Index

AUDIENCE :
- KIDS 6 - 12 YEARS.
- OUT-OF-TOWNERS.
- TRAVELING W/FAMILY FOR A LONGWEEKEND, UP TO 5 DAYS.

Printed in the United States
93831LV00005B/12/A

9 780960 776207